THE MEANING OF LIFE 2

More Lives, More Meaning

THE MEANING OF LIFE 2

More Lives, More Meaning

Gay Byrne
with Roger Childs

Interviews edited by Alice Childs

Gill & Macmillan

Gill & Macmillan
Hume Avenue, Park West, Dublin 12
www.gillmacmillanbooks.ie

© RTÉ 2014
978 07171 6492 9

Typography design by Make Communication
Print origination by Carole Lynch
Printed and bound by CPI Group (UK) Ltd,
Croydon, CR0 4YY

This book is typeset in Linotype Minion and
Neue Helvetica.

The paper used in this book comes from the
wood pulp of managed forests. For every
tree felled, at least one tree is planted,
thereby renewing natural resources.

A CIP catalogue record for this book
is available from the British Library.

5 4 3 2 1

CONTENTS

PREFACE

Sir Alex must have been quaking. Just when he looked set for imperious domination of the 2013 non-fiction Christmas bestsellers list, Gill & Macmillan came roaring into the fray with, er, an anthology of transcribed religious interviews by yours truly.

All right, let's be honest: *The Meaning of Life* was always likely to be more the Sligo Rovers of the book market than the Manchester United. Nevertheless, I am pleased to report that enough copies were sold to raise a significant sum for Crumlin Children's Hospital, which is why, when the invitation came to publish this sequel in 2014, with charitable proceeds to be shared between the Peter McVerry Trust and Christina Noble's foundation for Asian street children, I was happy to agree. I imagine the publisher of Brian O'Driscoll's memoirs is already quivering.

"Have something to say: the words will follow," wrote Alexander Pope, channelling Cato the Elder. It is a reassuring maxim for anyone contemplating a blank page and a publisher's deadline. But what *do* I have to say? Or, rather, what do I have to say about *others* having their say?

This book is to be published soon after I turn eighty, which means, inevitably, that some will want to read into it a valedictory note, if not a moribund one. Gaybo's swan song.

Tough. This particular Child of Lir is not quite ready for the taxidermist. While I still have enough energy, I shall continue to emit the occasional honk.

Of late, I have been flapping my way round the medium-sized venues of our thirty-two beloved counties, regaling the adoring masses with stories, gags and songs accumulated over my "three score years and ten" plus ten. It is a phase of the performer's life they call *anecdotage*.

Unfortunately, in October 2013, it cost *The Meaning of Life* one of its biggest potential scalps to date, when, at short notice, I was offered a half-hour interview with none other than the former leader of the free world, President William Jefferson Clinton. On the evening of his fleeting visit to Dublin, I was due to perform my one-man show in Galway and

I know the Galwegian temperament far too well to stand them up, even for the President of the United States. Hell hath no fury, etc.

You therefore won't find in these pages any of the reflections of Arkansas's most famous son, although I don't think you will miss them. There are too many other pearls of wisdom to be harvested from the twenty human oysters featured in these pages. These very different figures were generous enough to share with me on our television show the beliefs, values, thoughts and experiences that have shaped, or been shaped by, their lives. Even more generously, they have now agreed to let me reprint some of them, and I am very grateful.

As ever, there is a small, unseen army of people without whose dedication and kindness these interviews would never have made it to screen, let alone page. I hope they will forgive me if I don't even try to name them all, for fear of failing to name even one of them. The two exceptions I will make to that rule are Roger Childs, the Series Producer, to whom all complaints and legal actions relating to this book should be directed, and his wife, Alice, whose editorial chisel reduced these twenty interviews to perfectly sculpted and coherent chapter length.

I should also acknowledge the support of RTÉ in allowing me to carry on interviewing people for the enlightenment and distraction of the Irish viewing public for nine series and counting. For a simple formula, which has been described as "radio interviews on the telly", *The Meaning of Life* has proved to be remarkably enduring — perhaps because so many of us are still looking for meaning in our lives and are willing to believe that some others *might* just have found it.

Ah, but have they? Well, you decide.

GAY BYRNE, AUGUST 2014

|IMELDA MAY

Kissed by a Saint

You simply won't find anyone in Ireland who doesn't love Imelda May. I know. I've tried, and my extensive, if unscientific, research into the matter failed to unearth a single person who was less than smitten with the Liberties Belle.

So, what is that quality that makes Ms May such a darling bud?

Search me, but I know it instantly when I meet it, and in her case I first met it when she appeared on my *other* TV show, *For One Night Only*, in 2011. Her status as a "National Treasure" was instantly secured. For days afterwards people were stopping me in the street to tell me how wonderful she was. Not that I needed telling. I was pleased to discover, when we met again in October 2013, that she had experienced much the same reaction herself.

She should be used to it by now. The first time she felt that sort of adulation was when, as a small girl, she returned home to the Coombe from a family holiday in Rome, having been kissed on the cheek by Pope John Paul II. (You see, even he was smitten.) Neighbours queued up to touch the famous cheek, as if it were a relic of Padre Pio.

By the way, you didn't misread me there. I really did say that the Clabby family — for such is her clan and maiden name — went to Rome on holiday, back at a time when *no one* from inner-city Dublin, and hardly anyone from Ireland, went "foreign" on holiday. (My own folks never made it further than Bray.) And this wasn't the Clabbys' only trip: all five offspring were annually shoehorned into the family Rover, under a roof-rack piled as high as the Liberty Tower with luggage, deck chairs and sleeping bags, and off they went, by road and ferry, to France, Spain or even Morocco, like the Griswolds on vacation.

It was from her parents, Tony and Madge, that Imelda inherited her unique voice — somewhere on a spectrum of russets, reds and golds that spans Judy Garland, Dusty Springfield and Amy Winehouse. They also gave her her "try anything, talk to anyone, fear no one" zest for life, her striking looks, her bold creative flair and her still rock-solid faith and values. Oh, and that accent, which should be preserved in aspic in the National Museum as one of Ireland's aural jewels.

Tony was a painter — more of the Dulux than of the Rembrandt variety — but was not afraid to express his artistic talent in their two-bedroom home, the walls of which he adorned with giant poppies and dandelions to such a "mad" extent that neighbours used to knock for a gander. Madge still "drowns" him every night, as she sends out holy water in the vague direction of each of their children.

They are perfect role models for Imelda in her own marriage to her rockabilly soul-mate, Darrel Higham, and in her recent role as mother to young Violet. That Imelda remains close to her parents was either inevitable or a miracle, since she shared their bedroom until she was fourteen.

"God help me. I'm mentally disturbed because of it!" she shudders at the memory.

∼

GB: Tell me about that home and what sort of a household it was . . .
IM: A madhouse. Really!

GB: Was it generally considered in the Coombe that it was a madhouse?
IM: Probably [laughs]. I just loved it. I thought it was great fun.

GB: And there was music.
IM: Always music, always dancing, always people. My dad was a dance teacher, so obviously he'd be playing music and practising his dancing at home.

GB: And does your mum sing?
IM: Mam sings beautifully, yeah.

GB: You were never rich, but you were never short?
IM: Exactly, yeah. My mam and dad worked very hard. We never had much, being so many of us, and my dad worked in the Corporation — the "Corpo" — as a painter and decorator. But we never wanted. Mam and Dad never smoked or drank, so they'd save their money, and they always wanted to bring us on a holiday. And so we went to France, to Italy and Spain.

GB: Very unusual, Imelda.
IM: Very unusual. I know. I remember we took a day trip to Morocco when we were in Spain. Dad saw a boat, a day trip off to Morocco, which *nobody* went to then — North Africa. And I remember Dad saying, "Right, here's your choice. Do you want to eat tonight" — like, we'd go out for a meal — "or will we just get rolls and go to Morocco?" And we were, "Morocco!" and not knowing what it was.

GB: A day excursion.

IM: Yeah, it was brilliant. I couldn't thank my mam and dad enough for the excitement we had.

GB: How much religion was there in this mad household, and how mad was this religion? I'm talking about holy pictures and medals and Mass and all of that.

IM: All of it. All of it. Very religious family.

GB: Family Rosary?

IM: Family Rosary, Angelus every time it came on, Mass, Grace before meals, night-time prayers . . . Yeah, all of it. Great really, yeah.

GB: How much of that has stuck to the present day?

IM: A lot of it, actually, has stuck. Not constantly stuck, because as a teenager I thought, I've had enough of this, and went mad like most teenagers and went off, did my own thing. But, slowly, I kind of came back to it. Yeah, not as intensely, I suppose, as Mam and Dad. They have pictures and Rosaries everywhere. And Mam drowns Dad at night with her holy water bottle. She guesses where various countries of people are and everyone gets drowned.

GB: So, now take me to school then. What school was it?

IM: St Brigid's, Holy Faith, in the Coombe.

GB: Were you studious?

IM: I put my head down and got on with it. I wasn't a brainbox and I wasn't a dunce. Not that anyone's a dunce. My mother was always good, and she said, "Do your best. Whatever your best is, do your best and you can be proud of yourself."

GB: And the nuns weren't particularly awful or anything?

IM: Some were awful and some were fabulous. Like anybody, nuns are people too! [Laughs.]

GB: Now, your mother is on record as saying, "We always knew she would be special at what she did after a trip to Rome . . ." — you certainly got around, girl! — ". . . with the Girl Guides ended up with Imelda being cradled in the arms of Pope John Paul II."

IM: Yeah, and he's a saint now, isn't he? I got kissed by a saint. He kissed me.

GB: How did that come about . . . ?

IM: That was another one of the mad family excursions. I think it was my sister. The Girl Guides were taking a trip to Rome, and my family, being the way they were, would say, "Great, we'll all go!" And it was great, terrific. And we went up to the front. And then he went past and just picked me up and gave me a big kiss and put me back, and then the whole of the Liberties rubbed my cheeks for ages after, blessing themselves . . .

GB: This is the spot that was kissed by . . .

IM: Yeah, yeah, yeah . . . I was probably about six or seven, and they all kept rubbing my cheek and blessing themselves afterwards.

GB: It must become a bit of a bother.

IM: I thought it was very odd, yeah. [Laughs.]

GB: And at what stage did you realise that you could sing?

IM: I always sang at home. My sister encouraged me, Maria, a lot. And then, in school, they knew. They'd get me to do the harmonies. When I went into secondary school, I had Sister Hilda. She was brilliant. I brought my guitar in, she'd encourage it.

GB: And I know from your brother Fintan you got the tapes of Elvis and Gene Vincent and various other people, and you took to rockabilly at a time when it seems to me your gang would have been into Wet Wet Wet and Culture Club and Duran Duran and all of that sort of thing. What was it about rockabilly that got into you, as it were?

IM: The wildness.

GB: The wildness.

IM: I loved it. Yeah. I loved all the other stuff as well, all the Rick Astley and Bros and Duran Duran. But then I discovered rockabilly and blues and jazz . . .

GB: Billie Holiday . . .

IM: Billie Holiday, Howlin' Wolf, Gene Vincent . . . Judy Garland I loved. That changed me. That moved something in me that I hadn't felt before with music. It definitely got me. And I got it.

GB: Now, I'm also anxious to establish the fact that, for those people who think you arrived like a meteor already finished and ready, you slogged for fifteen years or thereabouts before you got there . . .

IM: Yeah, yeah.

GB: You must have had a ferocious conviction that this is what you wanted to do and nothing else.

IM: Yeah, I loved it. It's exactly what I wanted to do. The making of music — I found a great fulfilment in it. And fire, yeah — passion and fire drives me a lot. I'm very ruled by my heart in many ways. And I just steamed ahead with it, because I couldn't *not* do it.

GB: You couldn't *not* do it.

IM: Yeah, that was basically it. It was never a quest for fame.

GB: But I know you cleaned toilets and you waited at tables and you did double shifts in the nursing homes. You were looking after old people . . .

IM: Launderette, garage, yeah, loads . . . I wasn't making enough money doing it, so I had other jobs going along. But I always knew whatever job I had was a sideline, and I'd tell whoever I was working for. It was always shift-work, so I could change my shifts if I got a gig in. But making music for me, especially when I got into writing, that was, like I said, something that I found I *had* to do. And not so much a dream of, you know, "One day I'm going to make it." I just wanted to make music. I loved being on stage as well. There's a magic that happens between an audience and an artist, a singer or the band, and it's just for that couple of hours, and it's a huge joy. You can feel it, and it feeds back and forth. The happier the audience get, the happier the band get, the happier the audience get, and it feeds and feeds till the end of the night. And it's just a little bit of magic.

GB: And when you look at *The X Factor* and similar shows, you see all these kids trying to fast-track to fame. How do you react to that?

IM: It saddens me.

GB: Saddens you? Why?

IM: I think they're missing the point. *X Factor* things can be somebody striving for someone else's idea of success. I think a lot of people are striving for fame. Some people might think it's the answer to everything. But if you're famous for nothing, what's the answer? What's the question? What do you do with your life? I think it should be about making music. It should be about fulfilling your potential. If you go on *The X Factor* for a thrill, great, go for it. If you're going on to something like that to completely change your life around, what was so bad with your life in the first place? Secondly, why do you want it to change?

Because, for me, the journey is the joy. It's the people you're meeting along the way. It's the music that you're making. You're talking about "meaning of life." You have to enjoy your day every day. I like to enjoy each day.

GB: Now, speaking of the journey, let us move on to Mr Darrel Higham. He's English, but we can't have everything! Now, he must have been really kind of smitten, let's face it, when we hear about the efforts he made to come from London to see you.
IM: Yeah. He chased me.

GB: He chased you. Yes, and . . .
IM: Yeah, we met at a weekend in London. It was all to do with music, of course, and it was a gig. We got on really well for the whole weekend. And I left him with a little kiss and then I said goodbye and I went home. And then he, all of a sudden, had gigs — *loads* of gigs — coming up in Dublin, funny enough, yeah. [Laughs.] And he was on his way over. And the story goes that he hadn't got enough money for his ticket, so he sold his car. And the rest of that story is he's always saying to me, whenever we have a row or anything, he tells me how much he misses that car. But there's an end to that, because he just found the car on eBay.

GB: The car?
IM: The car, with the registration number, in someone's garden, with a tree growing through the ground of it and out the roof, and he's in the middle, him and his friend, of doing it up.

GB: I'd say your position is a very precarious one once that car comes back.
IM: Probably, yeah. I'm out, the car is in.

GB: Anyway, you remember the kiss that you left him with to go home. You knew then, did you? Come on, you knew . . .
IM: I'm not giving anything away. He says *he* knew. I like to let him think that . . .

GB: Did he say that?
IM: Yeah, he said he knew as soon as he saw me that I was the one.

GB: They all say that. Don't believe that, for heaven's sake.
IM: I don't, but I like to hear him saying it! [Laughter.]

GB: Are you one of these people who believes there's only one person in the world for you, and you're the only one person in the world for him?

IM: Yeah. The honest answer: I think we are made, definitely, me and Darrel, are made for each other, definitely. However, if anything was to happen to me, I would like him to fall in love again. Not too much, just a little bit. [Laughs.] So, I think there *can* be somebody else.

GB: And do you think your mother would have the same attitude about your dad?
IM: No.

GB: No?
IM: No, no. There's definitely just the two of them. I remember, once, we were messing around and said to Mam, "If you ever found out that Dad had done the dirt on you, like, would you throw him out?"
"Oh, yeah."
"But," we said, "what if it was fifty years ago and since then, you've had a great life together, what would you do now?"
And she said, "He'd be out the door." [Laughter.]
I said, "Even now?"
"Yeah," she said . . .

GB: Still!
IM: Yeah. And he roars laughing. He knows. But he's not interested. He's mad about her; she's mad about him. It's great.

GB: Come back to Darrel . . . and his touring with you . . .
IM: Yeah . . .

GB: How does that work out? I'm thinking of a little touch of claustrophobia or getting in each other's hair . . .
IM: No, that works really well, actually. We love working together. We probably kill each other more at home than when we're on the road. I can't nag him about emptying the bins. [Laughs.] No, it works. It works really well, because there's a bunch of us, but everybody gets on really well, and I want to make sure that everybody's happy and that they all feel that they're valued and treated well, because they are. So I'd be the boss . . .

GB: Of the band . . . ?
IM: Of the band.

GB: And now and then you have to crack the whip, do you?
IM: Oh, God, yeah. Yeah. Not very often, but every now and then they all laugh if they hear me going up to one of them saying, "I'd like to

have a chat." They all go, "Oooooh!" but I'll make sure that I'll say, "Is everything okay with you? You seem a bit grumpy. What's going on? Can we, can I, fix it out?" Because it can be hard, especially, you know, you're five weeks on the road, you're in a tour bus, all together — there's eleven of you in, basically, a caravan on wheels, missing home, missing their wives, missing their babies. It can be very hard and sometimes somebody can want to kill someone else. But Darrel runs the business with me and I couldn't do it without him, so he'll say, "You just go to bed. Put the baby to bed. You go on and I'll sort that out." And that's heaven to me. He's brilliant.

GB: Okay. Now, I was thinking, when the breakthrough did come, after all those years and so on, it certainly came at a fair old rush. I'm thinking of *Later with Jools*, your performance at the Grammys, spots on *The Late Late Show* and then duets with Bono and Jeff Beck and Lou Reed. Did any of that go to your head?

IM: No. No, how could it? You're just meeting people. Everybody is just a person. Well, certainly my family would slap me down if it did, and certainly the area where I'm from, the Liberties, they wouldn't take any of that. So, no.

GB: I'm thinking that, in the week that Lou Reed died, another great talent ruined by addiction and drugs and all of that, and you're in the middle of that kind of world now, and yet you've remained stable and sane. And so has the band, and so has Darrel. Why do you think that is?

IM: I know exactly why that is.

GB: Yes?

IM: There's a few reasons. One, there's my family, the way I was brought up, you know. I've had a great, solid, happy upbringing. Secondly, my husband being with me on the road. He's my rock, absolutely my rock. I couldn't do it without him. Thirdly, that things happened when I was older. I made all the mistakes I wanted with nobody watching, so, musically speaking, you know, you could write a rubbish song, but there'd be only ten people in the audience, so it didn't matter. [Laughs.] Fourthly, I have a great band and we're good friends. And, fifth, I have very strong faith. You see, I always have my cross on me, miraculous medals and all, and if I have any worries I can … [taps her medals] They say I have a direct line.

GB: Because that brings me precisely to the next [point] . . . What is talent, Imelda, as far as you're concerned? Where does it come from?

IM: It comes from your heart and your soul. Passion: talent is passion, I think. It's all linked. I have a belief that everybody has something that they're really, really good at. And it's a question of finding out what that is. So, if you don't feel that you have a talent that you're really good at, you just haven't found it yet. And I'd like to instil that in my daughter — that she has to find that — and I'm sure I must have got that from my parents, that I think everybody is really good at *something*.

GB: And is there any sense that you have that this is a gift from God to you?

IM: I heard somebody say, once, to me that your talent is a gift from God, and what you do with it is your way of paying him back. So, I like that. So I do think talent is a gift from God. It's like the hundreds and thousands on top of life: it can make life colourful and interesting and sweet, you know?

GB: Come back to God. What is your image of God?

IM: I know it's a man. I know that. Just ask any woman about labour and they'll tell you that no woman would do that to another woman. [Laughs.]

GB: It was that bad, was it?

IM: Oh, God, yeah. And my religion came out then too.

GB: Yes?

IM: I was like a holy nut in there. I was screaming, "Jesus, Mary and Joseph! Somebody help me . . ."

GB: Oh dear.

IM: It was a tough forty-two hours. It was tough!

GB: Does that mean we are not going again under any circumstances?

IM: No, I will. Isn't that mad? But they promised me it wouldn't be as bad, because they know my history now, that I had a tough time. She wouldn't come out. She got stuck . . .

GB: God love you.

IM: Yeah, I thought I was on my way out, actually.

GB: And what do you think happens when you die?

IM: Well, I'd love to think that you meet everybody that you've missed. Wouldn't that be nice? I'd like to think that you get peace and calm and a bit of fun. I hope it's not dull, whichever end you go. But I do think you have to meet your maker at the end and maybe say a few sorrys and grovel a little bit, and then maybe meet everybody that you've missed. That's what I'd love to think.

GB: So your image of God, when you were in labour and praying and crying . . .
IM: It's a man.

GB: . . . what were you aiming your prayers at?
IM: I don't have a visual image, but I do have a very strong connection. I'll try to go to Mass . . . When I'm travelling it's not so easy. I do try and go to church. But mostly, I thank him for day-to-day things: that I'm healthy, that my family's healthy and that we're all doing well. So, I do have a very strong faith. Most of my friends don't. But it's funny that I get a lot of them come to me when something's wrong with them, and they'll ask me, "Would you say a few prayers for such and such?" And I like that I can do that for other people.

GB: And Darrel, is he a believer?
IM: Yeah. Yeah, he is, but he wouldn't go to Mass like the way I would. I very much believe in "each to their own." You know, you often get people who do believe in God, [who] can be a bit smug with those who don't, thinking that they know, and vice versa. I've had friends of mine who think they're very intelligent, that definitely God doesn't exist and only people who are a little bit backwards must believe in God. I don't sit on either of those sides. I do believe it could be a very lonely existence if you think there's nobody there, so I'm happy that what I have works for me.

GB: Now, the last two years have been comparatively quiet, because of the arrival of one Violet Kathleen . . .
IM: Yeah.

GB: I presume she has taken over the universe?
IM: Yeah. Yeah, she's the boss. Everybody called me Boss, and now they're all calling her Boss instead. Yeah, she runs the show, big time.

GB: And how would you say that motherhood has changed you?
IM: I don't know. I feel like the same person, but the love that you feel for a child is overwhelming — for my child, obviously. The love that I feel for her is just, yeah, all-consuming. And my whole priority is her.

And I feel so protective of her all the time, and everything is to make sure she is okay. And Darrel's the same. We're just mad about her.

GB: And may we assume that Violet will be brought up in the same faith?
IM: Yeah, I'll do my best to. I won't force it on her. I'll do my best to give her the best grounding that I had. I'll be telling her all about guardian angels and about God and Jesus, and I'll tell her all of that. You know, I do believe in the Bible. I think of the Church — obviously there's been a lot of troubles with it recently. I think there's an awful lot of great people within the Church still that must be having a horrendous time . . . say, priests and nuns that I've met that are really good people. I know they've had a tough time. And I wouldn't like to see them tarred with the same brush as the evil people that should be dealt with. So, yeah, my faith is very strong, and I will bring Violet up with, hopefully, a strong faith that she can lean on, when she needs it. And then if she doesn't want it any more, that's her choice, absolutely her choice.

GB: I promise you, this is the last thing, and it's always the last question on our programme, and that is: When the day comes — which I think and believe is a far distant future — but when you finally pop your clogs and you're up there at the Pearly Gates . . . You meet God, Imelda . . .
IM: Yes.

GB: What will Imelda May say to God?
IM: "Howya . . . ?" [Laughs.]

GB: We need a bit more than that . . . and so will God, I promise you.
IM: "I'm home!" No, I don't know. It depends on who you meet.

GB: It's God.
IM: No, I know it's God, but it depends on how he is. Like, you hope to think that he's very personable, do you know what I mean? [Laughter.] I'd say, "Thanks very much."

GB: For what?
IM: "For letting me be born, letting me born into the family that I was born into, for my health, mostly, for meeting a great husband, for having a healthy baby, for letting me find my talent and letting me learn from my mistakes without being too harsh on me. Thanks very much for a great life."

GB: Perfect.
IM: [Laughs.] Thank you.

PETER McVERRY

A Man for Others

Some believe life is shaped by accidents. Certainly, when the brilliant young Jesuit and academic chemist Peter McVerry happened upon a homeless nine-year-old child on the streets of Dublin one day in the early 1970s, he hadn't a notion in his head about devoting his life to the service of the poor.

Of course, another theory is that life is shaped by the way people respond to accidents. You see, other people had presumably noticed the same homeless nine-year-old that day but didn't drop everything and take him in.

Peter McVerry may not have been expecting the encounter, but he was ready for it. He did what was needed for that child, and for countless others subsequently, because of his very muscular understanding of what Christianity really means: "To be a follower of Jesus you have to proclaim a God of compassion, by being the compassion of God." It reminds me of the old Jewish maxim "First do, then believe," which itself rests on the principle that good actions are more likely to inspire faith than faith is to inspire good actions.

The awful thing is that it's impossible, these days, to write a sentence about a priest taking in a nine-year-old without feeling a shudder of unease. Well-founded unease in some cases, of course, which is why Peter's natural instinct to "suffer the little children to come unto him" would now make him vulnerable to suspicion, or worse, if we didn't all know him better. Fortunately, like the great majority of our priests and religious, Peter McVerry has long since earned his trust.

Few now would have any qualms about him, except possibly some of his Jesuit compadres, for whom his relentless self-sacrifice, not to mention his leftist pot-shots at elitist education, must occasionally be a thorn in the side. No one, however, begrudged him his Freedom of the City of Dublin in the spring of 2014, least of all the man who shared his limelight that day, BOD Almighty. The irony is that this was probably the only time you will ever see Peter in a Mansion House.

Although Father McVerry is never preachy, he is an exceptional preacher. If asked, and only if asked, he will explain with astonishing lucidity what the "Society of Jesus" is really about for him: it's not just a religious order but a model for society. Just imagine a whole society of Jesuses, top to bottom: Jesus the needy; Jesus responding to the needy. That, to him, is what Christ was on about with all that "Whatever you do for the least of my brothers . . ." stuff. And "Thy kingdom come" was not so much a vision of the next life as a challenge for this one. We already know what God's kingdom looks like. We just have to build it, here and now.

Peter's eloquence, coupled with his unfaltering willingness to walk the walk, is enough to make you think there might just be something in this Christianity thing after all. As that other famous Jesuit, Jorge Bergoglio, is currently discovering, humility, humanity and humour — "the three hums" — can be very persuasive tools of evangelism. Except our Peter got there first.

And on this rock . . .

⁓

GB: Now, what is most immediately striking about you, Peter, is that, whereas most of us are perfectly familiar with the biblical exhortation to mind the poor, visit the sick and treat every man as your brother and sister and all of that, very few of us live up to that ideal. You do. And I'm going to read what somebody wrote about you during the week, knowing that I was going to be talking to you. You live in a shared, spartan flat in Ballymun. You own next to nothing. You work fifteen hours a day, every day, without a holiday, amongst people who most of us would see as. society's hopeless cases. In other words, not only do you talk the talk, you walk the walk. And that makes you very different from the rest of us. What is that difference, Peter?

PMV: Well, I think I've just been very lucky and very blessed to be able to do this. I got involved quite by accident. I started off in the inner city in the 1970s, and we came across one young lad, a nine-year-old kid sleeping on the street. So, we decided we'd better open a little hostel. So, we opened a hostel for him and a couple of other kids who were in the same situation. It was not my intention to spend my life working with homeless people at that stage. But one thing just led to another. And I look back and say, "Gosh, I've spent nearly forty years working with homeless people. What a surprise." [Laughs.]

GB: Father Peter McVerry of the Society of Jesus . . . I normally wouldn't ask this question until later on in interviews, but, now that it occurs to me, what is, or was, Jesus to you, Peter?

PMV: What he is to me now is very different to what he was to me thirty or forty years ago. The dominant spirituality which I inherited was that Jesus came to give us moral laws, to lay down the laws by which we were to live our lives according to God's plan, and if we obeyed those laws, then we would be rewarded with a place in Heaven. I don't believe that's Jesus' mission. That doesn't appeal to me at all. And it doesn't make sense to me in relation to Jesus' life and, particularly, to his death.

For me, now, Jesus came into a people, the people of God, who were extremely oppressed. Most of them were very poor, and many of them were ostracised by their community and by their religious leaders, because they were failing to obey the law of God. This was not God's dream for the people of God, and so Jesus came, it seems to me, to create a community, to reach out to everybody, to ensure that everybody's needs were met, to ensure that people could live a proper, dignified human life and to ensure that nobody was rejected, unwanted or marginalised. So, for me, the mission of Jesus now is about creating the Kingdom of God on Earth, which has to resemble and reflect the Kingdom of God in Heaven.

GB: Was he divine? Was he the Son of God?

PMV: He was the Son of God, but in a metaphorical sort of way. We're using human metaphors and concepts to try and understand God, who cannot, obviously, be understood in human metaphors and concepts. Jesus was the Son of God, but he's not the Son of God in the same way that I am the son of my father. But he is the reflection of God on our Earth.

GB: That's not strictly what we were taught in the Catechism as young people.

PMV: I read the Gospels now in a very different way to the way in which I read the Gospels even twenty or twenty-five years ago. So, for me, Jesus was about *this* world, not the world to come. You know, when Jesus was going around in his public ministry, thousands of people followed him. They spent the whole day listening to him. Clearly, what Jesus was saying was not irrelevant to them. And today the Church's message, which is supposed to be the continuation of the message of Jesus, is seen as so irrelevant to so many people. Instead of thousands of people following Jesus to listen to him, thousands of people today, particularly the young, are walking away.

GB: And whose fault is that?

PMV: I think it's the Church's fault, because I think we have emphasised a Kingdom of God in Heaven — that our aim here is to obey God's commandments and we'd be rewarded with a place in Heaven. The Church has become identified, and identifies itself, as a Church of Services, whereas I think the vision of Jesus was that the Church would be a Church of *Service* — a Church that reaches out to people in need and includes them within the Christian community.

I mean, I'm very disappointed in the Church and, indeed, very angry with the Church, because I think the Church has so much to offer: the vision of Jesus to build a better world. I mean, every single human being is a child of God, loved by God with an infinite and an unconditional love, and I imagine God looking down at our world, and you have one billion people living on the edge of destitution. Every one of them is God's beloved child. How does God sleep easily [laughs] in a situation like that? The Church is about creating a community. When I talk in parishes I say, "Imagine if, in this parish, there was nobody hungry, nobody homeless, nobody lonely and not being visited, nobody in hospital who wasn't being visited, nobody bereaved who wasn't getting the support of the whole community. And in this community everybody felt respected and valued and loved. Wouldn't that parish be the Kingdom of God on Earth?" And I say, "'Course it would. And that's Jesus' dream for our world."

GB: And do you think there's a glimmer of that now in the new Pope, Pope Francis, that he's talking along the right lines, at least?

PMV: I'm very encouraged by what he's saying, very much so, yes. He's trying to get rid of all this pomposity and bureaucracy within the Vatican, which — I have always said it — that the biggest obstacle to the promotion of faith in Jesus Christ today is the institutional Church. What the Church is focusing on is laws and rules and regulations and obeying those rules, and if you don't obey them, then you're going to be excluded. That's not the Jesus I read about in the Gospels, and I think Francis is pointing us in a different direction.

GB: Now, most people would see the Jesuits as being the educators of the reasonably well-off, posh people, so are you seen as a thorn in the side, in any way, of your colleagues in the Society?

PMV: No, I wouldn't be at all. They know I'm opposed to private education, but they accept that.

GB: So there's a little bit of "Ah, sure that's Peter, don't mind him, he's grand."

PMV: No, I think the attitude would be "Look, we are delighted you're doing what you're doing, but glad *you're* doing it, and not me." [Laughter.]

GB: Wonderful! Mind you, you did benefit from that whole thing yourself, since you were educated at Clongowes. Insofar as they turned out that character, "a man for others" in the Jesuit orthodoxy, they didn't do a bad job . . .

PMV: Well, I got a good education there, but my involvement in what I'm doing now had nothing to do with my education at Clongowes.

GB: Nothing?

PMV: No. I would have been a very mainstream Jesuit until the day I went to live in Summerhill, in the inner city. And that totally and radically changed me. I hadn't got a clue about the world. I mean, I grew up in a very comfortable world. When I went to Summerhill, first of all I was absolutely shocked. I had no idea that people lived in those conditions. And what shocked me even more than the conditions that people lived in was the fact that I had been living in Dublin for so many years and I hadn't even been aware that people lived in conditions like that. So, yeah, I was very naïve, and my understanding of God was very naïve.

GB: Okay, hold on to that thought for a moment. I want to go back to your parents. I know your mother was a Welsh nurse, a convert to Catholicism, and your father a GP from Belfast and Newry, so you were reasonably well off, shall we say?

PMV: We were very well off.

GB: Was it a fiercely Catholic household? I'm thinking of the ardour of the convert.

PMV: Yes, my mother, like many converts, became more Catholic than the Catholics themselves. So, Mass on Sunday was a must. The family Rosary in the evening time was a must.

GB: And did you get your work ethic from them as well?

PMV: I did, yes. My father was a GP. And I remember the phone constantly going at night-time, and sometimes going twice in the night, and my father would get up and he'd go off to see his patients, and I never heard him complain. So I think I got a sense of commitment to others and a sense of wanting to be of service to others from my father, and I got my faith more from my mother.

GB: Now, you're going from this interview, I know, into the church in Gardiner Street to say your usual Wednesday lunchtime Mass. Do you say Mass every day?

PMV: No, not every day. I say Mass every Sunday, up in Wheatfield Prison. That's my regular. But I don't say Mass every day. I don't see it as a private devotion.

GB: And, as far as you're concerned, what do you do at Mass?

PMV: My understanding of Mass, again, has changed very radically over the years. The understanding of Mass that I grew up with was that you went to Mass in order to worship God, present on the altar in the form of bread and wine, so it was an act of worship. Now, I understand the Eucharist very differently. At the Consecration, the priest repeats the words of Jesus: "This is my body, which will be given up for you. And this is my blood, which will be poured out for you." And at the Last Supper, he invited the Apostles to follow him.

So, for me, celebrating the Eucharist, I remember, first of all, how this community that I belong to, the Christian community, started. It started through the total self-sacrifice of Jesus on the cross. He gave up everything for us, including what was most precious to him, his own life.

So, I go, first of all, at the Consecration, to remember that; and, secondly, to commit myself to following him in his total self-sacrifice. When I go out of the church, I have to give myself, my body and my blood, for the sake of my brothers and sisters, just as Jesus did for me.

GB: That leads me on to the thought: would it be possible for you to do the work you're doing if you were not a priest? You're free of family commitments, you're free of professional aspirations and ambitions, you're free of all of those things. That's what the priesthood does for you . . .

PMV: It's what the priesthood *can* do for you, yes.

GB: *Can* do?

PMV: I would see my vows as freeing me to do things that I might otherwise not want to do. So I'd see my vow of poverty as allowing me to go places and do things that I wouldn't want to do, maybe, if I had wealth. If I had a big BMW car I don't think I'd be living in Ballymun. I'd be looking out the window every night to see if it was still there.

GB: And were you ever perturbed by thoughts of women and marriage and children and all of that?

PMV: Yeah, of course, yeah. I mean, obviously, the desire to have children and to see your children growing up . . . But, as I say, it was for me a decision: if I had children, I couldn't do the work that I'm doing now in the way that I'm doing it now. When I joined the Jesuits, you had to be celibate, so it wasn't any big decision for me. You just went along with it. But now, I understand why I *had* to be celibate: to free me to do what I'm doing. And I'd have to say I haven't regretted a moment of it. I've never, even for a moment, considered leaving the Jesuits.

GB: And was there a *eureka* moment that you realised that, in order to make Christianity work for you, you had to get down and dirty, as it were, amongst the people around this area?

PMV: No, there was no *eureka* moment. It was actually they who converted me. It was the people I was working with who challenged me, first of all — challenged my values, challenged my faith, made me ask myself, "What is this Christian faith that I have committed myself to?" They've changed my whole relationship with God. I grew up thinking God was a judge, God was up there looking down, writing down all the things you were doing wrong, and eventually, some day, you go before God. I don't believe in that God any more. I don't believe in a God who judges us. I believe in a God who forgives us. God's forgiveness is greater than our sinfulness.

GB: What about the bad lads, Peter, the awful people of the world who do dreadful things to other people? What happens? Is there a come-uppance?

PMV: One of the things I have learned from working with young people is never to judge *anybody*, because I've seen the horrific circumstances that some of the young people that I'm working with have grown up in. I've seen the violence, the abuse, the sheer neglect — a young person, just a few weeks ago, telling me, at thirteen years of age, he used to sit in the kitchen watching both his parents injecting heroin. If I were to judge one of those young people and say, you know, "There's a little junkie robber, there's a scumbag," I'm actually judging myself, because I know, if I had been born into their circumstances, I would be exactly the same as them. And if they'd been born into my circumstances, they would be the priest coming up to visit me in prison.

GB: Many people would say that in running this free-and-easy, non-judgemental kind of life, that you are actually indulging these people, to a great extent, to continue in their ways.

PMV: Well, everybody else is judgemental, so there's no point in me adding my little judgemental bit. I don't think we're allowing them to continue in that lifestyle. We're certainly offering them opportunities and encouraging them, but we will be there for them, whatever.

GB: Speak to me about hope and hopelessness. Many of the people that you're dealing with would be totally hopeless and you will fail with many of them, no matter how much work you put into it. What gives you hope and what keeps you going?

PMV: What keeps me going are the people I'm working with. The little you can do for some people means an awful lot to them. And what they have taught me is what the hardest part of being homeless is. It's not not having a bed for the night. The hardest part of being homeless is living 24/7 with the knowledge that you are considered to be of no value, or that society really doesn't want anything do to with you — they would much prefer it if you disappeared.

Yeah, we give people accommodation. We can give them drug treatment. We can give them counselling. But what we're really trying to do is to give them the message that they're just as important and just as valuable as anybody else. And if we weren't giving them that message we may as well pack up and go home, because the rest isn't worth it. It's the relationship they remember and value most — a relationship in which they felt cared for, in which they felt important and in which they weren't being judged and condemned. And we can do that for homeless people and it doesn't actually even cost money to do that.

GB: And when you speak of social equality and equality of opportunity and social justice, do you really believe in those things, Peter?

PMV: Do I believe they're going to happen? No! [Laughs.] No, certainly not for a long, long time. But I believe that's what we should be striving for. You know, in 1996, when the Celtic Tiger was just beginning, we had two-and-a-half thousand homeless people in Ireland. In 2008, when the Celtic Tiger was just finishing, we had five thousand homeless people in Ireland. During those years, when we had more money than we knew what to do with, the number of homeless people doubled. I mean, that's a disgrace. €100 million would solve the homeless problem in Ireland. So it's a question of values. What is it we really value? Because where we put our money reflects our values. During the Celtic Tiger years, if I had asked the Government for €64 million to solve the homeless problem, they would have laughed at me and said, "We haven't got €64 million." Then the recession came, and the banks asked the Government for €64 *billion* and the Government said, "Here you are. 'Course. You need it; we'll get it." [Laughter.] The banks *had* to be bailed out; homeless people don't have to be housed. And that's the difference.

GB: Does that make you despair?

PMV: It makes me angry. We could solve the homeless problem if we really wanted to, but we don't really want to.

GB: For centuries, as you know, the poor have been consoled, fobbed off, with the idea that everything will be righted in the next world, that the poor will be elevated and the rich and wealthy and powerful will be put down. Is that any part of your message to your people?

PMV: None whatsoever. The pie in the sky, "Everything will be all right in Heaven," is not part of my religious belief. That is where the Church has really gone wrong: it has focused our eyes on Heaven. And the religion that is given to people is actually a very self-centred religion. It's about me — me wanting to get to Heaven. What do I have to do to get to Heaven? God's dream for our world is a dream where everybody can live a proper, dignified human life as a child of God and the Church's mission is to make that a reality.

GB: So, then, the age-old question: why does God allow these terrible things to happen? Why are there homeless? Why does he not put a stop to it? And why doesn't he intervene?

PMV: God does intervene. Why does God allow them to happen? God *doesn't* allow them to happen: people allow them to happen. We create the problems of homelessness and poverty, we human beings. God is the source of love. God is pained and God suffers. And God intervenes, but God intervenes through us, and that's what the Christian community was supposed to be about: God's intervention in our world to create a better world, through self-sacrifice — *not* pursuing my own wealth, *not* pursuing my own comforts, *not* having a good life for myself, but sharing everything I have.

GB: Well, riddle me this, going back to Jesus again: he came on Earth, and he suffered and died to save us. To save us from what . . . ?

PMV: Why did Jesus suffer and die? That's the question.

GB: We were constantly told that he came to save us from Original Sin. I remember a *blitzkrieg* mounted against me when, once, I said I hadn't done anything wrong. Why was he dying for me . . . ? To save me from what?

PMV: I don't know what Original Sin means. It means nothing to me.

GB: Nothing.

PMV: Jesus came to save us in the sense that he came to tell us how to live together and, in that way, save us. For me, Jesus was crucified because he presented a new way of life that challenged the power and the wealth of those who were benefiting from the old way of life. And, in doing that, Jesus proclaimed a different God. The religious authorities at the time of Jesus proclaimed a God of the law. Jesus broke the law, and he proclaimed a God of compassion. So, to be a follower of Jesus, you had to proclaim a God of compassion, by being the compassion of God.

The poor and the homeless offer us the greatest gift that anybody can offer us: they invite us to open our hearts, to include them in our love. And if we expand our hearts to include the poor and the suffering and the homeless, then we become more loving persons, and therefore we become more fully human, and therefore we become more fully divine.

GB: Do you pray, Peter? You do, of course.

PMV: I do pray. Not enough, but I do pray.

GB: What is the manner of your praying? And how do you pray and when do you pray, and why and what for?

PMV: My prayer is very simple. I just sit in a chair and say, "Thanks." I feel I have been blessed in life. I've been given a good family. I've been given a good education. I've been given good opportunities in life. I've been given good health. I've had a very, very happy life — wouldn't want it to have been any different, and that has all been a gift given to me by God.

GB: And in the documentary which was made about you, you said the work satisfaction is fantastic.

PMV: 'Tis. I just feel I'm making a difference. The meaning of life is either about yourself and having a good time and building up your assets or it's about other people. We're here to make the world a better place than when we came into it. We're here to try and reduce some of the suffering that exists in people's lives. And I feel I'm achieving that in a small way, in working with homeless people, and so the job satisfaction is great.

GB: And insofar as you might think of taking a holiday, have you any idea what that holiday would be?

PMV: Yeah, I used to go on holiday. I mean, for a long time I didn't, because we never had any money, and I just couldn't get away. And then, as the organisation developed, and we began to get state funding, it allowed me to get away.

GB: What did you do?

PMV: I went as far away as possible! I loved going to Asia.

GB: Asia.

PMV: The first time I went to Asia it was to go and do a Buddhist retreat, which I really loved. Something about Buddhism attracted me and still does attract me: its tolerance for everybody, its respect for life, its focus on simplicity of lifestyle. I think we have just so much. The monks that I met in the Buddhist monastery out there live such an austere life, and they didn't even believe in an afterlife! [Laughter.] They believed in reincarnation.

GB: So, you do believe in an afterlife?

PMV: Oh, I do believe in an afterlife, but the one thing I believe about the afterlife is that there's no point in trying to imagine what the after-life is going to be like, because it's going to be totally different from anything we could ever possibly imagine.

GB: Suppose it's all true, all the Catechism which we were taught, and you get to the Pearly Gates, and there He is. What will you say to God?

PMV: I have a question for God and the question will be: "If it was so important for us to believe in you, why did you make it so bloody difficult? I mean, half the world doesn't believe in you, and the other half that does believe in you have all sorts of different thoughts about you."

And I think God's answer will be: "I didn't want you worrying about me and whether I exist and what sort of God I am. I wanted you worrying about my children down on Earth." And indeed, all religions have that emphasis on *love one another*. I think that's what God is interested in and I think that's what God will say to me when I put that question to him.

|MARY ROBINSON

And Here's to You, Mrs Robinson

I'm going to let you in on a secret. Our esteemed former President — the first woman to be elected to Áras an Uachtaráin — has a reputation for being slightly cool and aloof, with little of the banter and mucking-in informality that so endeared her successor to the public. Do you know what it is, though? I have realised she is simply shy. Her formidable brain and education may have carried her to the highest office in the land and, subsequently, on to the international stage. But no one teaches you how to feel at ease in a room with strangers or how to make small talk. And it doesn't come naturally to everyone.

Mary Robinson is much better at big talk than small. These days she is one of the Elders, a high-powered international club of elder statesmen and women convened by Nelson Mandela and bankrolled by Richard Branson, which tours the world addressing political leaders about the best way of solving humanity's many challenges. Give her a stage at the UN and she will wow you with her eloquence and her mastery of complex issues of law or human rights or the environment.

To me, though, the question is always "So what?" What difference do all those speeches make? Has any despot ever thrown open his gaols and torture chambers, because of the rhetoric of a speech on New York's Upper West Side? Has even one factory cut its emissions, or one airline — including Sir Richard's — reduced its flights, because of a conference on climate change? "Fine words", as the saying goes, "butter no parsnips," and so, by extension, I would guess, they also feed few hungry families, lighten few carbon footprints and stop few wars.

And yet when Mary Robinson sits down opposite you it is very hard not to be impressed, not only by her intellect but by the steadiness of her gaze and her unflinching honesty. I wanted to find out what makes her tick. What are the beliefs and values that fuel her formidable moral engine? Very graciously, on a snowy day in December 2009, she was willing to answer any question I cared to ask.

༄

GB: Take me back to Ballina and describe for me the Bourke household when you were a little girl.

MR: [Laughs.] It was a happy and busy household, because my father was a beloved doctor in the town. My mother was also a doctor, but when five of us came in quick succession and my grandfather was living alone and not in good health, she devoted herself to family and activities in the town. She was very fulfilled. It was interesting for me that, although she gave up her professional life, she felt that her life was very full and very meaningful. And, as I say, it was a busy house, because my father's surgery was in the house and I think a lot of my human rights I learned from the way my father had so much time for people.

GB: And religion in the household?

MR: Very much so, yes. It was a very religious household. My grandfather and grandmother were extremely religious, daily Mass-goers, and the cathedral was just across the road from our home.

GB: Would you say it was forced upon you or you just fell into it . . . ?

MR: Born into it and grew up into it and there wasn't any question.

GB: In the hierarchy of small towns — parish priest, doctor, local TD, dentist, midwife, da, da, da — you were pretty near the top of a hierarchy . . .

MR: Yes, I think so.

GB: Did you feel that?

MR: To a certain extent. I think there was a certain class element, whatever you call it.

GB: And at what stages did you become aware of that?

MR: I think more when I was in Mount Anville, because when I went to boarding school in Mount Anville, there was a day school, and we never connected.

GB: And were they lesser folk?

MR: In an implicit way. And it was very strange.

GB: What about finishing school in Paris? Coming from Ballina and going to finishing school in Paris, that must have been something special?

MR: Well, it was very interesting, because I was seventeen at the time, and I landed in Paris on my own and went to the Foyer de Sacré-Cœur, which was the residence, run by Sacred Heart nuns, that I was staying in.

We had very good teachers, because they came from the Sorbonne, and we had terrific courses in history of art, literature, philosophy, and it was an education beyond belief. And by the time I finished that year I was actually dreaming in French. I'd really immersed myself in the culture.

GB: Were you ever thinking about entering the convent?

MR: I was indeed, yes. In my last year in Mount Anville I was quite determined to be a nun. Both my father's sisters were nuns, one in India, Sister Ivy, and she had been writing letters back to my father that had a big impact on me. She went from the elite Sacred Heart, after Vatican II, to the poorest of the poor, and I thought it was a much better life for me. I was very influenced by the idealism of Christianity and of the Catholic faith.

GB: But you weren't *recruited*, particularly?

MR: No, no, on the contrary: I was *un*-recruited. I was told, "Mary, we're very happy to know that you are thinking about it. I know you're going to France. Go to France and if you're still of the same mind, come and see me when you come back."

GB: And was she right?

MR: She was right.

GB: You came back and it had gone?

MR: No, no. Well, I think being in France also had an impact.

GB: At what stage, then, did you decide that you wanted to do law rather than medicine?

MR: I never thought of doing medicine, although I greatly admired what my father was doing. I was influenced by my grandfather at an early age. I had a special relationship with him, probably because I was the only granddaughter. And we had conversations about law, about life . . . and books would come — he was a great reader — and I just loved these conversations. He explained to me about the cases he had taken — usually the small guy against the landlord or whatever — and so law was a natural way to learn how we could change the system — a kind of inner sense of justice.

GB: So, you decided to go to university then, at some stage, obviously? Trinity. A brave step then. In Dublin, we had to get special permission from John Charles to go to Trinity. Otherwise it was a mortal sin.

MR: Oh, from Mayo you had to, too.

GB: And at what stage did you begin to waver from your Catholic faith?

MR: I'm not sure that I would describe it as wavering so much as, during that year in France, when I had the opportunity to study the philosophers, I had a much broader sense of the world, basically, than I'd had growing up in Ireland and Irish convent school. I went from being deeply religious and horrified to be offered a glass of wine to being extraordinarily interested in the questions of the philosophers and all of that — very deeply engaged in a journey that I think I'm still on, a journey that didn't take me away altogether, but, certainly, within that, I began to see more and more problems with the Catholic Church in particular. The treatment of women within the Catholic Church — that was becoming very self-evident.

When I became Auditor of the Law Society in Trinity, I chose to do my inaugural address on law and morality in Ireland. I said that we should legalise contraceptives and the contraceptive pill, that we should have divorce in Ireland, that we should legalise homosexuality. And that was all in 1967. That area of space was one where the Catholic Church was intruding in a way that I was conscious was, again, not, to me, the appropriate balance. There was a realm of private conscience where people should be enabled to take their own decisions.

GB: How did your parents cope when you started your various campaigns? Contraception, for example. What was the reaction in Ballina?

MR: My parents were deeply affected and hurt by the fact that I was promoting a change in the law in an area that deeply troubled them, even though they were both doctors. They were so paid-up, in a Catholic sense, that they didn't really want to think the law through. They wanted to uphold the teaching of the Catholic Church, and at the same time they loved me deeply. They were terribly affected when the Bishop in Ballina, from the pulpit, said this was not appropriate etc.

GB: And did he name you, the Bishop?

MR: Yes . . . Well, I mean, it was clear.

GB: Everybody knew.

MR: Everybody knew. Yeah. I'm not sure that he named me, but everybody knew. I wasn't there. [Laughs.]

GB: And then did you suffer vilification because of that . . . ?

MR: Well, during that period I became vilified as Senator Mary Bourke, and I was quite taken aback. I was very troubled by it. I was getting hate letters, you know, awful letters, and then signed "A Catholic priest", and garden gloves cut up and sent in the post — this sort of thing. And Nick and myself were planning to marry at the end of 1970, and Nick realised that I was being affected, and he actually burnt a lot of the letters, which is a shame . . .

GB: Unseen, you mean?

MR: No, no. Well, seen by me, but unseen by anybody else. And then Nick and myself got married, and I took his name because we'd had to fight to get married. And I laughed, because, I said, "Now, I'm no longer vilified. I'm no longer Senator Mary Bourke." But, of course, the tag carried forward to Senator Mary Robinson.

GB: Now, go back to Nick and the marriage. More trouble, on account of he was Church of Ireland and you were Catholic, in Ballina . . . and your parents . . . ?

MR: No, I don't think that was actually the key at all . . .

GB: Oh . . .

MR: . . . because my parents were actually very broad-minded in that sense. They had lots of Protestant friends. It was much more, I think, that my parents were engaged in what I would call "over-love." You know, I was the only daughter, I had done very well at school, very well at university, I was a senator, I was a professor — nobody was good enough. And I was a contemporary of Nick's — we were in college together, in law — so they knew that Nick was a friend and they knew that Nick had lots of girlfriends. I mean, he got a first-class honours in his first year, and then he started to do posters of political cartoons and graduated with a third — not the profile that my parents felt was right for me. And I waited for a while to see if I could convince them, and the more I waited, the less convinced they were. They thought they could stop me. So, I thought, "Right, we have to go ahead with this."

Thirty-nine plus years later, I made the right decision. And it was painful at the time that my parents and, in fact, none of my family came, except one first cousin. But, in fact, my father had a terrific relationship with Nick, and my mother was still alive when our first child, Tessa, was born and, obviously, called after her.

GB: And so everybody in the end said, "What was all that about?"

MR: In a sense, absolutely, yeah. And within less than three months after the marriage.

GB: And what effect did that have on you, all of that . . . ?

MR: I think, in particular, the decision to go ahead with the marriage and not have my family there was a very tough one and a very important one. And also when I took the name Robinson, because some of my contemporaries *weren't* taking the name. I took the name very much. And, in a way, it's why "Mrs Robinson" means something to both Nick and myself, in a private sense. To take the name Robinson meant I was going down the voting from *B* to *R*. Remember how important that is in voting terms! But, actually, more than anything else, it was part of the bonding between us.

GB: Okay, come back now to the day someone told you that they wanted you to stand for President of Ireland. Was that an amazing moment . . . ?

MR: It was more of a life-changing day than I appreciated. And it happened to be Valentine's Day, which was interesting, the 14th February, 1990.

GB: I don't think you're a naturally gregarious person. In fact, I think you're rather shy, and glad-handing people and mixing with people mustn't have come easily for you?

MR: It didn't! And I had a cold sort of moment of wondering, "What is this going to do to Nick, to the family, etc.?" It was around about that time I realised an important thing: if I was in this to win, the Irish people were entitled to know who I was, in a way. That meant that I had to give more of myself. And I very deliberately took down some of the inner protections that were there and showed more of myself. And I realised that what I was doing was showing more of the mother in me — my mother — because she was like that — she was outward-looking, gregarious — and I was reflecting, "I'm more like her now." This is part of me that I've kept to the family. You know, humour, warmth, seeing the funny side sometimes. And the more I did that, the more I got back extraordinary response. And from then on I was in there to win and had a sense "This is do-able."

GB: But it strikes me that you would much rather have been an executive President?

MR: I'm not sure about that. No, I don't think so . . .

GB: You don't think so?

MR: . . . because an executive President would be political. I, essentially, like the moral voice. It's the legal-moral that interests me more than the political-executive.

I was extraordinarily aware of the importance of the office of President and that I had the opportunity to open it up in a particular way. I mean, at least, Charlie Haughey gave me the means to do it through a reasonable allowance, which has been increased greatly, much later.

GB: How did you get on with him, by the way?

MR: We had our differences, and he tried to bully me. Charlie Haughey tried to put me back in my box. He got a legal opinion that the President couldn't do all the things that I was doing, and he came to see me. And, of course, it's my field, so I talked about the constitutional law. Eventually, he flung the opinion on the ground in the room and said, "Ahhh! Lawyers! You know, you buy your lawyer and you get what you buy." We came out of the room, and I was the one smiling. [Laughter.]

GB: Were there things that you could have done, or would have done, or might have done, or should have done, when you were President that you didn't do and you now regret?

MR: The one thing I regret was the early resignation. It wasn't four months: it was 12th September, and the inauguration would have been on 3rd December, because that was when mine was. I didn't take a holiday, so, if you add that, I would have been entitled to about a month's holiday. It was about, at most, two months.

GB: You went straight into the other thing?

MR: I went straight in the same day, because I was getting a lot of pressure from Kofi Annan. The previous High Commissioner had resigned suddenly, just after I had decided not to have a second term. And then Kofi Annan took me into his study and said, "Mary, I need you."

And I said, "Well, you know, December is my date."

And he said, "No, I need you before that. When can you come? I need you for the General Assembly in September."

And I said, "All right, I'll come."

Now I know more about the UN — the UN is *always* in crisis! — I would definitely not have left. I feel that people got the impression I wanted out of the Presidency, into the bright lights. That was not the case.

GB: They took it as an insult?

MR: Yeah. And I actually would have loved to have done another three or four years as President. That was why it was so hard to take the decision. And that was my mistake.

GB: Is there any sense in you, Mary, of loss, giving up your religious beliefs, when you go back to when you were a girl in Ballina and in the school and wanted to be a nun and all of that? Is there any sense of losing an old friend in all of that?

MR: Not really, because I don't know that I've lost an old friend. I'm certainly on the outer fringes, if you like. I still have a very strong sense of spirituality. For me, God is love. There is more to life than the absence of belief in God. Some of the highest achievements of people have come from belief, and I used to explain to the children that we have an attic in our upper mind, and that's where we have our own personal beliefs and journey. And I have an attic in which I have that belief.

GB: But you wouldn't be a practising Catholic?

MR: Not in the sense of everyday practising, but I go to church. You know, I don't go of necessity, but I actually have not rejected the importance of religious belief. But it's very much with the freedom of not feeling any compulsion or any sense of sin.

GB: Do you pray?

MR: I do, but I do it in places that are very special to me, like the slipway on the lake of our home. And I have just very short, kind of spiritual encounters.

GB: Are you praying *to* anyone?

MR: Yes. I'm not quite sure what the entity I'm praying to is, and it's not a human entity, because God isn't a human entity. God is love.

GB: What image is in your mind then?

MR: I think it's an image of the meaning of life . . . of the spirituality that connects us. I still am seeking for truth. I am extremely at home with deeply spiritual people, some being very close friends of mine . . . and of different kinds of belief. I have an extraordinary sense of the Dalai Lama. I've met him quite a lot. I believe profoundly in the kind of way that he can live. But I'm not saying that I'm a Buddhist or anything. Also, when I'm in African countries and I meet these priests and nuns — because usually the Irish ambassador will hold a reception. It happened recently in Malawi and in Tanzania, and I met again, as I had met them when I was President, in African countries, these priests and nuns who have been thirty-five years, forty-two years . . . You just look into their faces and you know that they have an additional element in their life which is transcendent. It is their faith, and it is the fact that they live it. And I have never rejected that. I still aspire to the highest beliefs and morality of the Christian faith.

I'm very comfortable and indeed comforted by the cadences of a Mass, of the Christian religion, of the Gospels, and I always will be. It's deeply in my DNA. To me, the simple Gospel is a wonderful standard that we all can aspire to live up to.

GB: But what do you think Jesus was?

MR: I think Jesus was a God we haven't lived up to. [Laughs.]

GB: Do you think he was divine, as in "the Son of . . ."?

MR: Very possibly! He certainly is, to me, the highest form of what *we* can be.

GB: Does the Devil exist? Sorry, let me put that another way. When you would have been dealing with Mugabe and the chaps in Tiananmen Square who ordered that . . . ?

MR: Certainly, evil exists. There's no doubt about that, and I have had to confront that, and I have a sort of memory bank, an inch below my mind, so I can recall it very easily, of man's inhumanity — it's usually *man's* — to man, woman and child — usually woman and child. And that has been troubling, obviously.

GB: The Chinese Premier asked you at one stage, did he not, whether religion was a force for good. And you said, "Yes, it is."

MR: It was an extraordinary meeting. I was UN High Commissioner for Human Rights at the time, and because I was a former President I got access to their President, Jiang Zemin. I had been to Tibet; he had been to Tibet. And then, suddenly, through translation, he asked me a question, and then he broke into English, and he said, "I'm particularly interested in your answer." And I had to wait for the question to be translated. And the question was: "Given the advances in human science, I'd like to know, as High Commissioner, whether you believe that religion has any role in the modern world?"

And I said, "I very much agree about the advances in science. Look at the mapping of the human genome," which had just happened.

And he was nodding — as an engineer — nodding with satisfaction.

And I said, "But if you ask me, as High Commissioner, I believe that religion is, if anything, *more* important in the world today, not necessarily always for the good, but very *often* for the good."

And he did not like that answer.

The next time we met was after 9/11, and I reminded him this time of our conversation, and he immediately said, "But those who carried it out were not religious. They were in Germany. They were drinking. How come?" And it was very interesting. You know, it was a conversation that carried forward.

GB: Why did you reason that?

MR: That religion was important?

GB: Yes.

MR: Because it's very obviously so. If you're working in human rights you understand the extraordinary power for good — or not so good — of religions in the world. The Universal Declaration drew on those religions for the standards and the vision of the Declaration, and it's the spiritual adviser, it's the Church that is in the communities and is there always. So religion is extraordinarily important to human rights. But, unfortunately, many religions, from their origins, have subjugated women. It's a common thread in many of the religions.

Now, in my capacity as an Elder, as one of the Elders with Nelson Mandela, we engage together in how we might address the inequality between men and women in our world, because women in so many societies are seen as second-class citizens. We have decided that we must invite religious leaders to become champions of the full equality of women. And that will mean huge changes in the Churches over time, in the mosques, in many religions.

GB: As you say, you have your work cut out for you . . .

MR: Yeah.

GB: Is there any indication that anybody is listening to you about all of this?

MR: Funnily enough, when we put a strong statement about this on our website, as Elders, there was a flood of response, particularly from women's groups, saying, "Thank you. We need a moral leadership on this issue."

GB: Yes, but that's from women's groups . . . Is there anybody in the Churches, in the authority of the Church, listening to you and doing anything about it?

MR: Well, the strongest voice among the Elders pushing this was former

President Jimmy Carter, because he and his wife, Rosalynn, challenged their local Baptist church in Atlanta that it did not involve full equality, and they didn't get anywhere. So they left their church and went to a more progressive Baptist church. And so he feels extremely strongly about this. And Jimmy Carter, on behalf of the Elders, did a video for a recent meeting of the Parliament of the World's Religions in Melbourne, and I understand that that was much discussed and much talked about.

What we're seeing — and it's a very human rights issue — is the distortion of religion or cultural practice, based, very often, on religion and its harmful traditional practice. Usually *that* is used to subjugate women.

GB: We'll come back to the Elders in a moment and the United Nations . . . You know that the world is divided between those who think the United Nations is wonderful and well intentioned — brotherhood and sisterhood of man, and so on — and those who think it's a great big talking shop but it doesn't actually *accomplish* anything. What is your answer to that?

MR: I use what Winston Churchill said about democracy, that it's the worst system, except for all the others. It's the worst system, but we don't have another, and it is in constant reform. It very badly needs to be reformed.

GB: And who is fighting change?

MR: The sovereign countries, of course. And I fought this a little bit as High Commissioner. I always said that, as UN High Commissioner for Human Rights, I served the first three words of the Charter of the United Nations: "We the peoples . . ." Governments interpret their sovereignty as being somehow *their* possessive state sovereignty, whereas I believe it's the sovereignty of the people, and the governments serve the people. And if they are not serving the people, well, they are abusing that sovereignty. And that's why human rights doesn't stop at borders — the whole mandate of rapporteurs etc. to go in and look at what's happening in a country. But, still, when you have a Security Council with certain countries having vetoes, exercising constantly in a certain way, that distorts power.

GB: That gets back to who is listening to you in all the talk. And is this reluctance to change badness or just incompetence, or stupidity, or what?

MR: I think, when you have a body that represents 192 countries in very complex contexts, you've got to balance *all* the interests — the small islands and the Chinas and the United States. And that is not easy . . . And I worry that it's gone so complex it's hard now to get decisions. And we need global decisions, because they're often better for the poorest countries than bilateral, regional-power treaties.

GB: What do you think will happen when you die, Mary?
MR: I had the experience of watching my brother Aubrey die at the age of forty-one, of cancer, and that took away my fear of death. We were all with him at the end — his father, a doctor, watching his son, a doctor, dying. The last thing he did was to blow kisses to us, and he died with a smile.

Even more so, I was there when my father was dying — a deeply religious death, and he was waiting to go to where he wanted to go.

And so I have faced death. I almost died on a Soviet helicopter, as High Commissioner, coming out of Grozny. I was shot at, in Israel, when I was serving as High Commissioner. I fly a great deal. If death comes, death comes. So, I don't fear death at all, and if I can in some way be regrouped, as we are promised, with all of my beloved family, nothing will make me happier.

GB: When you were being shot at and about to die, what did you do?
MR: That's interesting. We went around the corner rapidly, and I telephoned my father. Nick wonders why, and I said, "Because he will be more distressed. You will cope better." [Laughs.] And that was troubling to Nick until I talked it through. I said, "If I had been able to have two conversations you were the next on the list. But I always felt you would cope better. *He* would be absolutely shattered and probably become ill and wouldn't be able to cope."

GB: One last question: suppose it's all true, Mary, all the stuff that you were taught in school and in your home, and you eventually get to meet him at the Pearly Gates — what would you say to him?
MR: First of all, I don't think that's going to worry me [laughs], and, secondly, I assume that it will be an extraordinary experience and, you know, "the beauty of the world hath made me sad, this beauty which must pass." God created this beauty. It can only be, obviously, a very interesting experience.

BRIAN CODY

The Quiet Man

When I was first asked to write this book, Kilkenny's all-conquering Manager, Brian Cody, was in hospital recovering from heart surgery. Typically, he had asked for no media intrusion and no fuss. He is a very private man in a very public role, but it seems that the less he says, the more people want to hear him.

Back at the start of 2011, the *Meaning of Life* team had sent him more than one interview request, but got no response. When he did finally answer, it became clear that this reticence was more out of bemusement than rudeness. He simply could not imagine why I would want to know his views on the meaning of life.

Brian's only condition for the interview was that it should happen in, or near, Kilkenny. He has moved no more than a dozen miles in his entire life from the community where he was born and if I wanted to talk to him, it was definitely going to be a home match. We met at the Mount Juliet estate.

Sportsmen and women are often quite dull interviewees. The single-mindedness which makes them excel in their chosen fields, not only on championship-match days but in the lonely week-in, week-out grind of training, leaves little room for wider reflection or experience. Brian Cody, however, has a hinterland beyond sport. He is not only a family man but a primary school principal – a true pillar of his community.

St Patrick's De La Salle is a Catholic boys' national school and it quickly became clear, while talking to Brian, that this matters to him, not because he's a Holy Joe evangelical, but because his own life – indeed, his success – is built on the rock-solid foundation of his Catholic beliefs and values.

He is no theologian. He doesn't claim to be. But he does believe what he teaches to the First Communion and Confirmation classes at St Patrick's BNS. As with the Cats hurlers he sends out on the field each week, I suspect the lessons he teaches those boys will stand them in good stead for life.

GB: I know I am talking to a Kilkenny man, born and reared. Tell me about your childhood.

BC: I come from a family of nine children: four boys, five girls. My father worked in insurance and my mother, as most women did at that time, looked after the house. She was a housewife. Very, very happy childhood. My parents were very straightforward, decent, good people who wanted the very best for their children at all times, and they ensured that all of us got a very good education.

GB: Your parents obviously were involved heavily with the GAA and the James Stephens Club. So there was really no option for you, was there, but to become involved in hurling?

BC: Well, I suppose there was, because I became more heavily involved than any of the rest of my brothers or sisters. I went to school in the local school, in Sheestown, and finished my education, when that closed, in St Patrick's De La Salle, where I teach and have taught from the day I graduated from college. And I went on from there to St Kieran's College. So my life has been wrapped up completely, I suppose, in that area, in that community and in that club.

GB: Go back to your parents. Was it a very religious household?

BC: Not dogmatically religious. My parents certainly were very religious people. Certainly, Mass was very important, and Confession would have been important as well, and prayer. They were not old-fashioned, in the strict sense of forcing stuff down your throat. But certainly the Sacred Heart lamp was there, and the holy water was inside the door. Very much an ordinary Catholic household.

GB: I have the image that, on long summer evenings, you'd be out there belting a ball around the place, doing something with a hurling stick . . .

BC: Absolutely, yeah. I mean, at the time there was lots of other families around the place, and we would meet up in the local field and we'd hurl, while it was bright. I spent a lot of time myself playing hurling against the wall and with my brothers. Something just caught me straight away and I loved it and I tried to develop as much as I could at it.

GB: Do you remember your first all-Ireland?

BC: I do, yeah. I played all-Ireland at minor level first, and under-21 and senior as well.

GB: You have the sport talent in spades, as they say. Do you think that was given to you — a God-given gift? Did you feel it necessary to nurture it and bring it on?

BC: I suppose it is God-given. We all have various talents, and you nurture that talent. But once you develop it and work at it and have a commitment to it, certainly then you can find out how good you can be at it. And I wanted to find out how good I could be at hurling, and I wanted to be as good as I possibly could be.

GB: Your friend Father Tom Murphy went on to the priesthood. Did you ever get the urge yourself?

BC: No. At St Kieran's College, there were many teachers who were priests, and there are some terrific people there. But I think, from a young age, I felt I was going to be a teacher. Maybe it was the sense of being able to be out in the yard playing hurling with the lads. [Laughs.] But it was something that came to me, I'd say, early enough, that I would like to be a primary teacher and there wasn't much of a contest when it came to making my mind up. You know, growing up, there were great players in my club, great players playing for the county and a massive excitement about it — you know, sixty, seventy thousand people in Croke Park. And what else would you want to be?

GB: I know that your senior playing career was cut short because of injury, and I wonder, when your identity is so bound up with something like that, when you finally realised "I can't do that any more," were you sad, depressed, angry, resentful?

BC: Definitely sad. Depressed? No. Angry? Not particularly, no.

GB: Hard to live with for a while?

BC: I'm not particularly a hard person to live with . . . [Laughs.] I suppose, really, the difference there is that, long before I finished playing, I was involved with looking after teams, looking after young teams, coaching players. So there was a natural extension to my hurling involvement straight away.

GB: Your remark that you're not too difficult to live with — I'd like to check that with Elsie some time and get her opinion on it! But did you actually meet through sport? I know she was a camogie player of considerable merit.

BC: In a sense, it was through sport. Our club had won an all-Ireland club final and we were celebrating on the night and she happened to be in the same premises, and she headhunted me straight away. [Laughs.]

GB: Was it love at first sight?

BC: Certainly from her point of view, I'd say. [Laughs.] It was, of course, love at first sight! No, no, we hit it off straight away and that was it. That was the start of our relationship; we got married a couple of years later.

GB: Instantly, through sport, I suppose, you found you were compatible in that respect and in respect of various other things as well?

BC: Yeah, there was a common bond there. But that wouldn't be enough to sustain a relationship or a marriage, for sure, so there were other elements to it, obviously. It's an amazing sort of an institution, really, marriage. You know, the fact that you can meet somebody and decide "Lookit, we're going to spend the rest of our lives together." So, it's an interesting journey to go ahead and fulfil that.

GB: Now, we'll move on to St Patrick's De La Salle, and you're Principal there. It seems to me that in many ways the gifts required to coach sports-people and to run a school would be kind of in the same area. Yes? No?

BC: Yeah, I would agree with that. There are many similarities between what I do in work and my involvement in sport.

GB: Do you think you're a natural-born teacher?

BC: Yeah, I think so. I think teaching is something that I can do very easily. I didn't have to force myself. It's about getting on with people and treating people well, I suppose.

GB: We were looking up the website and you say you hope to develop the pupils, not just academically, but in spirit and character. And you go on to say, "We hope to foster in them a deep sense of Christianity and love and a healthy respect for the beliefs of others. Values we hope that will lead them to a happy and fulfilling life." That's fairly well putting your colours to the mast.

BC: Yeah, it is. I think it's a fair enough thing to do. I mean, you put your colours to the mast in whatever you do, if you want to do it properly.

GB: And is there provision in there for non-national and other spiritual beliefs and so on? How do you cope with that?

BC: Absolutely. It's about the individual, developed in every child. Our school has a Catholic ethos and we fulfil that absolutely, and I think it's only right that we should, and we're proud to do that. We also, of course, facilitate every child who comes to our school — and some of them are quite happy to be part and parcel of the exposure to that. And if the opposite is the case for any children, that's facilitated as well. And we have, obviously, a certain number of children who come from various backgrounds and ethnic situations, and we learn so much from them, and our pupils learn from them, and vice versa.

GB: You taught Confirmation class for a while, did you not? That would be the standard, orthodox Catholic theology. Is it getting more difficult to encourage children to stick with their religious beliefs now, at a time when, for example, they see Confirmation as a sort of a passing-out ceremony? How do you cope with that?

BC: Yeah, I would agree with you there, for sure. You know, I taught sixth class for quite a number of years and, unfortunately, for a certain amount of our children — children all over the country — Mass-going would not be part and parcel of some of their lives. They have this great party — they have this great passing-out parade, as you say — and I always think it's a pity that the parents do not give the children the opportunity to be exposed to Sunday Mass as part of their build-up to the Confirmation and to the First Communion as well — you know, carry on with it after the sacrament as well. But it's their right to do it as they will, I suppose.

GB: The Church has had a fair few knocks in recent years. You're well aware of that, God knows. The scandals and a lot of the damage is self-inflicted, needless to say. How did you cope with all of that yourself?

BC: It's very sad, obviously, to see what has happened. And the abuse that has happened was criminal, without a shadow of a doubt, and it has impinged and affected so many people and so many families, and it's horrific to see what has gone on. And at the same time, how can I sort of make sense of belonging to, if you like, a Church like that? How can anybody?

I suppose I don't see the Church as being the priests. I don't see the Church as belonging to any individual, and it's not the preserve of anybody. It's all of us. It's what we believe in, ourselves. And it hasn't lessened my own sense of belonging to the Church. But I can very easily under-stand how it would affect young people now, growing up, say, at secondary school level — how they could question how this could be right at all.

GB: It strikes me that you're a fairly straight-down-the-middle, ortho-dox Catholic. Would that be right?

BC: Yeah. Ordinary, straightforward. I would think so, yeah. Very definite Catholic family, with strong Catholic values, and I was never tempted in any way to deviate from that. And part and parcel of my duty in school was to pass on that Catholic faith and tradition to our pupils and to prepare pupils for the sacraments and such like.

GB: Do you mean you saw no need to question that very deeply?
BC: Very possibly, that's true. I never met a stumbling-block that said to me, "What's it all about?" or "Why am I doing this?" or "Surely, there must be more to it than this . . ."

GB: So you'd go along with the Virgin Birth, the Immaculate Conception, the Death on the Cross, the Resurrection — all of that?
BC: As a middle-of-the-road Catholic, yeah.

GB: So, what is Jesus to you, Brian?
BC: That's a good question. Jesus was somebody who was a very, very good person. Jesus was a person who came on Earth, who gave wonderful example, and you can't particularly pick arguments in what he preached or what he suggested was the right way to live. So, he was a very, very straightforward, ordinary, forgiving, good person, who is the backbone, I suppose, of our Catholic faith.

GB: Was he divine?
BC: Yeah, yeah. Divine, yeah.

GB: And do you feel him as a presence, in any way, in your life, or was he a historical figure?
BC: Ah, no, I'd say he was a presence in my life, certainly. I've never looked upon him as historical. Jesus is the epicentre of the Catholic faith and I'm a Catholic, and I think, whatever it is you're involved in or you give yourself to, there has to be a commitment to it. Commitment is something that I'm wrapped up in in my life, with regard to sport, obviously, and my family and everything else. And I don't think it's possible to flit in and out of something either. I mean, I'm a straight-forward, down-to-earth Catholic and Jesus is at the very centre of that.

GB: And what is the Mass to you?
BC: Mass is something that I very definitely would go to every Sunday. It's a private time for myself, I think, where I can just put the rest of the things aside. Not always, because if you're playing a big match day, you're probably playing the match during the Mass as well! But you do

realise that it's a special time, a special moment. It's a divine moment, if you like, where, regardless of maybe your mind wandering, you do zone in, and you are very aware of the importance of the sacrifice itself. And it's something that I have never deviated from either.

GB: And do you believe in the Real Presence at Mass?
BC: I do.

GB: In preparing for this interview, we talked to a lot of people about you. They describe you as a man of strong values, good deeds, not a lot of words. But what comes across is somebody who is sort of shy and self-effacing. To me that doesn't seem possible, to be shy and self-effacing and to be coaching sportspeople. Would you talk to me about that?
BC: The most important element of a team is, I always call it, spirit — the spirit that's within the team. Everybody is completely committed to what we're doing: we buy into the same sense of values and the ambition to just drive things forward and to be the very best. I wanted players in the set-up who didn't need a huge amount of motivating or who didn't need to be told, "You can't do this, you can't do that." They were self-motivated, to a great extent.

You see, the players, the higher the standards you set — the more demands you make on them — the more they like it, because all they want to be is part of a set-up that's going to give them the best chance to be as successful as they possibly can be.

GB: And all of that is building towards that one Sunday in September, in Croker?
BC: That's the ambition. That's the lofty ambition, if you like. But, I mean, not getting there isn't failure either. We have been lucky, in the sense that we have the possibility of getting to that Sunday in September, which is, without a shadow of a doubt, the place everybody wants to be. But as long as they're getting the maximum out of themselves, that's success without trophies.

GB: But then, how do you cope with failure, like last year [2010], when the dirty was done on you by Tipp, to everybody's surprise?
BC: It's a huge disappointment, but I'm very realistic. We got to the stage where we won four all-Ireland finals in a row — terrific achievement. And then, suddenly, it was as if this team was going to go on — win and keep winning for ever. But, I mean, that's not sport, that's not life, that's not reality.

GB: What did you say to them when they didn't win?

BC: Well, not a lot can be said, but what I did say to them was "Lookit, we have won. We've had great success and we won with a bit of dignity and a bit of honour. We're going to lose with great dignity and with great honour."

GB: You spoke about your mind wandering at Mass, but on the other hand you've been known to lead prayers with Father Tom, your good friend, on all-Ireland Sunday. In that situation, are you praying for a win?

BC: I've never prayed for a win, to be honest.

GB: Never?

BC: No, I've never . . . and when I hurled, either. I've just a sense there's more important things to be praying for than to win in a hurling match. The morning of the all-Ireland final, I go to Mass. I do not pray for victory at all, because I think it's sport. And it's everything to us, and it's wonderful, but . . .

GB: There is a limit.

BC: There are limits. There are limits, yeah.

GB: How do you imagine God, when you do pray?

BC: I suppose I have this sense of Jesus Christ, and I pray to him. I talk to him. I just speak ordinary thoughts — words that, to me, are important.

GB: And do you believe that prayers are answered?

BC: Yeah, I do . . . I mean, sometimes they're not. How do you pick and choose when they are or they're not? When things go wrong and we have a crisis, straight away we pray, "Please, God . . ." and all the rest of it, and "Thank God . . ." when things go right. But certainly it's one of the things that annoys me, to an extent, is that when there is a crisis and when things do go wrong, for so many people, straight away, they pray. And then, when it's sorted, the sense of any kind of a commitment to their Catholic religion might just go out the window again.

GB: This next one is a bit off the wall, but Christianity is — one of the important aspects of it is — to hold out a helping hand to life's losers, whereas sport is all about winning. How to you reconcile that conflict?

BC: You could be right about being a bit off the wall, Gay, all right. [Laughter.] Sport is competitive. To fulfil yourself completely in sport, you've got to be competitive and determined and drive to always get the better of the opponent. And that's what it's about. So to go out and to even consider having the slightest bit of sympathy for the loser, as you call him, goes contrary to everything that would be right about sport.

GB: Did you find losing hard? And did it teach you anything?

BC: I think that's the great thing about sport — great sort of preparation for life's trials and tribulations, because life doesn't all go sweet and rosy for everybody. You have setbacks, and it does help very much in the formation of character for all the things you've got to put up with.

GB: Speaking of which, I know you're close to Mickey Harte, and you knew Michaela, and when such an unspeakable tragedy comes into somebody's life, did that rock your faith in God in any way?

BC: It rocked everybody, I think, and it shook everybody, and it horrified everybody. And Mickey himself, everybody knows, has a great sense of faith, and that's what's essentially keeping him going now. And Michaela had that as well. So you meet tragedies in so many different ways. That's the most unspeakable one I think I've come across, unfortunately. But if we were to kind of pin all of those things on God or the futility of beliefs, or suddenly let that shatter everything we have been brought up to believe about the afterlife or whatever — no, it hasn't rocked that element of my life at all.

I think the greatest sense of relief that so many people have is their faith, and you go to the funerals of so many people and you see the central element of it is the Christian burial and the Mass and the words of the priest. And that brings some sense of understanding, possibly, to those who are mourning. But it's the one thing that they want to hang on to, that sense of knowing that there is something further than this, and the hope and the expectation and the belief that some time, somewhere, there will be a reunion.

GB: Do you believe, then, that the people you loved and who loved you, who have died, do you think that they have a watching brief over you and can influence your well-being?

BC: Well, I suppose we pray to those people, and certainly I would speak to my parents . . . and I had a brother who died, and friends. And you would always, you know, go to the graveyards and spend a bit of time there and it's a great sense of relief. You don't see them — they no longer can be physically part of our lives — but emotionally and mentally they're still there for us.

GB: Do you think that they can help you . . . ?

BC: Oh, I would think so. Certainly they spent their lives helping us, you know — our parents. They devoted their lives to helping us, and they would never have any other sense of anything but commitment to their children's lives, and certainly that would still be very, very strong.

GB: Do you believe in Hell?

BC: I'm not sure I do, no. I can't envisage Hell being part and parcel of something that Jesus Christ advocates, you know, with the whole sense of a forgiving Father and everything else. I don't see God as up there with a pen or a pencil ticking us off and saying, "Lookit, you passed today" or "You didn't pass yesterday."

GB: Heaven — do you believe in it?

BC: I do, yeah. I believe in Heaven, whatever it's meant to be. A sense of something that's an extension of this life, if you like — that there is an afterlife. We often speak about Heaven on Earth as well. Sometimes it's the first Sunday of September, as well you know! But, yeah, there's something there.

GB: Last question: If it's all true, and you eventually get to the Golden Gate and you meet God, what do you think you will say to him?

BC: "Thank God." And I would be very, very happy to be there. I don't have any sense of fear of what's waiting up there, or out there, for me at all, and I'll say, "Lookit, thanks be to God, we're here. What's next?"

As a postscript, it is worth noting that the Brian Cody interview attracted one of *The Meaning of Life*'s highest audiences – several Croker-fuls, to use GAA currency. I had thought it a very straightforward conversation and so was surprised to learn that the feedback from colleagues in RTÉ Sport was that this had been a startlingly revealing interview with the great man. Perhaps there's a lesson there for all of us media blabbermouths: sometimes the people with the fewest words are the ones to whom the public believe it is most worth listening.

I am delighted to see that Brian has made a full recovery. This particular Cat clearly has at least eight more lives to go.

IAN PAISLEY

Dr No

There was a time when the name Dr Ian Paisley was one with which, in certain households, you could threaten your children, if they didn't go to bed. Such was his bogeyman status.

More seriously, Lord Bannside, as he is now known, is regarded in some parts of this island as the great defender of freedom, faith and Protestant, Unionist identity. In others, he is known, on more polite days, as "Dr No" — the man whose barking intransigence seemed, at times, to lend weird sanctification to the Loyalist cause, no matter how often he condemned paramilitary violence. He was the last, and certainly the most audible, obstacle to the Good Friday Agreement of 1998.

But things — and people — change. He later became the First Minister of Northern Ireland's power-sharing Executive. As he had promised Bertie Ahern and Tony Blair, when he eventually came on board the peace process, he did so *absolutely*. He is a man of his word. And he got his reward. Few could have believed the spectacle of the "Chuckle Brothers" — the former IRA commander, Martin McGuinness, and his DUP *bête noire* — leading the international charm offensive to rebuild their fractured nation. It takes a big man, as they say, and Ian Paisley is certainly that.

Only now, he's also an old man and not always in the best of health. When we met, in 2010, he had already been in and out of hospital, as happens to men in their eighties. His delightful artist daughter, Rhonda, is now much more his protector than his diary secretary and warned us that there would be a cut-off to our interview: "Daddy doesn't do long interviews like he used to . . . and he's got another engagement afterwards."

As we later discovered, his subsequent "engagement" was with his pillow. Lord Bannside needed an afternoon nap. And who could blame him? I just wish we had known that that was our competition when we allowed our interview to be curtailed.

I had a long — perhaps too long — list of questions for Lord Bannside and he is a past master at filibustering: answer the easy questions at length and you might not even have to face the more difficult ones. Having said which, I know he is not one to duck any question. It is up to the interviewer to marshal their thoughts into the allocated time and, like many a Drumcree policeman, on the day we met, there were times when I felt decidedly out-marshalled.

The location? Well, where better to interview the Rev. Dr Ian Paisley than in what was for years his bastion church on the Ravenhill Road, the huge and very impressive temple to his evangelistic prowess on Belfast's south side. This was before the rather unseemly coup that saw him removed from that particular bully pulpit.

I tried to ignore the fact that there was an accidental Tricolour of book spines directly behind his head during our interview. My English producer was subsequently more squeamish, thinking that viewers would assume we were making some sort of infantile or mischievous point, and so the spines were duly re-coloured in "post-production".

It was Dr Paisley's relationship with one particular book, however, that most fascinated me. He is one of the few people I have met who believes, firmly and absolutely, that every word in the Bible is true. Not just true, but factual. This is not a book of poetry or metaphors: the seven-day Creation, Noah's flood, the parting of the Red Sea, everything, right up to the Ascension of Jesus, happened just as the Good Book says. The Rev. Dr believes that the Bible is a historical account of God's interaction with humankind. It is also the pole star by which he has steered his entire life, from the moment of his very precocious "conversion".

GB: Now, it strikes me that, with not only one parent but two as preachers, you must have been brought up in a very religious household. Tell me about that.

IP: I wouldn't say it was very religious. The only thing that would have been remarkable would be that we always had a time of prayer in the morning and a time of prayer in the evening. But otherwise it was a normal home with normal duties and the normal chastisements that all children need to have to bring us up in what my father called "the fear, nurture and admonition of the Lord."

GB: Your mother, by all accounts, was a formidable woman.

IP: She was.

GB: Tell me about her.

IP: Well, she was of Scotch extract. She was a tremendous lady, with great skill, and ran a very tight household, but ran it well. And, of course, money in those days was a rare commodity, and preachers . . . [Laughs.] They thought the preacher just lived on manna from Heaven and didn't worry too much about their salaries. But I learned that money was not everything, that you can have money and not be happy, but you can be penniless and be happy. I learned that, and I have enjoyed it ever since.

GB: Your daughter, Rhonda, paints your childhood as kind of not exactly filled with fun and skit and sport and games. Would that be so?
IP: Well, not really. After school hours I did what all other boys did. We played our marbles. And our ways were simple, but they were happy.

GB: You didn't go to theatre very much . . .
IP: No, not at all.

GB: Didn't go to cinemas?
IP: No, no. We were cut off from that.

GB: Sundays must have been a very busy day for your parents, obviously.
IP: Yes.

GB: How did you spend Sunday, looking back on it now?
IP: Well, on Sunday, I woke up and then I went to a Sabbath School at around ten o'clock, and that lasted for three-quarters of an hour. And then I went to the morning service at 11:30 a.m., and then I had the afternoon fairly free, except when we had special meetings in the church. And then we had an evening service . . . and usually a half-past eight service after that, where we would go out to hear my father preach.

GB: Then, at six years of age, I know you had a special spiritual experience. Tell me about that.
IP: Yes. Well, my mother ran, on Tuesday evenings, a special meeting after school. She took that service herself and spoke. On 27th May — I put it down on a little bit of paper, if I can find the bit of paper . . . Wouldn't need to look for a paper at the Judgement Day . . .

GB: [Laughs.]
IP: [Finding his slip of paper.] It was 29th May, 1932, in Ballymena Baptist Church, and she pointed me to Christ, and I received Christ as my Saviour and my Lord. Now, she had spoken that day about the lost sheep and the lost lamb, and it went right home to my heart.

GB: Can you describe that to me?

IP: Yes. I was broken in heart. I was weeping, because I felt that I had sinned.

GB: But you were only six?

IP: Yes, but I have a deep experience of that. I had broken God's law.

"*I came to Jesus as I was, weary, worn and sad;*
I found in Him a resting place, and He did make me glad."

And my whole life changed. And, of course, as a boy, I was just like any other boy. I was bad at times and needed the ruler. My mother used the ruler, and she used to give us a good smack. [Demonstrates enthusiastically.]

GB: So, you were slightly rebellious on occasion?

IP: Oh, yes, I was indeed. I was no saint. I was a sinner, saved by grace. And I'm no saint now. I'm still a sinner, saved by grace.

GB: And so, at what age did you decide that you had a vocation to the ministry?

IP: Well, I finished school, the Technical High School in Ballymena, and was going to the Agricultural College, because I was very interested in that. And before I was going to go to college, I decided that I should go down to my father's people and live with them a time, on the farm, to get a practical idea, because I was going to go that way. So I went to Sixmilecross and lived with a family there, friends of my dad's, and I went to the bog to cut turf. And I had a feeling in my heart that I had better make a decision: what was I going to do? Was I going to go on and do something in agriculture, or was I going to change around and start being a preacher? And I felt very strongly that I had to make the decision on the Lord's side. And that's what I did.

GB: I'm going back to 1951, now, and you met this woman, Eileen.

IP: Yes.

GB: Where did you meet?

IP: I knew her oldest brother, Billy, very, very well. We met occasionally . . . and then more occasionally, and we both fell in love, one with the other. I don't know what she saw in me, but I saw plenty in her.

GB: But you got engaged within three weeks, I was told.

IP: No, not quite.

GB: Not quite.

IP: But we were engaged from the beginning ... [Laughs.]

GB: But is it not true you were engaged to another woman at the time?

IP: No. The time that I started going out with Eileen, that was off.

GB: That was off.

IP: Oh, yes, it was.

GB: That's just as well!

IP: Oh, it is, indeed. No, that was mutually off.

GB: Well, it was a beautiful union. I know you've gone past your golden wedding anniversary, and you have five children: three girls and two boys. Were you a strict daddy?

IP: [Laughs.] Well, they told me I was far too strict.

GB: Yes?

IP: And I, of course, used to laugh at them and say, "It's well you haven't a daddy like most people or you'd have marks on your legs." [Laughter.] No, I was strict, because I was brought up in a strict home. And, of course, I believed that that's a good way to be brought up. But I loved my children and my children loved me, and we never had any disputes in the home. But, as a father and as a mother, you have to just watch that you don't become a bully, and you try to make Wee Ian what Big Ian was. It's not done. Children have to be brought up in "the fear, nurture and admonition of the Lord", but not in a harsh way.

GB: They had a hugely different upbringing to your upbringing.

IP: Oh, they had, indeed. And, of course, they had also the fact that I was a sort of marked man and hardly a post got to the house that there wasn't threats to me.

GB: So, they suffered because of your high profile?

IP: Oh, they certainly did.

GB: Let's talk about your beliefs. On your website, you say that your mission is "to promote, defend and maintain Bible Protestantism".

IP: Yes.

GB: What is that?

IP: It's Bible Protestantism! [Laughs.] It's a religion of the Bible, and I think that this [holding up his own Bible] is *the* Book. And I believe it's

God's Book, and I believe that I should follow it and should exhort people to follow it . . . but that they must do that of their own free will and accord.

GB: And do you believe that that is literally true?
IP: Yes.

GB: Literally?
IP: Yeah, literally true.

GB: Do you mean Adam and Eve . . . ?
IP: Yes . . .

GB: Noah, the flood . . . ?
IP: Yes . . .

GB: The burning bush . . . ?
IP: I believe the lot, from Genesis to Revelation, from the first Amen to the last Amen. I believe it all. The Bible is God's Book. It has stood the test: it has been burned, it has been sawn asunder and has been attacked. The heaviest of brains that agents had have been used against it, and they're forgotten. But the old Book still reigns, and I preach the Book and believe in it, practise it, and mourn when I don't keep it the way I should.

GB: Did you ever have any doubts about your faith?
IP: Oh, of course I had. But I believe that all I have to do is to rest upon what the Book says and some day we'll see that vindicated.

GB: Now, you know the way people, especially in America, say that all the troubles in Northern Ireland have been about religion . . . ?
IP: Yes.

GB: What do you say to those people?
IP: [Laughs.] Well, if I was in good form I would say, "And all the troubles in America were about religion." [Laughter.] No, but I say, "Well, I don't think that you are in position to pass judgement." My neighbours, many of them, are Roman Catholics. They don't look on me as an anathema, nor do I look at them. They're all right people. And I say, "Do we have good fellowship together?" So, we do. We don't see eye to eye on Gospel work, and our theology is different, but it doesn't mean that we don't live with them.

GB: But you've said that the violence comes from the Roman Catholic Church.
IP: Yes.

GB: Did you mean by that you actually believe that the Catholic Church is backing, was backing, the Provos and the Republican movement?

IP: Well, it would look like it, in some cases. But, I mean, I think that the Roman Catholic Church in Ireland did always back a severance of this part of the island from the rest of the United Kingdom, and they were really declared nationalist, in that sense. But then, of course, there were nationalists that were not gunmen. There were nationalists that were good, respectable citizens and did well for their people. So, they weren't all gunmen.

GB: I know that you have many Catholics in your constituency and I know that you look after them very well and you get on very well with them and so on. And yet you've, on occasions, gone out of your way to make insulting remarks about what they believe in. You held up the Host, in the Oxford Union, and mocked it, and so on. And you must have realised, because you're a gentleman, that that was causing huge offence.

IP: Well, of course, you've got to understand I'm an Ulsterman. And in regard to the incident that took place, the thing was that it wasn't the Church, but it was the doctrine that, in the Mass, it becomes the actual body and blood of Christ. And that to me is repugnant . . .

GB: Transubstantiation . . .

IP: Yes, Transubstantiation. Oh, I would utterly reject that. God has chosen bread to be the memory-giver of Christ's body and the wine to be the memory of his precious blood. And there is nothing miraculous about the communion table. The Lord said, "Do this in memory of me." Well, if the Lord's there bodily, you can't remember him. [Laughs.]

GB: And did your Catholic constituents react to that occasion with the Host and to other things you've said about the Pope, whom you describe as the Antichrist?

IP: Yes. Well, I was not the first man that said that. I had this Protestant doctrine, and every one of the Protestant Churches have that in their confessional. And I'm with the big league in that one. [Laughs.] But the point is I don't say those things to annoy Roman Catholics: I say them because I believe that I must tell them the truth, as I see it.

GB: And in the unlikely event that Pope Benedict would walk in through the door of this church now and meet you face to face, not with anybody else involved, just meet you face to face, how would you cope with that, do you think? How would *he* cope with it?

IP: [Laughter.] Well, if he came as a sinner to the Saviour . . .

GB: Yes . . . ?

IP: . . . I would rejoice. But the Pope will not be coming.

GB: But if he did . . . ?

IP: Well, you're putting up something that's not going to happen. [Laughs.] I'm too wise an old fella now to fall for that one.

GB: But would you greet him and shake his hand . . . ?

IP: Oh, I would find great difficulty in shaking his hand.

GB: But why? "Faith, hope and charity, and the greatest of these is charity . . ."

IP: Yes, but the Pope makes claims that are outrageous. And also, let me say, I am not at all happy about the way that he personally has dealt with the paedophiles . . .

GB: Quite.

IP: And I didn't like, on the Pope's visit — he never said he was sorry. He said he was sorry for the people, but he never said, "I am sorry." And I feel I have a duty and I have to condemn and say, "Well, I can't accept that." And certainly, I will be persecuted for righteousness' sake. The early Protestant reformers were nearly all burned at the stake. So, I mean, who am I to say that I deserve a different ending? [Laughter.]

GB: Getting back to Northern Ireland again: Gerry Adams said on this programme that he was provoked into the Republican movement because of your threat to remove the Tricolour from a Republican club on the Falls Road, if the police didn't do it. Did you ever fear, during all the Troubles, that your words worsened the situation rather than improved it?

IP: No. I think that my words put determination into the Protestant people not to allow themselves into a situation where part of their remnants would turn to violence. And we very nearly had a far bigger returning of violence than we had among Protestants.

I mean, in the early Troubles, there were very severe deaths caused, and I didn't want that. And I felt that, if it got strong leadership now, they're not going to go to the dregs. But, of course, at the tail ends, some terrible deeds were done by Protestants. And those deeds, if you check the books, I was the first to denounce them and to say, "I'm not on that side." And I don't know how many Roman Catholic funerals I attended. I was attending them all the time, to show where my real doctrines lay.

GB: Taking your lead from the Bible, what, to you, is evil? And do you believe that the Devil exists . . . ?
IP: Yes.

GB: . . . and that he is, throughout the world, creating evil?
IP: Yes, I believe the Devil exists, for I've done business with him. People have tried to kill me and I received a letter one day from a man who said that he would kill me, and he would see to it that I'd be killed. Three nights afterwards, I was attacked on the Albert Bridge and, fortunately, the bullet missed the car and hit one of the big stone buildings and I escaped. But I must say to you: that man that did that got converted and became a very devout Christian and is still walking in the paths of righteousness since. So, he was changed completely by the grace of God.

GB: Going back to Bertie Ahern and Tony Blair and how well you got on with all of those . . . and the "Chuckle Brothers" — the picture of yourself and McGuinness, which would have been unimaginable ten years ago. Your illness struck you in — what, '04, '05? You went off to hospital and so on.
IP: Yes.

GB: Did something happen to you at the time of your illness? It seemed to onlookers like me that there was a huge transformation from your *dissenting* voice to your *assenting* voice, after your illness — that you were a much more mellowed person and much more friendly and well-disposed.
IP: Well, the real crux of the matter is . . . I was negotiating with the various people and I said, "Look, I want to make it very clear to you that you'll not make a Roman Catholic of me." And I said, "I have great faith in my Lord, but I don't think every *Sinn*-er is going to be Born Again." But, I said, one thing: "If you can persuade me that the IRA will give up their guns, I will be prepared, in those circumstances, in a properly elected Stormont, to sit down with them to run this country."

Now, I think that it was a pity that we hadn't had a stronger British Prime Minister, for I believe that he could have succeeded in that. But he believed from the beginning it couldn't be. And one day he rang me seven times to try and get me to change this. And I said, "Look, I could change it, but there'd be no change on the ground. We want a change on the ground. So, we've got to have that."

"Well," he said, "you can't have it."

"Well," says I, "that's because you didn't put your back to it." Says I: "If you had put your back to it, you could have had it," and I said, "Look, don't ring me ever again. Day over."

GB: You said that.

IP: Yes. "You don't ring me until you have a different story."

Well, he realised then and he went back to the IRA.

And of course, they said, "Oh, can't do it."

"Well," he says, "I have to tell you, then, there will be no settlement." And he said, "It might even be worse for you fellas."

And, anyway, he then rang me back, and he said, "They are now thinking along the lines that you have said."

So then, we were to meet, as you know, at Stormont. And when I went into the room that day, I didn't know what they were going to do. I didn't know whether the Head of the IRA would say, "Ian, I'm going to sign up." And he sat there. [Laughs.] I can see it to this day. I had the document in my hand and I handed it over to him, and he looked at me and he looked around the room, and I said, "Now, what's going to happen?"

He said, "I will sign it."

And he signed it. And I must say, and I have to be absolutely honest, they have kept their word. They did do that.

GB: You're eighty-four, God bless you . . .

IP: Yes, Amen.

GB: . . . and you've encountered death on innumerable occasions, and you think about death.

IP: I do.

GB: It's appropriate for a man of your age to think about death.

IP: Yes, that's right.

GB: Are you afraid of it?

IP: No, no. Christ died for me. Therefore the death that I die, and all Christians die, is a death in hope. It's not a hopeless thing.

GB: And do you think you will see your parents again and your loved ones again?

IP: I will. I will see every one that had faith in Christ again.

GB: Is there any possibility that you might end up in the other place?

IP: No, because I have God's word for it. "God so loved the world that he gave his only begotten Son that whosoever . . ." — "whosoever" is a very wide throw of the net — ". . . whosoever believeth in him should not perish, but have everlasting life." And that's where I am resting.

GB: Do you believe that Hell exists?

IP: Oh, I certainly do.

GB: And who goes there?

IP: Those that have rejected the Lord Jesus and refused to accept him as their Saviour and their Lord. My affair is to be right with God myself and get as many people to be right with God. But I can't force you, take you by the scruff of the neck and throw you into Christ — can't be done. I wish it could! I'd be busy all day.

GB & IP: [Laughter.]

IP: I'd have to take lessons to get better muscles! [Laughs.] But all I can say to you is this: He has said, "Ye must be born again." Have I been born again with him? And if I have, then I have great peace in my heart.

GB: And when you finally come face to face with him, what will you say to him?

IP: All I will say is, "Thank you, Lord, for saving a wretch like me, and deliver me from Hell in bringing me to Heaven, and I just want to be beside you and to look upon you and to love you and serve you. Give me the worst job in Heaven and I'll do it." [Laughs.]

GB: Thank you very much.

IP: Amen.

Postscript

In preparing this book, we were required, as a matter both of courtesy and of law, to approach all our contributors, to ask their permission to reprint excerpts from their interviews. At first, no word was forthcoming from the Paisley household, so my producer, Roger Childs, eventually telephoned his son, Ian Jr, who said, "Daddy's simply not well enough to deal with your request, Roger, but you can rest assured that he will make no complaints. He will see Gay's book as an extension of his ministry."

And so should you. I wish the doctor peace. He has earned his rest.

J. P. DONLEAVY

One of a Kind

'Struth . . . !

In an instant, I understood the secret of J. P. Donleavy's longevity and remarkable good health: he has been cryogenically frozen.

His house — a crumbling, stately pile, perched amidst acres of its own farm and parkland in Co. Westmeath — is surely the coldest place south of the Arctic. The roaring fire, which he had dutifully made up in expectation of visitors, only barely thawed the cobwebs in the fadedly grand drawing room. By the end of the interview, my limbs were like tundra.

"Mike", as James Patrick Donleavy is known by those closest to him, for reasons that would require too much explanation, greeted me in the kitchen, where he was hand-squeezing oranges for his daily glass of elixir. Clearly, it works. An undefeated boxer and gifted athlete in his younger days, he told me on the day we met that he still runs at least a mile a day and keeps his bodily pipes from freezing totally by shadow-boxing. At eighty-six. (He is now eighty-eight.)

He was once handsome in a way that some women find exciting and others simply scary. He told me that the grubby, turf-stained deerskin jacket he was wearing was a present from "the richest woman in the world", an ex-girlfriend who thought nothing of paying thousands of dollars for an original modernist painting masquerading as a coat.

Not that Mike is short of a bob himself. He has sold tens of millions of books — most famously, or infamously, *The Ginger Man*. Even putting to one side its considerable literary merit, this, his first novel, was guaranteed commercial success as soon as it was banned by the Catholic Church. His son, Philip, is now trying to make a movie from the book and seems to have succeeded in enrolling Johnny Depp in the enterprise. For years, a movie was impossible, because Philip's father was in litigious dispute with the novel's original French publisher, Olympia Press. Mike eventually solved that problem by buying the publisher. Well, that's one way of doing things.

He has a reputation as a recluse, famously not turning up for his own book launches and art exhibitions. (He's always been resolutely amphibious when it comes to literary and visual arts.) It was therefore a pleasant surprise to discover that he is actually very congenial. The only sign of reclusion was that he nearly lost his voice after about ten minutes in conversation. "It's the first time I have spoken for this long in about two years."

Although he was raised as a Catholic, in the leafy part of the Bronx — I know, that was news to me, too — I don't think he ever really believed in God. Certainly, he says he can't *remember* having done so. If anything, however, that disbelief has *added* meaning to his life, rather than taking it away. It is all about the here and now. *Carpe* your *diems* and forget the hereafter.

I had read cuttings before the interview which, with any other guest, might have become unmentionable "elephants in the room": some years ago, Mike discovered that two of his children had been fathered by other men — two of the Guinness brothers. The revelation seems to have put paid to his second marriage. The finger-waggers and "told you so" brigade might point to this as perfect come-uppance for someone whose novels are almost a charter for promiscuity. Writers in glass houses, etc. . . .

However, when I tentatively raised the subject, Mike demonstrated nothing but moral integrity. He has only kind words for those children — still, clearly, *his* children, whatever the DNA — and their mother, who had visited him in Westmeath just a few days before us. Begrudgery and bejudgery are not really his style.

Instead, J. P. Donleavy's watchword seems to be "kindness", which matters to him far more than small matters of virtue or belief. Even when talking about Gainor Crist, the wilfully debauched and degenerate real-life model for Sebastian Dangerfield, the fictional "Ginger Man", what Mike recalls about him is his kindness: Gainor was once kind to him.

That little kindness has gone a long way.

∽

GB: I want to start by taking you back to the Bronx, New York, 1930s. As we sit here in your elegant place in Mullingar, in the heart of the Irish countryside . . . you've come a long way, as they say. How rough was it in the Bronx in the 1930s?

JPD: Well, it varied a great deal as to what part of the Bronx you were in. The Bronx could be a very rough place, but Woodlawn, where I grew up, was totally cut off from the Bronx. It was literally like a country town, and so all of that was pretty pleasant. It's quite a rural area.

GB: I'm told that your father was a "spoiled priest". Is that so?

JPD: He was at Maynooth. I know that much — that he was there studying and decided to leave and went to America. But that's the most that I do know about his background in that way.

GB: Now, my understanding is that your mother had some money from somewhere.

JPD: Uh-huh. My mother was often accused of being the richest woman in the Bronx. One thing I did know, though: she was a great philanthropist. There was a place called the Boys' Home, Father Flanagan's Boys' Home. She actually used to back those things, and people would come from all over America for her to disperse her sort of . . . [Parodies a gesture of largesse and laughs.]

GB: Dishing out money.

JPD: Yes, and hand it out to people. Especially, say, a new emigrant that had just arrived in America — she would always make a point of making them comfortable or meeting them or taking them somewhere.

GB: It sounds like a fairly posh upbringing.

JPD: Modestly so, yes. No one was very, very rich.

GB: Do you remember it as a religious household?

JPD: Yes, my father certainly kept to his own kind of interests. I didn't know a great deal about them. But my mother was always — I'd use the word devout — and paid a lot of attention to religious affairs, without people knowing too much about this. She didn't push it in anyone's face at all.

GB: Do you recollect going to Sunday Mass?

JPD: Yes, growing up it would have been the routine. It was like a social occasion.

GB: And there's no recollection of a daily Rosary, which was a great practice in Ireland?

JPD: No. I did hear of things like that and ran a mile. [Laughs.]

GB: [Laughs.] The Jesuits, as you well know, proclaimed: "Give me the boy at seven and I'll give you the man." Quite clearly, they failed miserably in your case. You went to a Jesuit college, but you were expelled, and you declared yourself an atheist at the age of thirteen. How did Irish Mammy and Daddy react to that, then?

JPD: Pretty badly, I think, because there was nothing I ever seemed to do which made anyone's image of me improve in any way. In fact, I was a very silent, reclusive person, really, growing up.

GB: When you declared yourself an atheist at the age of thirteen, do you think you knew what you were talking about?

JPD: I think that I was pretty certain of matters by about the age of fourteen. I felt that whatever I believed then was going to be *it* for life, which has been the case, actually.

GB: You stuck to your guns?

JPD: Sort of. Nothing much to stick to!

GB: Okay. You were too young to be active when war started, but you were drafted into the Naval Reserve, is that so?

JPD: Yes, I enlisted in the US Navy. You had to enlist in the Navy: you would be drafted into the Army, but the Navy was a little different. You literally had to want to be in the Navy, and so I enlisted.

GB: Did you see active service anywhere?

JPD: No, I didn't. And I wouldn't be sitting here now if I had gone up forward in the Amphibious Corps. I think one man survived, who came and visited me here in this house and knew that I had been in the Amphibious Corps. They were wiped out at Normandy, and so I just missed that happening.

GB: The random choice of nature.

JPD: Exactly that.

GB: So, arising out of the GI Bill of Rights, you were entitled to an education, but why Ireland, why Dublin, why Trinity?

JPD: My mother's interest had a lot to do with it. I had this picture of this ideal life that you can live in this unusual city Dublin [laughs], and I decided to come and have a look myself. I said, "Are there any universities in Ireland?" She said, "Yes, there's Trinity College, Dublin." And so I wrote off to Trinity, and they just simply said, "Come over."

GB: So, give me a picture of yourself at that time. You were nominally a Catholic and you were coming into a Protestant university. Also, you were a self-declared American atheist at a time when Ireland was heavily under the influence of the Catholic Church, and Dublin particularly . . .

JPD: Well, I became very conscious of that at Trinity. There might have been one or two Catholics, but they had to get a certain dispensation to even go to Trinity. It was a strictly Protestant operation in the middle of Dublin.

GB: I'm trying to figure out, as the old saying has it, did they see you as a Protestant atheist or a Catholic atheist?

JPD: Ah! I didn't know there was that distinction. [Laughs.]

GB: [Laughs.] Oh, there is that distinction, I assure you. Oh, yes!

JPD: I don't know where I would have fitted in, in that case.

GB: Okay, so what gave rise to *The Ginger Man*? . . . And what attracted you to Gainor Crist, the man who was Sebastian Dangerfield in *The Ginger Man*?

JPD: Well, I'm not sure. He had an elegance about his life. He somehow came into the orbit that we moved in, and we had the same congenial friends, and it was through these friendships that already existed that one just got to know him. But the first thing was that someone came up to me to borrow all my clothing. He [Gainor] went to get some sort of job. He was very elegant and could present himself and do most things, but he had to borrow clothing. I had quite a wardrobe that I'd brought from America, and so this friend borrowed all. And I went along and I saw him [Gainor] in a pub, when we were meeting up for the first time. And he was dressed in all my clothes.

GB: So you started to hang around together?

JPD: Yes, we saw one another. And he was always interested in everything around him. And, as I say, a very congenial gentleman.

GB: Quite clearly, you were one of the better-off students in Trinity at that time?

JPD: Yes. I was enormously well off! I can remember I would go each evening for a couple of glasses of champagne up at the Shelbourne Rooms. [Laughs.]

GB: Not bad for a student in Trinity.

JPD: Yes, indeed. I had my GI Bill of Rights, and my mother gave me an allowance. And it must have been the richest days I've known in Ireland!

GB: Boy, oh boy! And did Gainor Crist know you were writing about him?

JPD: Oh, he did, finally, yes. I remember I went over to Paris and we met up there, and he just realised I was writing this book, and he never minded at all and was just complacent about matters.

GB: Even after the book came out?

JPD: Yes, even when the book came out. He was intrigued and interested.

GB: So, here is this story, then, described by many people as straight-forward porn, debauchery, libertarianism, decadence. And yet you say that Gainor Crist was a sort of saint. Explain that to me.

JPD: The saintliness came . . . I remember, once, when we were caught — nowhere to stay, on a chilly evening — on a crossroads, and I remember it was a roundabout or something, but there was a grass mound where you could sit down. And I actually sat down. I was tired and I fell asleep. And I remember finally waking up and looking up, and Gainor was sitting about two, three feet away, and he was just sitting there. And his sweater — he'd taken it off and covered me, and he was sitting there. And I could see he was freezing. I was amazed. He just looked to my comfort, having fallen asleep on the side of the road.

GB: So, all in all, he would have been a generous soul, a decent guy?

JPD: Yes, that's true.

GB: Getting back to the book, when all the fuss was made of it, what did Mum and Dad think? How did they react to all of this?

JPD: Well, no one wanted to have it mentioned. I think, in Catholic churches all over America, at some stage it was proclaimed to be reading that you shouldn't read.

GB: What was your reaction to the condemnation? Were you worried by it, or did you rejoice in it?

JPD: Not particularly, because one realised that people — when you're stopped from reading something, everybody wanted to read the book.

GB: [Laughter.]

JPD: And so I had to give in! Brendan Behan was the first one to read the manuscript of the book, and he read it one day, out at my place in Kilcoole, where I had my cottage. And he said, "Mike, that book of yours is going to go around the world." [Laughs.]

GB: Wasn't far wrong. Did you like Brendan Behan?

JPD: Yes, I did. His life and his habits were something else, but there were two parts of him. He could behave in this terrible sort of way. If he wanted revenge on people, the things he did were unspeakable, and I've never spoken of them since. But he could be difficult.

GB: You were not a great drinker?

JPD: No, not terribly, because I was an athlete, and so I was so conscious of my condition.

GB: I knew him in later life, and he was a lovely companion and a very nice man to talk to when he was sober. When he was drunk, he was just such a pain. Did you know Patrick Kavanagh?

JPD: Yes, I did, yes.

GB: Did you like him?

JPD: Oh, quite well. Well, he was the first one, somehow. He made some pronouncement about my writing or something that I'd written and, as I left the room, someone made some objectionable remark about me. And Kavanagh spoke up and said, "Don't laugh at that man. He's going to be something, some day." And that caught me unawares.

GB: Well done, Patrick! I sat the other day, it just occurs to me, in Patrick Kavanagh's seat, by the canal.

JPD: Oh, God.

GB: Go back to that era and your feeling about Dublin and Ireland. You wrote about that time: "It was quickly dawning on me that Ireland, with its small, inbred population of active begrudgers" — I like that! — "was no place to survive long enough to become rich and celebrate it." Why did you stay, if that was your view . . . ?

JPD: I suppose I got used to the life, and, as you know yourself, it's a pretty pleasant life, Dublin. Congenial.

GB: "Congenial" is a very good word, indeed. So what happened, then, to this book, which was condemned by so many people and then suddenly became a huge success and very popular and everybody wanted to read it? . . . Indeed it joined "The 100 Most Influential Novels in the World" . . . What happened to bring about that change?

JPD: I suppose they began to circulate the book when repetitive editions came out. People might loan it to each other and so on.

GB: What were all those disagreements about with the Olympia Press down through the years? Did you become the owner of Olympia Press eventually?

JPD: Maurice Girodias, who founded the Olympia Press, had published the book, and he put it in a distasteful edition, listing all sorts of pornographic books in the back of my book. And so we fell out on that, and we entered this litigation, and it was so ridiculous. We were having actions all over the world: America, everywhere. It was a dreadful business. And then, finally, someone said that it had gone bankrupt, the company, and was up for sale, and we bought it.

GB: [Laughter.] So, you're squabbling with yourself.
JPD: When I started suing myself, I thought, "Now, I've got to straighten it out!"

GB: So, now you own the lot?
JPD: Now I own the lot.

GB: And all copyright?
JPD: Yeah.

GB: And all film rights . . . ?
JPD: I have to only stop suing myself! [Laughs.]

GB: Okay, that would save a few shillings . . . Are you interested in money?
JPD: Well, only as a course of survival, literally, realising that it does provide the space that we're enjoying here and so on. But not more than that, particularly, no.

GB: It's common knowledge that you had marriages to Mary and to Valerie, and both of those marriages are over. Does this make you an unbeliever, or a non-believer, in marriage?
JPD: No, I suppose marriage is something of importance, and in both these cases — both charming ladies who decided to, you know, move on to other matters and people, and so on.

GB: Not suddenly, presumably?
JPD: No, gradually is the better word, yes. [Laughs.]

GB: But you still believe in the institution of marriage?
JPD: Yes. I think it protects one person from another, yeah.

GB: Now, your two children were not fathered by you. They were fathered, with Mary, by Finn and Kieran Guinness.
JPD: Uh-huh.

GB: And yet you've remained good friends. Tell me about that.
JPD: Yes, I could never feel that it should make any difference, in the sense that if they were in my custody one would look after the children. And I was always immensely fond of children, simply because often they made good company.

GB: How shocking and how saddening was that whole episode?
JPD: Well, it was always a pretty painful business, yes, and you just wanted to save, as much as one could, the people or the children, especially, from any kind of trouble or damage that they might encounter.

GB: And did you?

JPD: I think, for the most part, yes, we did.

GB: Go back to your boxing days. How good were you, do you reckon?

JPD: Well, I never lost a fight, and I think that maybe someone invited me to go professional. [Laughs.] These were some of the best boxers in the world that I grew up with and a coach who was the referee for all the Joe Louis fights. He was my coach in the New York Athletic Club. And that had a room especially for boxing, and so it was a sport I took up. But I realised that you didn't want to get your head pummelled too much. [Laughs.] And so I slowed that up a great deal and took up wrestling. [Laughs.]

GB: Easier?

JPD: Well, yes, I think so.

GB: Many people would have regarded you as having been in the vanguard of liberating people from "the tyranny of the Church". Has Ireland become a better place through being liberated?

JPD: Oh, I think so, yes. I think it has, because there were a lot of very terrifying situations in Ireland. Religion was something where they could literally kind of control things that could make it hard for you. They could drive someone out of Ireland, if they liked, and so it wasn't that easy. One didn't want to see it ever get that strong that it could threaten people and, you know, chastise them.

GB: Do you think that the Church — organised religion — has any bearing on any kind of moral compass in one's life?

JPD: It's a formality, which is important, I think, in life. People forget that to congregate, say, in a church — the music, everything about it — it's a very beneficial part of life. I may not, in all respects, think that there's a God, or that any religion is the right religion, but I think it's very important in life. It formalises a lot of things in life for people to sit and contemplate on, which they wouldn't otherwise do.

GB: If God and organised religion and the Church does not give you a moral compass in your life, what does that for you? By which I mean, what motivates you to be good, rather than the opposite?

JPD: Well, I regard it as just a practical matter. If you, say, walk down the street and punch someone, then you could expect to be punched back. I mean, it's a matter of survival of the society. In other words, you do something to somebody that might provoke them to do it back to you. And so you *don't* do it to them.

GB: "Do unto others as you would have them do unto you . . ."
JPD: Yes, I think that covers it.

GB: And you do the right thing, because you consider it to *be* the right thing.
JPD: I think this would be the word: the *kindest* thing. If the word "kind" could fit in there somewhere, that would be my priority.

GB: So, as far as you're concerned, who was Jesus? And what was he?
JPD: Well, I don't know a great deal about that. I kind of look upon it as a historic matter and haven't taken that much interest to go into it very deeply. So I just look at the whole aspect of the various religions that exist and respect them all.

GB: You respect them all, but you've no time, personally, for any of them.
JPD: Yeah, I don't take up my own position in any of these, no.

GB: And, as far as you're concerned, there is no such thing as God up there in the sky?
JPD: Only in people's minds, I think. I mean, you have to think it over. I could be making a mistake! [Laughs.] One gets interested in astronomy and, of course, astronomy is the matter where they're now coming up against this really kind of strange awareness about what's happening *out there.* [Indicates the heavens.] They don't know any more where it ends or what goes on. There could be ten million worlds just like this one.

GB: But you don't think that there is a hand guiding all of that?
JPD: I don't think so, no. But that's one of the best questions of all, the one you just raised now. What might be moving it? That's a question I don't think anybody has ever settled.

GB: You're in pretty good nick for a man of your age. Tell me about your fitness routine.
JPD: Yes, I do some calisthenics in the mornings, and, generally, through the day, I might do a little bit of shadow-boxing and things. But then I get out on the road here, and I get to jogging maybe a mile, a mile and a half, two miles. It might change each day. And so I make sure that I cover — oh, two or three hours of rigorous exercise, or reasonable exercise, every day.

GB: At our stage in life, one tends to think of death a little more than heretofore. Do you think of death?
JPD: Well, yes, occasionally. It doesn't seem to worry me at all.

GB: So, what do you think happens when you die, if anything?
JPD: I don't think anything much happens. It could be blank out there, or in there, or whatever. No one, I think, has satisfactorily come up with something that does go on afterwards, or when your focus of awareness ends, and at that point I don't think anything is happening.

GB: Light switch goes off.
JPD: That's it.

GB: End.
JPD: Yeah.

GB: And when you say that, do you wish you had faith that you'd go on to something better?
JPD: No, I wouldn't wish anything that I thought wasn't correct or true. You see, probably, having a scientific background, or having read science at university, my attitude has always been: what the practical thing tells you, you just go by that.

GB: So, what is the meaning of life, as far as you're concerned?
JPD: Well, to stay living as long as you can. I think survival is the matter that all of us think most of — just to keep living and stay alive.

GB: Okay, final question . . . which we ask all our people on this programme. Just suppose that what the Jesuits taught you all those years ago about the whole theology of the Church is true, and that there is a God and there is a summoning to judgement on the last day, and that there are Pearly Gates or something similar . . . and you arrive at them when you die, and you are confronted by him, her or it. What will you say?
JPD: "How's it going?"

GB: [Laughter.] Is that the best you can come up with?
JPD: It might be the best I could come up with, I'm afraid. [Laughter.]

GB: All right! Thank you very much.

EMILY O'REILLY

The Little Girl Who Found
Her Voice

"Speak up!" For some, that phrase can be an admonishment; for others, an encouragement. For Emily O'Reilly, the first woman to become European Ombudsman, it has at times been both.

She is an apt choice for the "voice of the voiceless" role of Ombudsman, whether here or in Strasbourg, because she herself has experienced voicelessness, quite literally. When she was five, she was hospitalised for a long period, far from home and family, as her poor parents, at their wits' end, tried to help her find her speaking voice. Her eyes still well up at the memory of the homesickness and silent isolation she felt during the long weeks of therapy.

It seems to have worked, though. She is certainly not stuck for words now. Our conversation rattled along for over two hours, during which Emily completely forgot about and missed an appointment with one of our European Commissioners — possibly not the best start to her new job.

She famously jumped ship to public advocacy from journalism at the suggestion of Charlie McCreevy, who, one suspects, might have been motivated by a desire to turn one of the most effective critics of Bertie's Government into a public-service wonk. If so, the plan failed dismally. Emily proved to be perfectly willing to use her new position to bite the hand that had fed her, if she ever felt it needed biting.

It is a useful, but rare, trait for a champion of civic rights to believe that there are more important things than being loved. That was also a characteristic of Emily's journalism. She was willing to speak uncomfortable truths about all sorts of powerful groups and people, and she was even willing to dent the halo of her martyred journalistic peer Veronica Guerin, fully aware that, as a consequence, she would become a pariah in certain hack circles. It is not that she wants to be disliked or that she fails to anticipate the fall-out from such actions: it is more that she feels the fear and does it anyway. How else do you explain the decision of someone with a pathological fear of flying to take on a role that involves constant shuttle flights to Europe? Or the choice of a mute infant to pursue a career that involves relentless public speaking?

This cool, unflinching, bloody-minded courage first caught my eye when Emily broke the story of the pitiful death of the Granard schoolgirl Ann Lovett and her baby in 1984. I well remember the resentment we faced on *The Gay Byrne Show* when we followed up on that story on air; but it was Emily who first lifted the stone, not only on Granard's dirty secret but on the whole nation's. It won Emily awards, but few friends, I suspect. To paraphrase Othello, however, she undoubtedly did the state some service.

Ah, but might she yet do it even higher service? And would she want to? Rumours abound that she may run for the Áras in 2018, when she tires of high-flying in, and to, Strasbourg. Interestingly, she didn't scotch the rumours, or even deflect them, when I asked her about them during our chat. But neither did she try to use our interview as an early hustings. She will win few votes from *mná na hÉireann*, I suspect, with what she revealed about her attitude to women. Once again, though, she put being truthful before being loved.

I suspect that one reason she is able to do this is that she gets so much love at home that she doesn't need to crave anyone else's. Her husband clearly adores her. Of course, she'll take other people's approval and affection, if it is offered, but not at any price. Her philosophy is perhaps best captured by Keats's maxim:

Beauty is truth, truth beauty, − that is all
Ye know on earth, and all ye need to know.

∽

GB: Mentally, you're already making arrangements for your flight to Strasbourg and packing your cases to be the first female European Union Ombudsman. And it occurs to me that you've a grand job here in Dublin and a lovely family and a lovely home, and you hate flying . . .
EOR: [Laughs.]

GB: . . . so why on earth are you taking on this ferocious responsibility?
EOR: That is an absolutely brilliant question! When I first learned that there was a vacancy, and a few people had said to me, "Would you consider . . . ?" and all of that, I said, "No, I won't," for all of the reasons that you have just cited. I have five children. The youngest is thirteen, the eldest is twenty-three, and it wasn't so much that they would miss Mummy, but Mummy would miss them. It was my own neediness for the children. And then, instead of seeing it in a negative way for the family, I started seeing it in a positive way: it might be an adventure, it might open doors and ideas and thoughts for them. And then, leaving

aside all of those domestic considerations, it is an exciting job, and I suppose it appealed to that part of me that still wants and needs to be challenged.

GB: We'll come back to the job later on, but first take us back to Tullamore. Your late dad worked with the ESB, and your mum had and reared you and your three siblings. Was that a happy household in your memory, growing up?

EOR: It was. It was very standard for the time: you know, very nice parents, the whole Catholic school thing. We weren't terribly well off. If there was unhappiness at all for me, it wasn't within the family. I was a very shy child, and that caused me a lot of difficulties. I had a speech difficulty when I was very young. It wasn't a stammer, but nobody could understand me apart from my mother. So I had just turned five, I think, and I was sent to Baldoyle Hospital, which was a hospital for children who had physical handicaps and people with intellectual disabilities as well. I was just dumped there one weekend afternoon . . .

GB: From Tullamore?

EOR: . . .And my parents had probably been told just to leave me there and not to tell me what was going on, but it was quite a traumatic time. It wasn't that anybody was cruel to me, but the first morning that I was there I was being brought to the speech therapist, and I remember they had to drag me down corridors, and I was screaming and crying. And some time ago, my mother gave me some letters that I had written to her at the time. And I mean I could have cried for the child that I was. You know, it was "Dear Mammy, thank you for . . ." whatever it was she sent me. "I don't cry now any more . . ." I thought, What a tragic image . . .

GB: And did you have a hard time arising out of that in school? You were bullied a bit . . .

EOR: I was, yeah. I mean it was typical. You know, shy, little, nerdy child. I was quite bright, and I was really exceptionally good at English. When I was seven, I had the reading age of a sixteen-year-old, and I would read eight books a day. Now, I'd love to say it was Bunyan and Dante — it wasn't. It was Enid Blyton and everything [laughs], but I just absorbed, absorbed, absorbed, because "out there" was a bit scary.

GB: Okay, the family moved to Dublin, and you were in the Firhouse National School and then with the Sisters of Mercy in Ballyroan. That was rather more pleasant for you, was it not?

EOR: It was. At the age of about thirteen or fourteen I gave myself a good talking-to and willed myself out of my shyness. Not completely, but I can remember a moment, sitting on the wall outside the school one evening, saying to myself, "Emily, this is getting you nowhere."

GB: "Pull yourself together and get over this . . ."

EOR: Yeah, exactly. It made me realise that, in order to achieve anything in your life, ultimately you have to do it yourself.

GB: That's an extraordinary discovery in itself.

EOR: No, it isn't. I sometimes feel, when people talk to me about how I got on, I'm not amazingly clever or amazingly good-looking or amazingly anything, but I do have, I suppose, the will to do it and not to make excuses if I can't. So, when I see a goal, I *just* see the goal. I don't tend to see the barriers, whereas some people will itemise the barriers, every step of the way.

GB: I know you did Spanish and English in UCD, and you taught in France, and you did various other things. At what stage did you decide "It's journalism for me . . . I want to be a hack"?

EOR: Well, I'd done the BA and HDip, and I had not been a stellar university student at all. And when I reflected on the people and the things that had interested me, it all pointed to journalism. It was writing. It was the people I had hung out with in college. It was a great interest in politics and current affairs, which I got from my dad. And all of that pointed in one direction.

So, to cut a long story short, I'd sent a CV, such as it was — heavily enhanced, I would imagine — to Conor Brady, who was the then Editor of the *Sunday Tribune*, later Editor of the *Irish Times*. And he made me, immediately, their Education Correspondent. [Laughter.]

GB: And you knew as much about education . . .

EOR: Absolutely.

GB: [Laughter.] Oh dear, oh dear! . . . I think that what put you on the map was the Ann Lovett story from Granard in Co. Longford, the little girl who was found dead in the grotto with her dead child beside her. Tell me how that came about and what effect that had.

EOR: That was in the early spring, 1984, and I was in the newsroom one Saturday morning. Brian Trench, who was the News Editor at the time, called me over to his desk, said, "Emily, I've just got a phone call, a tip-off from somebody anonymous, that a young girl was found dead with a baby. She had just given birth in a place called Granard. Would you check it out?"

GB: I have long been convinced that your breaking that story was actually the start of the uncovering of that whole child sex-abuse thing.
EOR: You are absolutely right, because I remember that this was just after our great pro-life amendment campaign, when we were being reassured left, right and centre that, of course, women having babies would be cared for and nurtured, which was not the case. They either died, their babies died or they were shunted into Magdalene laundries. It was if we had this beautiful Catholic carpet, and underneath that was anything that didn't fit: colour, race, gender, sin. But, yes, that did begin that, because after that, people started looking under other rocks. It also gave people permission to talk about what had happened.

GB: Okay . . . To more cheerful subjects. Along came Mr Stephen Ryan. In what circumstances, and how? And was it hot-diggedy-do, straight away . . . ?
EOR: Well, Stephen was working in the *Sunday Tribune,* and I had returned to the *Sunday Tribune* after a period, and he was this force of nature within the office. He was doing the design part.

GB: What do you mean by the "force of nature"?
EOR: He was very vibrant, very tall — six foot four. He is now completely bald; at the time he had long hair, bright shirts — wonderful life-force, really.

GB: Was it an immediate thing or was it a slow, meandering build-up?
EOR: I think it was certainly fairly immediate for him. For me . . .

GB: Has he said this?
EOR: Yes, constantly. I was twenty-eight or twenty-nine. He was a few years younger. He keeps telling me he sort of took me off the shelf and dusted me down. I suppose what attracted me to him was he was quite different to me: he absolutely complements me. And I'm not sure that I would ever have been enabled to do what I do without him. And I think I can say that he absolutely loves me. You know, even when I'm looking

my worst, he will still say something that makes me think he is completely blind . . . And long may that continue!

GB: Well, twenty-six years later, and five kids, it seems to be working reasonably well. May we deduce from that that you are a fan of marriage?
EOR: Erm . . . I think this is an area that is a complete minefield now-adays. If you say you are, you box yourself into a conservative, smug, Catholic little corner. And I think people always speak from their own experience. But children do love their parents being together. I mean, there was one of *my* children, and I remember somebody remarking that in this child's particular class, there was something like eleven kids whose parents had separated. And they had separated at a point when their children were still quite young. And, okay, there but for the grace of God . . . but, in my experience, children are very conservative creatures. They like things to remain the same.

GB: Going back to the children, did becoming a mother, having children — does that change your opinions and your attitude and your outlook?
EOR: I think it has to, if you are a thinking, sentient human being at all. If change means reflecting on how you're doing things and reflecting more on how the world is doing things, I think that probably came about, for me, when my older children were kind of out of young childhood, entering adolescence, thinking, "Oh, my God, that was the easy, big feeding and changing and minding stage . . . Now comes the tough bit." And "What sort of a world am I — are we — sending them into?" I suppose that coincided with the Celtic Tiger piece. A lot of people went crazy, and a lot of secular, material value became upper-most, and this became almost like the new religion. You know, the sort of people who were lauded, the type of success that was lauded . . .

GB: Did you try to bring your children up the way your mother brought you up? Catholic Church and so on . . .
EOR: I did, yeah, absolutely. They were all baptised — Holy Communion, Confirmation as well. I suppose, in a way, it was lazy, in that I was mimicking or mirroring what Mum and Dad had done for us. It's almost as if you had this kind of handy, off-the-shelf religion or way of doing things that was easy to access through the schools . . . even though, actually, they went to Church of Ireland schools and local school.

GB: Did you say they went to a Church of Ireland school?
EOR: Yeah. Where I live, in Howth, the local one to us was the Church of Ireland school, on the Burrow Road . . .

GB: Because it was handy?
EOR: It was handy, and also my observation of how religion is taught in any school — Catholic, Jewish — it's very lightly done.

GB: Nowadays, you mean?
EOR: Nowadays.

GB: Not in your day . . .
EOR: Oh, God, no. Certainly not. It went on from dawn to dusk. But, anyway, I don't think it particularly mattered where they went. They did Catholic instruction outside of the school for First Holy Communion and all of that.

GB: All right. Now, apart from the journalism, you have written three books. The first was *Candidate*, about Mary Robinson. The second was *Masterminds of the Right*, an exposé of how the Catholic Right operates in Ireland, especially in the Knights of Columbanus. Then there was *Veronica Guerin*, and you took a fair amount of flak about that. And the message seemed to be, from going ahead to publish that book, that being liked is not the most important thing in life — that you felt you wanted to do this, and you had to do it . . .
EOR: I thought it was a simple proposition. Woman journalist dies, shot dead — international news, political upheaval — unprecedented. You write a book about it. But that wasn't the narrative.

GB: That was not the nub.
EOR: No. A story takes hold, and there's only one story. Veronica was a secular saint. She had gone to rid the town of crime and drugs . . .

GB: Bandits!
EOR: . . . all of that, and she was brutally killed. Now, a lot of that is true, but a lot of that is a romantic fairy tale. I mean, Veronica was a hungry journalist with flaws. I mean, she did tell lies about certain things; she did obscure the truth; she did operate in a way that wasn't entirely ethical. It got results! So I came up with my own narrative — the facts of which were never disputed — and all hell broke loose. So, whatever . . . It was a brutal, tragic time for Veronica's family. Whatever happened to me paled into insignificance. I did what I did. I don't regret it. I remember

somebody saying, "Never speak ill of the dead . . ." Well, I mean, there goes history. [Laughter.]

GB: I want to read you something. *"She's a blonde. She's gorgeous. She's married to a great guy. She has five terrific kids, a magnificent house, was never dented by the job . . . and still comes to the Press Ball in high-heel shoes and a backless dress."* That appealed to me very much, I must say. *"She has it all . . . No wonder people resent her."* What is that resentment about?

EOR: I don't know. When you put it all out there, yes, it sounds pretty damn good, but that's the swan piece. You know, nobody ever sees the legs going like the clappers underneath, in a slightly more ungainly way. Even the backless dress thing . . . that was a Press Ball, and I had just had one of my children, and I remember I was wearing a cream dress, and I thought I looked very nice. And I came downstairs and Stephen was at the end of the stairs, and, as ever, he said, "Emily, you look lovely. You look gorgeous." And my mother-in-law, Lord rest her, was at the bottom of the stairs . . .

GB: Oh dear!

EOR: . . .And she looked me up and down and said, "Yes, Emily . . . I think you need to do more tummy exercises . . ." [Laughter.] At which point, elegant Emily flounced out of the house.

GB: So much for backless dresses and high heels . . . !

EOR: Yes. So much for backless dresses . . . and harmony in the home.

GB: Now then, P. J. Mara described you as "blonde ambition". I don't know whether he was complaining about the "blonde" or the "ambition" bit, but let's talk about ambition for a minute. What is ambition for you, and what's your measure of success?

EOR: Well, it's funny. Sometimes I'm portrayed as somebody who's constantly thinking about my next move. I mean, God forbid. I'm just thinking, "Does Superquinn stay open until half nine?" or "Can I get that thing from the dry cleaner?" or "Where did she hide the recorder?" All that stuff. But what I *do* do, when I do have a job, I just try to do it well.

GB: Get on with it.

EOR: So, I was competent in a lot of jobs and, as a result of that, I either got another job or somebody came and asked me, "Would you like this job?"

GB: Okay, the Presidency, then. It's been mentioned in connection with you. Or rather you've been mentioned in connection with it.

EOR: About two years into office, I made a speech about a lot of what I'm speaking about here: Celtic Tiger, values, all that sort of stuff. And from that time on, people were saying, "She's running for the Presidency." And it became a complete pain.

GB: "She wants to be President!"

EOR: "She wants to be President." And I didn't. And I never discussed it with anybody — not my husband. It was never an issue. I did not think I had accomplished enough in my life to justify being President of this country.

GB: But now?

EOR: I don't know. Perhaps if I was approached, or if I thought to do it independently, then I would see where I was in my own life and whether I could contribute anything worthwhile.

GB: Sure. So, the other thing I want to check out with you is that you have said that you're a "man's woman" rather than "woman's woman". Is that so?

EOR: Well, I think that was something that was said. I wouldn't entirely disagree with it, as long as people understand what I mean by it. I think my experience, when I was young — and I was a bit picked on in school — did alienate me a bit from women. And in my life I've found men simply to be more straightforward. I can trust men in a way which, perhaps because of my childhood, I don't feel that I can trust women as much. And I will say some of my best pals, my closest pals, are men.

GB: Okay, leave that. So then, you become the Ombudsman. You take on vested interests. You take on organisations, including the Church. You take on people of influence and power. And therefore you'd better be pretty clear in your own head about your own moral compass.

EOR: Well, I was a little leery about that, because I thought, "What if I wake up on a Monday morning and my moral authority isn't feeling that strong or I'm not feeling terribly moral? or whatever." But certainly, as Ombudsman, you do have to be independent. And if you think that you are going to be compromised because you cannot be independent — you cannot be impartial — then I think you have to leave the job.

A friend of mine says, "You have to live it, not laminate it!"

GB: [Laughs.] Then Glenties, MacGill School. As a contrast to the Celtic Tiger, you recommended that people might go tip-toeing back to the Church, or Churches. Now, I know that it wasn't the Monday night Novena you were recommending, or the First Fridays, but what had you in mind there?

EOR: I've always thought that, to be fully human, we all crave some sort of transcendence, something that takes us out of the mundane, material nature of our lives. And the question is: are we just a random piece of flotsam and jetsam that just so happened, by a quirky combination of chemicals, to have appeared as a microdot in the universe, or is there something guiding all of that? I have no idea.

I think why people believe — sometimes, despite themselves, in their intelligence — is that there is a craving, a need, to believe in something — a refusal to believe that this is all there is.

And I remember reading a poem by Seán Ó Ríordáin called *Saoirse*, and he was talking about freedom of the mind and freedom to think, and what a tyranny it was. And I'll always remember he envied "the little people with the little thoughts". You know, religion is the opium of the people. Because if you can comfort yourself, whether it's with religion or whether it's yoga or belief in a spirit or whatever, you begin to think way beyond our own tiny little paltry existence. It's just almost unthinkable.

GB: Talking of transcendence, what, or who, was Jesus, as far as you're concerned?

EOR: A very real and immensely humane individual. And I've always been able to separate out the idea of God from the person of Jesus Christ, as mediated to us through the Bible. And I've never found anything, actually, on which I disagree with him.

GB: Was he the Son of God? Was he divine?

EOR: I've no idea. But I'm talking about the man, the person, who lived those thirty-odd years, and what he said on Earth in relation to how we should live and how we should be and how we should deal with each other and how we should forgive.

GB: You know what you were taught. You no longer believe what you were taught by the nuns . . . ?

EOR: I neither believe nor don't believe. I guess I'd probably go more towards the *not* believing than believing.

GB: Okay. Do you pray?
EOR: Erm . . . Occasionally, yes.

GB: To whom and what and when and why?
EOR: Well, again, I mean it's the easy, off-the-shelf piece.

GB: What?
EOR: God. "Please, God, let this happen . . . Please, God, let this not happen." It's not down on my knees and structured prayer.

GB: You don't sit and recite the Our Father, the Hail Mary . . .
EOR: No. In times of trouble I will look up at the sky and say, "Please . . ."

GB: And do you go to Mass?
EOR: Sporadically.

GB: Do you go to other services?
EOR: Sporadically.

GB: Were you ever attracted to any other faith? Buddhism, Muslim, Jew, Church of Ireland . . . ?
EOR: No. I have enough to be going on with, wrestling with this particular one . . . Church of Ireland — I kind of like Church of Ireland. I have a theory that a lot of Catholics move to the Church of Ireland, because their churches are prettier, their services are shorter . . . Sometimes the Church of Ireland communities can be, because they're so small — I mean, you probably noticed this in Howth — they're very united communities, they all know each other, you know? And maybe that is something we've lost.

GB: Your father died . . .
EOR: Eight years ago.

GB: . . . and you wrote somewhere that he did not go quietly into that . . . ?
EOR: No.

GB: He didn't *want* to die.
EOR: No, he didn't. Dad was eighty-one when he died, but in his mind he was twenty-five, I think. He did not want to leave this life; he did not want to leave my mother. Whatever about us, he certainly didn't want to leave her. And he lay back on the pillow and he said something like,

"Emily, so where do we go from here?" And I think, in a way, maybe, that was the big question. And Dad and I had a really close bond — really close relationship — and he knew I wasn't going to flam him. And I just said, "No idea, Dad." And that was it. Now, he died peacefully, but I'm not sure he was entirely peaceful in his mind. He wasn't accepting of it. And that was his absolute right, as far as I was concerned.

GB: So where is he?
EOR: He is around. I think of him, Mum thinks of him, we all think of him — the children.

GB: Any stronger presence than that?
EOR: I'm not sure. I don't visit his grave. I do occasionally, at Christmas, or sometimes maybe a birthday, but I don't feel he's there.

GB: What I'm asking you is what do you think happens to us after we die?
EOR: I think we are just put into a grave and that's it, really.

GB: Switch off.
EOR: Yeah. I don't believe we go to Heaven and you'll meet your loved ones. Whenever I think of meeting my loved ones, I think, "Well, I hope God knows which ones I loved. I'm not going to be landed into eternity with the ones I couldn't stand!" [Laughter.] But that's how I feel now. I might change.

GB: Final question. Suppose it's all true, what your mother and father believed in, especially your mother, and you get to the Pearly Gates and you are met there by God. What will you say to him, her, it?
EOR: I think I'd ask him how he thought it was all working out . . .

GB: Okay. Thank you.

JOHN LONERGAN

Believing in People

J ohn Lonergan divides public opinion. To some, the former Governor of Mountjoy epitomises all that is right and decent in Ireland. Humane and humble, passionate and compassionate, he somehow managed to do one of the toughest jobs in the country with gentleness and fairness.

But there are also those who see him as Ireland's answer to "Porridge's" Mr Barraclough: a liberal, so woolly that his own wool was regularly pulled over his eyes. "Never mind Lonergan's bleeding-heart utterances about prisoners' rights," the argument goes. "What about their innocent victims' rights? And what about the unrepentant lags, smuggling drugs and mobile phones into 'The Joy' to enable them to continue their 'outside' activities 'inside'?"

John Lonergan takes both views of him with a pinch of salt. He is not vain enough to pay much heed to adulation and he is far too well versed in the links between poverty and crime to believe that people in prison deserve all the toughness we can throw at them.

You might think that Lonergan's career in the justice system was vocational, but in fact it was more a case of *needs must*. As an out-of-work Tipperary school-leaver, he answered an ad in his local paper for trainee prison officers and never looked back — a life sentence, from which he has now secured early release.

When we met for this interview, I was not surprised to discover that John's social ethics were inspired by Canon John M. Hayes, founder of Muintir na Tíre and sometime parish priest of Lonergan's native Bansha. That figures. Practising a highly pragmatic form of "muscular Christianity", Muintir na Tíre promotes community solidarity as a route out of poverty, and it resolutely tears down barriers of class and wealth. Pope Francis would approve.

What was surprising, however, was that when I started to probe John Lonergan's beliefs and theology in detail, I discovered that he hasn't really got any. God? Unlikely. An afterlife? Probably not. Jesus? A really good guy, but probably no more than that. Catholicism? An all-too-human institution, whose members mostly fail to practise what they preach.

I gather that, since that rather candid articulation of non-belief, quite a few people have written to Lonergan, or stopped him in the streets, trying to revive his Christian faith. They care about him and want him back in the club. It also upsets some believers to discover that they don't have a monopoly on virtue, that you don't necessarily need a faith to be, or do, good.

Having said all that, John Lonergan clearly is a man of faith. Every time he trusted a prisoner not to abuse privileges or leniency it was an act of faith – and one not always rewarded. Instinctively, he understood that prison is a place where no one trusts anyone. In order to break that cycle, you have to be willing to take the risk of believing in people – even people who give you plenty of reasons not to believe in them.

Judging by the number of Lonergan's reformed former clientele who still stop him in the street to exchange pleasantries and thank him for his kindness, some of those little acts of faith went a long way.

∾

GB: I'm going to start by taking you back to Bansha, Co. Tipperary. And, as they say, it's a long way from there to here, via Limerick Gaol and Port Laoise and Mountjoy. Tell me about your upbringing in Bansha.

JL: I was born in 1947, in the townland of Tooreen, which was in the parish of Kilmoyler, which is about three miles west of Cahir. There was eight of us in total: I have three brothers and four sisters, and we lived in a totally rural community. And, of course, my mother would have been the person who properly kept it all together, like all mothers in those days.

My father worked as a handyman-gardener with a family that used to reside in a house called Tooreen Wood House, which was a big house in the middle of a mature wood. And he used to work there for £4 9 shillings a week.

GB: Were you conscious of being poor?

JL: Not really.

GB: You never went without food?

JL: Never, no. Mainly because we were able to provide potatoes and vegetables, and killing pigs was a regular feature at that time, so you cured your own bacon. So, there was always the basics. But I guess, because of that, we were very content as well. Our ambitions weren't very high, and our expectations weren't very high.

GB: A religious household, I presume?

JL: Yeah, the very basic stuff, like Mass every Sunday.

GB: Daily Rosary?

JL: When I was a child, I can remember my mother — again, mothers! — my mother was always organising the Rosary, usually after supper at half six. It was almost automatic that you all knelt down around the kitchen and the Rosary was recited.

And that time as well, of course, women were very much suppressed by the Church. I have no hesitation in saying that now. They were very obedient. They believed the Church doctrine in relation to families and procreation and all that stuff, and so they felt that their job was to have children and to rear as many children as they had, irrespective of the circumstances those children were going to have to grow up in.

GB: Now, your father did join Muintir na Tíre . . .

JL: Yeah.

GB: And the founder of that was Canon Hayes, who was your parish priest — quite clearly, a man who had huge influence on you, yes?

JL: Yes, of course. I've often said it since, that I've no great time for the institution of the Church and what it has done, but individuals within the institutional Church were terrific people. And he would probably be the first person that I met who was a true Christian, in the sense that he believed in the philosophy of Christianity, which was around equality. And then, of course, his whole philosophy about the need for building viable rural communities — that was way ahead of his time as well, and he was very much on the side of the poor. I believe that is where the Church should find its strongest roots: looking after and fighting on behalf of the poor, those who struggle or are voiceless. He predicted the Celtic Tiger and the destruction it would bring with it, and that's hard to believe now, seventy years onwards, but he did.

GB: In what terms did he predict?

JL: He predicted that if we become a society obsessed with materialism, we'll create nothing but greed and selfishness and competition and *Mé-Féiner*-ism, and if we treat human beings as production units, we will have failed miserably. And sure, during the Celtic Tiger, that's exactly what we did. So, he was a visionary and he was a prophet in that sense.

GB: Now, were you an altar boy to him?

JL: No. I was subsequently. But I had a lot of contact over the years, as a young person, with priests, as a result of serving Mass, and I must say that every single one of them were nothing but gentlemen. I have nothing but the height of respect for them.

GB: How and why did you get into the Prison Service?

JL: Like many people in life, Gay, this was a pure accident. It wasn't by design, and it certainly wasn't anything that I had a vocation for. It was just in the papers. They advertised at that time — the old Civil Service Commission — and I responded to it. And then, on 8th March, 1968, I was asked to report to Limerick Prison, in Mulgrave Street, as a prison officer.

GB: Was that a rude awakening for you?

JL: Like most people then, I suppose, I had this basic perception and belief that the baddies were in prison and the goodies would be outside, and I wasn't a week in Limerick Prison working when that particular perception was shattered, because they had psychiatric problems, physical disabilities, addiction problems — mainly alcohol. Many of them were homeless.

GB: They were just thrown in there?

JL: They were sentenced, Gay, for the most minor things: wandering with intent, no means of support, drunk and disorderly, vagrancy. All oul stupid things, and maybe one or two fairly serious guys that might have robbed a bank or something.

GB: And what effect did all that have on you at that young age?

JL: Well, I suppose, you can go two ways when you enter a place like a prison. You can get hard-hearted and say it's too good for them. And I'm afraid lots of people fall into that category. You know, if they commit the crime, you do the time, and shut up and get on with it. I went the opposite direction, because I felt that these were fundamental injustices and that if people had different journeys in life — if they had different opportunity in life — many of them would never have been in prison.

GB: Were you very out of step with the other people of authority in Limerick at that time for your attitude?

JL: God, no, Gay. The very opposite, because, again, the public's perception of people who work in prison would have been pretty negative and pretty stereotypical as well, that they'd be fairly tough guys. In actual fact, what I met in Limerick was hundreds of the most caring people you could meet. It's amazing that they're there, and they work so hard to try to make life better for those who are in prison. You have the other type as well, of course: hard-liners who believe that prisoners have no rights and should be punished. But there are always the other side as well: people who make the biggest of all difference.

The Principal Officer — he was an Assistant Principal at this stage in the Department of Justice, a man called Richard McCronnach, or "Dick Crow", as we used to know him — he said to us, as a group of young staff in the early 1970s, "If you want to put your religion or your Christianity into operation in a meaningful way, there's no better place to do it than in a centre for young juvenile offenders." You see, prison is an amazing place. I've often highlighted that a prison operates mainly on the dynamic of *mis*trust. Nobody trusts anybody in prison. And I mean *everybody*, from top to bottom. Prisoners don't trust staff; staff don't trust prisoners. That's why they're always checking them, searching them — all that sort of stuff. Now, it's very difficult to grow and develop and reach your potential in an atmosphere of mistrust, even in your own home. Mistrust, by God, it will eat away and undermine everything. There's no relationship that could be sustained on the basis of mistrust.

GB: Arising from which, we often talk about the concept of evil, and to most of us evil is a concept, insofar as we very rarely encounter it, I think. Have you encountered evil, and what is your concept of it?

JL: Yeah, I've encountered people who have committed evil acts — no question about that. I had to. I spent forty-two years and met hundreds of thousands of people who have committed very minor offences, but also people who have committed horrific offences. And so I'm absolutely clear that human beings have the capacity to do evil. And many of us have committed evil acts, and they're not necessarily all criminal, but many evil acts are committed by human beings the world over. But I never met a completely evil *person*. And while I have met people who have committed acts — and, in some cases, they deserve to and need to be kept in prison for the rest of their lives, because of the danger they present in society — I've never met an all-evil person. And I always balanced that, Gay, by saying neither have I met an all-good person on the outside. So, I believe that all of us have the capacity as human beings to commit evil.

GB: Well, then, the next one is: why do some people end up like that and others don't?

JL: It all begins at birth, or perhaps even before birth. You know, some people, when they are born, they pull out a long straw: they are born into loving, caring parents, they're born with talent and, in many ways, they get a soft run through life. Everything seems to be just right for them. And, equally, on the other extreme, you have many, many people born with all sorts of difficulties.

GB: But there are plenty of people who come from an abusive and restricted background who choose not to do bad things.

JL: My comment on that, Gay, is that there are some extraordinary people. Human beings have an extraordinary capacity to survive. We know that from the concentration camps, for instance. Nelson Mandela is one example of a person who survived. Why? Because he was a very special person with very special strengths and abilities. Not every human being is equipped to the level that Nelson Mandela was equipped, in terms of human ability, human endurance, the capacity to cope.

For instance, if you were born to a family where your mother is addicted to heroin, and your dad is an alcoholic, you're not going home to a meal or to any warmth or to any love. You're going home to a hostile environment. Now, nobody would convince me but that that leaves a mark emotionally, psychologically, mentally — and physically sometimes.

GB: Are you hurt, John, when people say that you are a bleeding-heart liberal and you're far too soft? And then certain sections of the media have given you what one person called "the moral authority of the Dalai Lama" . . .

JL: Oh, God help us!

GB: Is that offensive to you?

JL: Yes, but one of the things that happens during life is that there are certain things you get used to. You must have, I believe, a philosophy for what you're doing or a vision or a belief that what you're doing is right. Doing the right thing is seldom popular; doing the popular thing is seldom right. The easy thing for me to do, when I was in prison and after prison, would be to flog them and to promote that philosophy "They're scumbags: lock them up." That would be popular. But it wouldn't be right.

GB: And yet, and yet, you do agree that the victims of these people — the people who have been mugged in the street or robbed or burgled or terrorised by them — that they are entitled to see that there is some retribution, that the regime which criminals are sent to should be tough?

JL: Yeah, I don't agree with that . . . I totally agree with the cry of the victims and the hurt and the pain of the victims. Of course, victims should be supported and helped. And, of course, those who cause the trouble and perpetrate the crimes must be punished. I believe fully that people who do wrong need to repay that wrong in whatever way. If that's imprisonment, fine. What I don't believe is that you can change people by force or by punishment. But you can help to change them. You can't force change, but you can nurture it.

I mean, some of the experiments we did in prison, like the drama projects and the work-party projects — all of that was done to demonstrate that, given different circumstances, given support rather than criticism, and focusing on the positive in the human being rather than the negative, that many human beings will respond. And through my lifetime in prison I saw that first hand, time and time and time again.

What is the objective of that? To stop them recommitting crime. If they're stopped recommitting crime, what are they doing? They're not creating more victims. So, in actual fact, you're helping victims. You're working in the cause of victims, even though victims themselves may not be aware of that.

GB: So, tell me this, then. In all of your experience, to what extent have you been treated as a fool or taken for a sucker, having your kindness, your empathy, flung back in your face?

JL: Very, very seldom. But I would rather be conned or codded the odd occasion than become a cynic. Of course, there would be people in prison who would try to pull the wool over your eyes, but one of the things that experience does for you is it helps you get on top of that and to become aware of that.

On the other hand, one of the most rewarding things for me would be — for the last two-and-a-half years, since I retired, I've met hundreds of people who have been in prison. Any day I walk the streets of Dublin or Cork or Limerick, in particular, I meet several guys . . .

GB: Your clients are all around you . . . [Smiles.]

JL: Men and women who come up to me and they're talking about their experience and they all usually mention the fact that they were treated with humanity. So, I believe that, while it's not popular, those are the little things that make a difference.

GB: Okay. Now, as well as prisons, you were co-opted onto various Church social bodies like Crosscare and Centrecare. Arising out of that, what have you learned (*a*) about yourself in this work and (*b*) about the workings of the Church?

JL: I suppose one of the amazing things was in relation to the established Church. I soon realised, in Crosscare in particular, the politics of the Church are every bit as strong as the politics of the general society. The bureaucracy that exists in the Churches is equally strong and as controlling as the bureaucracy of the state. It's amazing. The same principles apply and the same controls apply and the same restrictions apply on people to voice their concern. You know, if you don't play the party line, Gay, in terms of the state, you ain't going to go very far. And if you don't play the party line with the Church, I'm afraid the same is true.

And we have all the evidence of that: people who question, people who talk out, people who confront, who are not happy and express that view, they're not very popular, and there's efforts nowadays even to suppress them and to muzzle them. How is that compatible with an organisation that says, "We're here to promote social equality and justice and fairness for every man and woman"?

GB: So, where has this disillusionment led you? How are you fixed now in relation to the Church, your faith, your religion?

JL: In relation to the Church, personally, I've always believed that it's all about living it. So I'm not a big fan of the cosmetics of Mass and of Confession and Communion, because I believe that that's the easy, cosmetic part. It's not about what you do on a Sunday: it's what you do on a Monday and a Tuesday and a Wednesday. So, it's about making a difference to people, helping people, supporting people, and taking a special interest in those who struggle in life. I call them the underdog. I felt an underdog myself for most of my life, and I believe that it's important.

And, by the way, Gay, it's also one of the most rewarding things a human being can do: to make a difference to the underdog, to the struggler, because they will never, ever forget that gesture. And so, we think of the individuals in the Church who have done heroic work. But they're all individuals. The Church as an institution has done very little,

I believe, except suppressive stuff, control-freak stuff. But individuals . . . If you take people like Father Peter McVerry — the wonderful work he does. And he's also an advocate. Sister Consilio around addiction, Sister Caoimhín out in Ballyfermot — and I suppose my ultimate Christian would be the person I admire most in life, John Hume, the man who brought peace to Ireland. I have always claimed that he sacrificed everything for peace — his own career, to a degree, his own party, everything — because he believed that the bigger picture required reconciliation.

GB: It seems to me that it is not so much the abuse scandals which have turned you against the institutionalised Church: it's the politics . . .
JL: Oh, absolutely. I can totally understand the abuse side, because it's human beings. Just because they're priests or sisters or members of religious orders doesn't change the fact that, fundamentally, they're human, and in any body of human beings you're going to have wrongdoing and you're going to have sins committed. Of course! Human nature, that's what it is. There's no perfect human being.

So I'm not disturbed, except by the way it was handled, by the obsession with the established Church around the materialistic side of it: compensation. They got a lot of advice: "How do we save money?" — the last thing that a Christian Church should be concerned about! They were far more concerned about the protection of their assets and the money they were going to save, rather than the people.

And then the other thing that disturbs me about the Church, and this isn't very popular at all, is its total reneging on those of its members who committed the crimes, the priests and the other religious orders, the Brothers, that committed the crimes. Where does the Church stand in terms of forgiveness for them? Where does the Church stand in terms of reconciliation? The only example I can see is that it doesn't stand at all, doesn't forgive at all. There's no reconciliation. We still have Bishops, for instance, totally ostracised, simply because they did wrong twenty to twenty-five years ago. Where is the Church's example for being able to provide reconciliation for their own members? If you believe in it, well, then you must do it.

GB: Do you think we're a Christian country?
JL: I'm very much influenced by what is attributed to Gandhi many, many years ago, when he said, "I like your Christ. I don't like your Christians. Your Christians ain't like your Christ." I think that's still very true.

GB: You just said that you were an underdog yourself.

JL: Oh, God, I was, yeah. And I still feel a bit of an underdog.

GB: In what way?

JL: I can never identify with the establishment, even when I spent forty-two years working in prison. I believe that there was too much covering up, too much suppression. There was a spin doctor approach to most things, sending out the positives all the time, when there was very little, and suppressing the truth about the reality of overcrowding in prisons, lack of work, lack of activity, the huge injustices that were done to people in terms of the lack of facilities for them and the conditions they were subjected to. You know, you can go into that system, and if you're loyal to it, well, then you'll certainly be popular. But you also then have to cope with your own feelings. How true are you to yourself? And for me that would be very important, that you always have your own personal values and principles. And if you don't have them, I'd say, well then, you're nothing, really.

GB: So political, institutionalised Church to one side, do you believe in God?

JL: I have my doubts. Is there somebody up there that is controlling the whole thing . . . ?

GB: Well, is there?

JL: Is there an afterlife?

GB: Is there?

JL: I'm not so sure, Gay. It's very hard to find any sort of concrete evidence that there is, but I suppose we all, as human beings, live, to some degree, in hope that there is something. But I wouldn't bet on it, now. I wouldn't be very confident that there is an afterlife. But I hope there is.

GB: Do you pray?

JL: Very little.

GB: And when you're in difficulty or in doubt, do you ever address somebody up there to say, "Give me a helping hand." No . . . ?

JL: No, not really.

GB: And so, what about Jesus? I mean, you keep on saying, "Do the Christian thing," and Christians are merely followers of Christ. So, what was Jesus to you, then?

JL: I think he was just an extraordinary human being that had the charisma. And we have had some since as well, extraordinary human beings that had this ability, this charisma. People like Canon Hayes, Nelson Mandela.

GB: But is there any semblance of divinity in Jesus, as far as you're concerned? Physical resurrection? No . . . ?
JL: Yeah, I find that very difficult.

GB: You spoke lovingly earlier on about your parents. Do you think you'll see them again?
JL: No, I don't.

GB: So, this society that you envisage of equality and equal opportunity — is there any sign of that coming about?
JL: None whatsoever, Gay. There's less chance of it happening now . . .

GB: There is less chance of it happening now? I would have thought there is more chance of it happening now.
JL: Well, I think there's less, and out of all the examples that we have in the last, recent three or four years of recession there's all the indicators that those who are going to suffer the most are the poor, the sick, the old — all those who depend on social services and support from the state, all the most vulnerable . . . So, will we have an equal society in the next twenty, thirty years? I don't believe we will.

GB: Final question: In the extremely unlikely event that all of what Canon Hayes taught you and your parents believed is all true, and you arrive at the Pearly Gates and you meet God, what will you say to him, John?
JL: I will have questions for God. I will certainly want to know: "What were you at? Where were you getting your policies and philosophy from? What were you trying to do? And why all the suffering?" And, in some ways, I'd be saying to him, "Look, it's time you stepped aside for a while and maybe let somebody else do this, because there's so many things that I think that were wrong, in terms of the suffering and the injustices."

GB: John, you can't go round telling God he's wrong!
JL: One of the great difficulties of Irish society over the years was that we didn't ask enough questions. We didn't challenge enough. Actually, in my youth we were educated and conditioned not to question: "Shut

up and do what you're told, and do what we say, not what we do." And I think that one of the weaknesses in the Catholic Church, in particular, is that it suppresses those who question. That couldn't be healthy. And if God is this wonderful being that we're being told he is, well, then surely God would be quite tolerant and compassionate enough to listen to a humble being asking questions that many, many other humble beings would like answers for.

GB: God save you.

RONAN KEATING

No Matter What

*T*he *Late Late Show* has kick-started many entertainment careers, but few as memorably as Boyzone's, mainly because on that occasion it was a matter of the career taking off in spite of their appearance, rather than because of it.

Louis Walsh's newly-minted boy band had apparently been auditioned with the mute button pressed. Even he didn't know whether any of them could sing. In fact, that Friday night in 1993, the band was so new that they had no songs and no dance moves ready to perform. Small things like that, however, were not going to prevent the great Svengali of Kiltimagh seizing a *Late Late* showcase for his protégés.

The clip of Boyzone's improvised gyrations to a backing track has haunted them ever since. In my introduction that night, I said they had "no talent whatsoever: they don't sing, they don't write music and they don't play instruments . . . They will probably be very successful."

Well, I was partly right.

Out of pure good fortune, Ronan Keating and Stephen Gately actually had enough vocal talent — and the other lads had enough looks and moves — to survive their unpromising debut. They went on to record nine Irish and six British number 1 singles.

When I recorded this *Meaning of Life* interview with Ronan, in early 2009, in his home in Malahide, he was enjoying solo success as both a singer and a songwriter. He was a happily married family man and in a good place. Neither of us could have guessed what the next couple of years would have in store for him.

Stephen Gately's sad and unexpected death, later that year, prompted the Boyzone reunion tour, which, in turn, took them all away from home for months and led to Ronan's fall from grace. His marriage never really recovered.

It is not my place or intention to judge him. The Club of the Perfect has a very small membership and those of us who have not been invited to join should be careful how we evaluate the lives and deeds of our fellow non-members. My only observation on those subsequent events is that I did not see any of them coming. Neither did Ronan.

The Ronan Keating who spoke to me in early 2009 was, as I said at the time, "a revelation" — relaxed, thoughtful, articulate and self-effacing. He spoke sincerely and lovingly about his wife, Yvonne: his "rock", who had rescued him from anger and depression after the death of his mother,

Marie. He talked candidly about his difficult relationship with his father and his need to swallow his pride and repair it. He discussed his faith — actually a remarkably conventional form of Catholicism, imbibed on family trips to Knock and through regular childhood Mass-going. Somehow, it had survived the distractions and adulation of global superstardom and had helped prevent him losing the run of himself.

In short, I liked him. I still do.

~

GB: Going back to the start of your musical career and Boyzone and the celebrated appearance on *The Late Late Show* — you were fifteen or thereabouts.

RK: Yes . . .

GB: Is that what you always wanted to do?

RK: Always. It's all I ever wanted to do. I got a part-time job in a shoe shop, and my manager in there knew that — saw the advert in the paper — and he was the one that said to me, "You know, this is on around the corner. This Irish answer to Take That is auditioning tonight." So, people knew that's what I wanted to do.

GB: And was it that you wanted to be famous, or was it the making of the music?

RK: Oh, no. You see, that's the thing: today, everybody wants to be famous. For me it was to be on stage, to be singing, performing, to work with these world-famous producers and songwriters and to get the chance to sing with these people, all of that. Back then, I think there was always a mystery about bands and about artists, and that's what made *us* fans. Now we know too much about everybody, because of the internet and media and reality TV. So, a lot of that mystery is gone. That's why people are famous for fifteen minutes and it all just becomes disposable, and someone else replaces them pretty quickly. For me, I wanted to be in the industry because I wanted to be a singer.

GB: Go back now to your mum and dad and growing up. What sort of a background did you have, and was it a religious background or whatever?

RK: My mam was a devout Catholic. They went to Mass nearly every day, prayed every day. You know, we did all the things every Catholic family does. We dressed up and went to Mass every Sunday. We got our throats blessed, and we did Ash Wednesday. Yeah, so I had a great childhood. Good, Catholic Irish family, I guess.

GB: Your mother would have been devoted to God and Padre Pio and St Anthony?
RK: Yes.

GB: What about the Blessed Virgin . . . ?
RK: Yeah, Blessed Virgin. We went down to Knock a lot. We'd have regular excursions down to Knock, once a year at least. We'd pile into the gold Escort. I sat across the back window a few times, 'cause there's so many kids . . .

GB: Down to Knock!
RK: Do the couple of hours, do the Stations of the Cross and go to where the Blessed Virgin supposedly appeared, and then head home.

GB: And at what stage would you have said that you might have got doubts about things?
RK: As I got a bit older. I joined the band. I started to travel. Now, travel is an amazing thing and when you start to meet people, you witness other cultures and you think, "They don't believe in anything that I believe in. But yet they're totally sane and normal people . . ." You know, "Hang on a second here. We've been taught one thing, and who's to say who's right and who's wrong?" So, that's really when I started to think about it all. Now, I *am* a Catholic, a believer, and I'm not saying I've turned away from it, but this made me think about it, as I travelled.

I guess, when Mam died, I had a real issue then. I had a real problem, because this was a woman who devoted her life to God. And she was fifty-one years of age. I mean, she was a young woman when she died. That's not very fair. I went to a dark place for a while and I neglected God, and I stopped praying and I stopped speaking to him. But as time went on, I realised that this was exactly what my mother wouldn't want.

And that's not the right reason to go back — I know that — but these are the challenges that we're set. This is why God went into the desert for forty days and forty nights, you know, and the Devil came and tempted him. And, you know, there are lots of different issues. All the time I was battling with them, and then I started drinking, and you don't think clearly . . .

GB: Go back to touring with the boys. You were all in the same boat, all Catholic fellas and all brought up the same way, all the same background. Was there any kind of spiritual life or insistence on the part of *anybody* on going to Mass, wherever you were in the world? Was there anybody there saying, "Well, you know, it's Sunday. We'd better go . . ."

RK: [Laughs.] I wish there was! I wish there was! No, Sunday mornings were . . . recovering from a hangover from a party.

GB: Yes.

RK: No, it was such an incredible time on the road, but the workload was massive. And we didn't have time for anything. And if you turned around at seventeen years of age and said, "I want an hour off on a Sunday morning to go to Mass," they'd tell you where to go, you know, the record company and everyone else.

GB: Are you serious?

RK: Absolutely. You don't have a voice. You're put into a band, a pop band, a boy band. You're not allowed to stand up and speak, otherwise you're a rude little git. You know, you're getting too big for your boots. Now, I prayed every day. I never stopped praying. Every night, I lay in bed and I'd say my prayers before I went to sleep. And I still do today.

GB: But what about booze, drugs and sex and rock and roll?

RK: There wasn't drugs . . . There was definitely booze, all the time. But that was our release. That was the way, every evening, we'd finish work whatever time, and you'd have a few drinks in the bar.

GB: And none of you were Pioneers . . . !

RK: No, no, no. [Laughs.] My pledge lasted about a couple of weeks, I think! I was terrible!

GB: Go back to touring. Suddenly, from being nobody, you were all catapulted into fame and recognition and being idolised and all of that. Now, cutting out this terrible hard work where you didn't even have a Sunday morning off, how did you cope with that?

RK: It was funny. Actually, I'll tell a funny story after being on *The Late Late Show* that amazing night, with yourself.

GB: [Laughs.]

RK: We made eejits of ourselves . . . !

GB: I think your admission that you weren't a dancer is putting it mildly.

RK: [Laughs.] Mildly! It looked a bunch of lunatics in a corner of a nightclub on a Saturday night. I was working in Korky's Shoe Shop at the time and the next morning, Saturday morning, I walked down Henry Street, thinking I was the bee's knees. I was, "Did you see me last night? Hey!" I thought I'd made it. Little did we know we had a long way to go.

GB: How did you cope with that fame, that recognition?

RK: Yeah, I was fine. I mean, luckily, we were all five northsiders. We all had our feet firmly on the ground. Never once did we let anyone lose the run of themselves. And then, when we came home, our families wouldn't allow us to lose the run of ourselves in any way, especially my mother. I remember her calling Louis Walsh once and saying, "Who does your man think he is?" speaking about me. You know, "Too big for his boots now . . ." That was the grounding we needed, and that's why I think we're still about today and we get this second chance.

GB: So, during all the time of the fame and making your way as a group, you did stay in touch with the Church and faith and God . . .

RK: Yeah, always.

GB: . . . because Mum was there?

RK: Yeah. Well, every time I'd be home my bag would be full of miraculous medals, and there'd be holy water thrown at me as I'm walking out the door, constantly. And then, when you buy a new car, Mam would come out and bless the car and leave the bottle of holy water in it. We always had our bits and pieces.

GB: When did you get the first inkling that your mum was sick?

RK: I guess it was about 1996. She had an issue that she wouldn't speak to me about. Mam was old school, old generation. She would never go to a doctor to get her breast checked. You know, women didn't. Cancer was the big taboo. So, she knew there was an issue. She found a lump, and we found out it was malignant.

GB: So, she had the operation?

RK: She had the operation and eighteen months later, she had the all-clear, and it was a celebration in the family. I remember it well. Mam had gone through so much. She lost her hair. She was a hairdresser herself, so it was a big deal for her, losing her hair. But then she embraced it. She went off and bought wigs and enjoyed that.

We then found out that it had moved on to the spine. That was in late November, early December, and then she passed away early February the following year, so it was very, very quick.

GB: During all that time did you pray?
RK: Yeah, a lot.

GB: A lot.
RK: Yeah, 'cause she did. She went to Mass every single day. And I prayed for her, and she prayed, and we all prayed.

GB: And, Ronan, when you were praying, who were you praying to?
RK: I was praying to God.

GB: And what was your figuring of God?
RK: Visually?

GB: Yeah, who and what you were praying to.
RK: [Laughs.] I'm reading a book at the moment, actually, called *The Shack*. It's quite interesting and it's talking about this. This guy loses his daughter, and God appears to him. And God is a big black woman. And he says, "You're God? This is not what I expected. I mean, you know, the beard and the long white robe . . ." I have to say, I'd be pretty similar. I'd be thinking, the big beard, the whole lot, yeah. I mean, images of Jesus also . . . the Jesus that we know.

GB: And did you have devotion to any other saint or any other figure . . . ?
RK: St Anthony was Mam's, you know, and Padre Pio. They were the ones Mam would pray to a lot. Over the years, she owed St Anthony an awful lot of money. [Laughs.] She used to always say that.

GB: And did you not send her to Padre Pio . . . ?
RK: Yeah, and she went off with Keith's mam. They went off to Medjugorje. Listen, she was devout, like so many other mothers and fathers in this country. She was 120 per cent a believer to the very last day. She prayed the night before she died: "God take me. I can't take any more pain." And the next day she died.

GB: So then, your reaction immediately afterwards would have been anger against God, I presume . . . ?
RK: Yeah, absolutely. I was questioning my faith. I thought, "This doesn't make any sense to me. Why?" And all these people are saying these

things to you: "Only the good die young . . ." and "You know God wants to take the good ones . . . He needs them . . ."

GB: Rubbish!

RK: Absolute waffle. Don't come to me with that. So, I was angry and I had enough. And I definitely turned my back, for a while, on God.

GB: Tell me about the Foundation, now . . . this wonderful good that came out of this dreadful thing.

RK: Yeah, a lot of negative feelings in the family, and just anger and confusion. So we tried to channel all that negative vibe and energy into something positive. And Linda came up with this idea: "Why don't we start the Marie Keating Foundation?" We were going to help people that were in our position, 'cause we had to educate ourselves, very quickly, about cancer. None of us knew anything about cancer at all.

So, as soon as we found out that Mam had a lump on her breast, we educated ourselves overnight. And we realised that early detection is your best chance of survival. You know, if you catch it early, it can be cured. Already, there is a 6 per cent increase in the survival rate of breast cancer in this country in the last six years. That's a massive step. We're going the right way, thank God.

So, yeah, we've set this up. We've three mobile units on the road in Ireland, with oncology nurses on board. People go on board, they speak to the nurses, find out more about cancer, how to check themselves. And we can fast-track to a specialist in your area.

GB: Wonderful! Just helping people . . .

RK: That's all it is. It's a free service. It's education and awareness. That's it. We've had a hundred thousand people on board the units in Ireland alone.

GB: And you have given a great deal of your time to it. You've done the marathons and so on . . .

RK: Yeah, I have a lot going on. I have two marathons this year. I have Chicago, which I'm running with a hundred and fifty garda síochána in October, which I'm really looking forward to. I've walked across Ireland, twice — four hundred miles.

But the one thing we've done this year, which I feel is going to be probably our greatest achievement, is that we've brought our teaching into the schools. Seven hundred and fifty schools across the country have accepted it. It's part of the curriculum: SPHE. You know, you learn it at that age, it's there with you for life. And we can really change things in this country because of that.

GB: Roughly the total amount collected so far over the years for . . . ?
RK: In Ireland alone, we must have raised €4½ million over the last five, six years, which is fantastic.

GB: In the midst of all of this, you were still performing and travelling and doing your thing . . . ?
RK: Yeah. And when Mam died, I thought the answer for me was to get back straight into work again. So I did. And about a week into it I broke down.

GB: You missed your mum?
RK: Yeah, I did. I really missed her.

GB: Where do you think your mum is?
RK: She's around me. She's around all of us. I can feel her all the time. I mean, I can hear her telling me things. And maybe that's just a past voice — I know what her reaction would be to something. But I hear it when the time is right. I do feel her presence, protecting us, minding me — all of us.

GB: So, do you think there will be a day of judgement?
RK: I'm not sure about that, to be really honest. I'm not sure. I don't know if we get judged. I don't know if there is a Heaven and a Hell and a Purgatory and all of those things. I still haven't figured that out.

GB: You used to believe it?
RK: . . . Because it's all I knew, and that's just the way it was. It was drilled into you. When you're growing up as a kid, you fear the local parish priests, and I had a bit of an issue as I got older. You know, your priests are supposed to be your friends and they're supposed to be people that you can lean on and people that you can ask for help. But I remember, in particular, there was a priest . . . you'd be afraid of your life of the local parish priest. The kids would never go near him. And there were none of these allegations back then about child molestation or so on. You were just afraid of your life. And I thought, "You're not supposed to fear these people."

GB: And with regard to the whole abuse scandal with the Church, presumably your priest friends say, "Well, don't tar us all with the same brush . . ."

RK: Absolutely. And I'm not, by any means. And nothing happened to me, thank God, and anyone I know. I have friends who are priests. I do go to Mass, but I do stand back and listen to what they have to say and take some of it with a pinch of salt.

GB: And do you derive anything from going to Mass?
RK: I derive more from sitting in the church speaking to God myself than I would from going to Mass.

GB: Just an empty church?
RK: Yeah.

GB: What do you do when you're there?
RK: I pray. I pray to Mam. I pray to God. I pray to whoever I feel I want to speak to at that time.

GB: And do you feel better, coming out?
RK: Yeah. I mean, it's not like the only place I can speak to God is in a church. I speak to him all the time.

GB: Your talent and your gift for music . . . Do you think that that is God-given?
RK: Yeah, all of our talents are God-given. You can't be a believer in God and not believe that we are creatures of God and that what we have is given to us by God. So, yeah.

GB: And so do you see it as an obligation to use that to the best advantage?
RK: Yeah, in all I do. What I have as a singer, the opportunities . . . I have to help other people. I think we know the things that we're supposed to do. If you have the ability, you do it. You can't waste what you have.

GB: I hear your mother talking now.
RK: Yeah, right. Okay. [Laughs.] It happens!

GB: You talk about your mum all the time but not your dad?
RK: No, my dad is around me every day. I see him every day. He's here. My dad and I, we have a great relationship, now. It wasn't so good at times. But I was young and silly. You know, I made mistakes when Mam passed away. We had a falling out and we drifted apart.

GB: What did you fall out over?
RK: Ah, loads of different issues that I don't need to talk about publicly. But when you're twenty-one years of age, you think you know it all,

and you don't. You know feck all. And being a father myself really allowed me to realise the mistakes that I'd made, and I apologised and I said sorry to him and asked him to come back into our lives. And he did, thank God, and it's better than it's ever been. It's nice to have a da, you know?

GB: And were the kids essential to that reconciliation?

RK: Yeah, well, my son being born was a big part of that. I wanted my son to have a grandfather. I wanted to have a dad. I wanted my dad to see his grandson — you know, all of those elements. But I realised I had messed up, so it was me that had to fix this.

GB: Most young fellas go through that rebellious period.

RK: Yeah, but I mean I really pushed him out of my life . . . I really got it wrong.

GB: In what way?

RK: Oh, I drove him out of the house . . . I just didn't see him or hear from him, you know? We didn't speak at all. It was horrible. It's horrible to even think about it. I cringe at what I did. It's awful.

GB: Were you ever attracted to any other faith or religion or belief or spirituality?

RK: I love the idea of meditation. I love the idea of being able to focus and relax and get rid of all of those negative thoughts and feelings and stress in your life. We live with so much rubbish on our shoulders, in this day and age, that we need to release.

GB: What kind of baggage are you talking about?

RK: Just rubbish . . .

GB: Do you retain hurt and offence . . . ?

RK: Maybe it's a bad thing, but I have an ability to not hold a grudge and to let things go. I've had reason to hold grudges with people that are now very good friends of mine: Louis Walsh, you know, some of the lads in Boyzone. And I don't. Boyzone would not be where it is now, if I held a grudge. I wouldn't be in the band. I wouldn't be back and that would be a great regret, if I was to see the lads go ahead and do it without me.

GB: So, am I right in saying that, generally speaking, you're not a stressed person?

RK: I'm not a stressed person on one hand, Gay, and on the other hand I am. I get totally stressed about things I shouldn't get stressed about.

GB: Like what?

RK: Like my health, my kids' health, my family's health — my brothers' and sister's. I think about it all the time. I found a lump in my testicle about two years ago and I freaked out, totally. And it was totally normal, but, you know, I had myself written off. And that's a tough thing to do, to go in to your doctor and drop your trousers and let him feel your testicles. [Laughs.] It's not cool. It's not comfortable. But, you know, I had to do it. So I did, and it was fine, and everything is grand. But I worry about these things. And as soon as I have one thing over with — the stress is gone — I need to find something else to stress about.

GB: Okay, we're coming near the end. I don't detect any resentment against the Catholic Church, in spite of your trials and tribulations . . . ?

RK: No. But, again, maybe that lies in the person that I am. I don't resent anyone. I don't hold any grudges.

GB: Is that because you reckon you've been very lucky?

RK: Oh, yeah, I'm really blessed. Totally blessed. I have this opportunity . . . I don't have a problem with the Catholic Church. I have things that niggle away at me, but I don't. I admire priests and the work that they do, 'cause they're incredibly intelligent, spiritual, brilliant people. There are issues that lie within me, not within anyone else. I'll figure them out. I'll deal with them.

GB: And when you met the Pope . . . ?

RK: Yeah, that was pretty special. I felt I was in the presence of greatness when I met him. It's like meeting Bono, you know?

GB: [Laughs.]

RK: [Laughs.] But you do feel like you're in the room with someone really special. Like, I've been in a room with Michael Jackson and felt nothing — almost freaked out, in a way, and wanted to get out of the room. And then I've been in the room with the Pope. And I know these are very different people, but when you are in a room with someone like Bono, you feel like you're in the presence of greatness, 'cause he is a special character, as is [Bob] Geldof and people like that.

GB: What's the greatness about Bono and Geldof?

RK: Bono is probably the greatest rock-and-roll star in the world, yet he's done more for the people of Africa, for the planet . . . And that's an amazing achievement, what he's done for people. It's selfless . . . It's an amazing thing to do what he's done. I remember watching an interview, when he was in St Andrews — I think the G8 was going on up there — and he landed in a helicopter, and someone was slagging him off, you know, saying, "Here you are . . . Who do you think you are, swanning in and out?" And he said, "You know what? For every one like you that has a question like that for me, there is a million people in Africa that I'm helping and I'm saving, so I don't really give a f*** about you, right?" And it was great. It was brilliant. What he's doing matters. It really matters. I've been to Africa. I've been to Ghana. I've been out there on the ground. I've seen what has to be done, and I've seen what has been done, and it's incredible. And, you know, he deserves more recognition than what he has already.

GB: And Bob as well?

RK: And Bob is amazing.

GB: Well, you're doing it . . .

RK: Yeah, but I've so much to learn, Gay. That's the one thing that some people in my shoes get wrong, you know? Educate yourself. I'm not an authority on cancer in any way. I've a long way to go. I've a lot to learn. But I know what I know, and I'm trying to help people.

GB: One last question we ask all our interviewees: if and when the time comes that you meet God, what would you say to him?

RK: Well, I'm presuming you find it all out at that time . . . "Why? Why do these things happen? Why do we suffer? Why do people have to go like they go?" That's the unfair part, really. "Why do children have to die?" That doesn't make sense to me, and never will — until that time, I suppose.

GB: Thank you.

RK: Thank you, Gay.

MAUREEN GAFFNEY

Wisdom

Back in the last century, when I presented a daily show on RTÉ Radio, Maureen Gaffney, Adjunct Professor of Psychology and Society at University College, Dublin, used to join me regularly, dispensing good sense to the nation on practically any subject the nation and I cared to throw at her. Note that I say "good sense" and not "common sense", because I have discovered that good sense is not at all common.

The ancient Greeks decided that Wisdom was feminine. They even gave her a name: Sophia. In a rare deviation from its usual patriarchy, the Bible reached the same conclusion: Wisdom is a feminine aspect of the Judaeo-Christian God. This does rather raise the question, incidentally: if Wisdom is feminine, what does it say about the faith of our fathers that it excludes all things and people of the feminine variety from any position of power, influence or responsibility?

"What's this?" I hear you thinking. "Has Gay suddenly gone all feminist?"

Well, believe me, if you had shared a house with the three Byrne women for as long as I did, you too would not have needed to read Germaine Greer and Erica Jong to get in touch with your feminist side: it was a "convert or die" atmosphere worthy of the Spanish Inquisition, and I was an early convert.

Hence inviting Maureen Gaffney on to my show. As far as I – and much of the nation – was concerned, she was, and remains, almost the embodiment of wisdom. I used to say there should be a statue of her in O'Connell Street. Perhaps it is still not too late to mount a petition.

Ah, but wisdom is one thing. What about Maureen's beliefs? Despite our long acquaintance, I was strangely in the dark about this side of her and looked forward to finding out more.

What I discovered was a story of evolution, with all the apparent contradictions inherent in that. Having "left the Church" during her student years, much to her mother's dismay, Maureen found herself, a very few years later, begging a Chicago priest for a Church marriage to her beloved, John. Said reluctant priest would almost certainly have felt vindicated, had he heard that Maureen and John then decided not to baptise their two children. However, I hope he would also have had the grace to rejoice when, later still, Maureen accepted the warm embrace of the Dominicans and started going to Mass again, at Eckhart House in Dublin. The religious circle was finally made even more complete when Maureen's daughter decided, of her own volition, while studying at Trinity, to receive instruction and baptism in the Catholic Church. Maureen was thrilled.

So, what was all that about? She stepped out, then she stepped in again. Was this really any more than the religious equivalent of Lanigan's Ball: adolescent rebellion followed by mature rapprochement?

Actually, yes, there was more to it than that. Something very significant happened in the meantime: the Catholic Church — in which a clever, ambitious young Irishwoman felt she had no place in the late 1960s — has, in some small pockets, wised up. By which I mean, it has made a little bit more room for the famous feminine wisdom mentioned above.

Now, don't get me wrong. I am not saying that the Vatican has finally "got" women. You only had to look at the gender balance at last year's conclave to realise that it is a work in very slow progress. However, Maureen has clearly found a way, which she did not think was previously available, to be a smart, modern woman and a Catholic. And so has her daughter.

Perhaps this is no more than the *à la carte* Catholicism about which we hear so much. Certainly, when she talks about Church attitudes to sex and sexuality it is clear that she thinks that, from the Pope down, the Catholic leadership has simply "lost the plot". And yet that is no longer enough reason for her to wash her hands of the organisation. Almost in spite of herself, she has discovered that something in that Church also gives her a connection with the God in whom she never ceased to believe.

"You can come to the feast at any time," she said at one stage during our conversation, as she spoke about the parable of the labourers in the vineyard. And she has come. I only hope that the Church to which she has returned has enough wisdom and grace to keep her.

ᵔ

GB: I want to take you back to Midleton, Co. Cork . . . I have the impression that your parents were very young when they married, and money was not exactly in plentiful supply, yes?
MG: Yes. My mother was, I think, about nineteen when she married, and my father was twenty. They met during the Emergency. My father was in the Irish Army and had been drafted into Midleton, and my

mother, who had a very steady boyfriend at the time, fell madly in love with my father, and the two of them married within, I think, a year. They settled in Midleton, living with my grandmother. There was a huge shortage of housing at that time. So, when I was born, four years later, we were still living with my grandmother.

GB: And what about the tensions of that living accommodation . . . ?

MG: Oh, I'm sure they were awful. And it was relieved, but relieved in a very negative way, by the fact that my father couldn't get work in Midleton, and he had to emigrate, repeatedly, to get work.

GB: When he went away, where did he go to?

MG: He went to Dublin, he went to England. And he would come back, then, for periods as well. For the periods when he was away, I would live for the moments when he would come back. But, almost from the moment he would come back, I would be dreading the moment he'd leave again.

GB: What was this thing that your mother had about always trying to get a council house?

MG: Oh, my mother, when we were very young, was always trying to get on the housing list, which was very difficult, because at that time the only criteria, really, was how many children you had, and my mother had two, and I don't think she wanted any more. So, someone told her that she should do the twenty-six Rosaries. That entails saying the full Rosary and special prayers, as far as I remember, every single night for twenty-six nights.

GB: Twenty-six!

MG: But here's the great thing: as a test of your faith, whether you got your intention or not, you had to say twenty-six Rosaries in thanksgiving [laughter], which was a tremendous sort of little trick the Church had to kind of copper-fasten your faith. And, of course, she dutifully did that as well, and she claims that at the end of the process the key was forthcoming and we moved into our new house.

GB: It worked!

MG: Yeah, it worked. But I always think that if she had that much determination she was going to get the house anyway! [Laughter.] She was kind of conventionally Catholic, but she had absolutely no time at all for the Church's stance on various things.

GB: She wouldn't have agreed with the Church on contraception and stuff like that?

MG: Oh, most certainly not. Not that she had any access to contraception, of course, but that was a source of terrible debate in our house. I remember her telling me that, when she was a young married woman, when you went to Confession, what you dreaded was the priest saying at the end of your Confession, "How old is your last child?" And if your last child was more than two, then immediately you got the third degree: "What was it, were you trying to prevent another child?" And, of course, people were. So, no, she had absolutely no time at all for anything like that.

GB: What about the nuns? Did you have a good time with them?

MG: I loved school. I actually refused to leave, the first day I went to school. But the nuns were generally extraordinary women.

GB: And did you know then you were academic?

MG: Well, I did, yeah, because I loved school. And I absolutely loved — we had a choir — and to this day I love plainchant. Whenever I go into a cathedral, anywhere in the world, I can sing along with the best of them. I could still sing the Mass, you know. But there was little else to do, really. You know, apart from read.

GB: Okay, so eventually, then, university. And then about that time, when you were still a student, you were working in London part-time, and you decided to give up the Catholic Church. Thank you and goodbye.

MG: Yeah. I was working as a waitress in London and I missed Mass, one Sunday, because I had a shift that I couldn't get off. And I was kind of looking around to see was there anything I could do, was there any kind of afternoon service or something that I could go to. And then, I remember the moment when I thought, I'm actually not going to. I'm not going to go.

So I stopped, and when I went home after the summer, I announced to my parents, "I'm not going to be going to Mass any more, because . . ." as I put it grandly, "I've left the Church." [Laughter.] Of course, they were absolutely outraged . . . I think my father was kind of half intrigued, really. But they kind of settled. They never forced me. They argued with me about it, but my mother was more concerned, really, about what the neighbours would think.

GB: "You were missed at Mass on Sunday . . ."

MG: Oh, I remember her shouting upstairs, and she'd say, "Why can't you do it? You don't go to church, chapel or meeting." I remember this routine every Sunday. But they never made it impossible . . .

GB: It was the institutionalised Church that you objected to . . . ?

MG: Yes, yes, that I still object to, really. The next interaction I had with the Church was with John and myself, my husband and myself . . .

GB: Mr John Harris. When did you meet, how did you meet, why did you meet . . . ?

MG: We were in the same classes in college, and we knew each other, but, you know, we weren't going out together or anything.

GB: And?

MG: And then, when we left college a couple of months afterwards, we met again, and we saw each other with new eyes, I suppose, and that was the beginning . . .

GB: And how long after that did you tell John that you were going to be married to him?

MG: [Laughs.] We actually didn't get married for quite a while afterwards. We married when we went to . . .

GB: Chicago.

MG: We went to the University of Chicago, yeah. We were both graduate students there, and we got married there. That was my next formal interaction with the Church.

GB: Yes. This is the woman who doesn't want to know about the Church, now . . .

MG: Yeah, so we decided we wanted to get married in a church, and we wanted to get married in the Catholic Church, because I think of being a Catholic as being part of that community. I was born into that community. I have great affection for it. I share many of the beliefs. So, I thought, "Well, I can disagree with the institutional Church and protest about that, but I can still get married in the Church." Anyway, the priest took a different view.

GB: The American priest?

MG: Yes. He was very outraged by this, so he refused to perform the ceremony. But, anyway, we were having none of that, so we had I couldn't tell you, Gay, how many meetings [laughs] where we had these sort of huge disputes and dialogue and discussion about everything, until he relented finally, but with very bad grace. Now, of course, I hadn't been to Mass for years at that point, and he started the entire ceremony by saying an Act of Contrition . . . [Laughter.]

GB: He started with the Act of Contrition?
MG: . . . and he didn't stay or anything afterwards for the reception. But it didn't make a blind bit of difference to us. We had the best wedding ever. [Laughs.]

GB: I'm just trying to think about the theology of that. Perhaps he was welcoming sinners and he wanted to forgive you your sins, with the firm purpose of amendment, before he married you.
MG: Yes. Or, I think, he was trying to settle his own conscience about it. I don't know. But, anyway, he did it with a very bad grace.

GB: It occurs to me that you must have been amongst the first to believe that you could have a career and a family and all of that together.
MG: Our generation was the first, and it was very, very difficult. I spent the first couple of years — when the kids were small, in particular, you know? — every time I was at work, I thought I should be at home; every time I was at home, I thought I should be at work.

GB: Now, you didn't have the babies baptised into the Catholic Church . . .
MG: No.

GB: Why not?
MG: No, well, we decided that, since we weren't practising ourselves, that it would just be hypocritical to do that, so we didn't. It wasn't really an issue. The only time it became an issue was when the First Holy Communions came up — not with my son, obviously, but my daughter. I think she would have loved to have been flouncing around in her dress and all of that. But I think people have an intuitive sort of spirituality and a sense of the sacred.

GB: No, but I'm thinking of you not getting them baptised, and I'm just wondering, what was your state of mind?
MG: Well, I think I felt particularly alienated from the Church around that time . . .

GB: Why particularly around that time?

MG: Because that was the time when the Church was still exerting an enormous amount of, in my view, very inappropriate influence on the state. I absolutely hated what happened during all these referenda in the '80s . . .

GB: Oh, yes.

MG: I really objected to the tone of the debate — to the viciousness, really, of the debate. And I felt, and I still do, that the Church was absolutely entitled to make its views known and to impress upon its own flock what they believe to be the correct view on things. I believe they have no right at all to unduly influence the choices that the Government has to make about trying to accommodate a multiplicity of views in society.

GB: Of course.

MG: So that was my view then.

GB: So, tell me about Eckhart House and Father Miceál O'Regan and Sister Joan O'Donovan.

MG: Well, that was a hugely important part of my life. I can't remember exactly when I started going there first. It was an institute that was set up by the Dominicans, and it really is based on the teachings of Meister Eckhart, but is much more than that. And I'd heard very good things about it and I bumped into Miceál, as it happened, and I said, "I don't want any of the religious part of it. I'm only interested in the self-development part."

GB: [Laughter.]

MG: So he said, "Well, come along anyway." So, it incorporated a big focus on meditation and mindfulness and all of that, but it was done at such a high level — the level of intellectual rigour that they brought to their work, the philosophical background they brought there, the insights from other religions and the way they would sort of tie it together. And I absolutely loved it — I mean, just absolutely loved their whole approach. And it really helped me evolve myself as a person.

And every Sunday, at the end of all the stuff, they'd set up a little table, and he'd come in and he'd put on his vestments and, of course, I'd immediately depart. So, I remember, one weekend, we were doing, I suppose, really very deep work — you know, on ourselves, on our families, on our backgrounds, on our memories — and I was so moved by my own memories and that sense of solidarity and bonding that I felt with others . . . We shared deeply intimate things with each other. So, I stayed for Mass, without thinking of the implications. I just stayed. And it was like a veil was pulled. For the first time ever, I understood what the meaning of community — this kind of community of faith — might be. And I just felt completely uplifted. It's very hard to put words on the experience, but I remember sort of weeping with joy.

GB: Weeping?

MG: Mmm. And I think that it just was a revelation to me, really, and it was particularly a revelation about what breaking bread meant — what it really means to share that deep sense of community, of the Catholic, in the sense of universal, you know? — these kind of universal truths we were all discovering about ourselves. And Catholic in the sense that everybody was welcome. We all had our place there. It was a transcendent experience.

GB: Listening to you now, it was obviously a major, major experience.

MG: It was, yes. It was. I think, once I had had that experience, I saw everything in really quite a different light. And then I remember just thinking of a parable which I used to really object to when I was in secondary school. And it was the one about the labourers in the vine-yards, and the ones who came late got paid the same as the ones who came early.

GB: Getting the same amount . . .

MG: And I never understood that. I always thought it was deeply unfair. And I just suddenly understood what it meant.

GB: What?

MG: I think what it means is that you can come to the feast at any time. You can come to the Word of God at any time. That you can enter the House of God at any time, you know, either physically or meta-phorically, and join that community and be an equal. And that's how I felt there, after that.

GB: When your book *Flourishing* came out last year, there were various people describing you as the new guru, dispensing wisdom and meaning to life. Talk to me about psychology and religion. Is there a sense in which psychology is taking over from religion?

MG: Well, I suppose psychology and religion interface in lots of ways, because they deal with many of the same issues. A large part of religious belief and religious practice is all about living a good life, making good relationships, you know? Like, what it is to be a good person. A lot of psychology is about the same thing. So, it's about how you think about yourself, what gives meaning to your life. Meaning is hugely important: it's not an accessory. I mean, we have the part of our brain that's devoted just to that, just to seeking meaning, even when there isn't any, because it's good for human beings to have meaning.

The other hugely important domain of religion is how to live. And that's where I would depart radically from the Catholic Church in many respects. The way that Jesus taught us to live is unsurpassed. But the Church lost the plot when it came to sexuality, because the idea of understanding sexuality through the Catholic lens is to reduce it to something so simplistic and something so rigid and something so out of sync with the way people think about themselves. I think the thing, the plot, was lost, as it were, when artificial contraception was banned. It just made no sense to people. The idea that two people who love each other, who are in a long-term relationship, can't make a decision about when to have a family just makes no psychological sense. It is counter to everything we know about intimacy, about how people grow and develop together and the role that intimacy has in that. Their stance on homosexuality, in my view, is unconscionable. Sexuality is a deep part of our identity. So, I fundamentally disagree with them about that.

And I think once people made up their minds that they weren't going to go along with the Church's extraordinarily rigid and intolerant views of that, then it opened up a whole vista for them in terms of, well, "If I have to make up my own mind about these things, you know, then where does that leave me about other issues?" And I don't think they look to the Church for answers. They look to psychology. And, again, I want to make the point that the two are not irreducible. But I think, until the Church develops a more mature, psychologically informed view — and, I would say, compassionate view — of sexuality, there's always going to be a kind of hands-off attitude to their teachings.

GB: Do you think the teachings of Jesus have been monstrously distorted?
MG: Hugely. I mean, I know it's a cliché to say it, but I think he would find himself a stranger in his own Church.

GB: Since you mentioned him . . . Who is Jesus? What was he, as far as you're concerned?

MG: Well, the question that always comes after that is "Do you believe he was divine . . . ?"

GB: Yes.

MG: . . . Or do you believe he was just a prophet?

GB: I was about to ask, but start at the first one first.

MG: I think we all, every human being, has a spark of the divine in them.

GB: No, no, no, no. That's not that we're asking.

MG: I know, but let me finish . . .

GB: Who do you think he was?

MG: I do think he was divine and sacred in a very special way.

GB: Was he the Son of . . . ?

MG: Was he the Son of God? Well, I think really what "Son of God" means to me — I can only say what that means to me — is very much how I expressed it, that I think there was much more of the divine about Jesus. I think he was more than just a prophet, more than just a charismatic leader or a preacher. And I'm sure the Buddha was as well and, you know, all of the other great prophets. But the one I'm concerned about is, I suppose, the Christian tradition.

GB: Would you believe in the Resurrection?

MG: In the same way, I think, that I understand the Resurrection to be the defeat of death, really. That it's sort of the assertion of immortality — the assertion of the transcendent of life eternal. I think he embodied that . . .

GB: But you would be shaky about the actual, physical Resurrection?

MG: I wouldn't say "shaky". I would say "understanding it at different levels". But having said that, do I believe it's just a metaphor? No, that wouldn't capture how I feel either. No, I think there is a mystery about these things, and I don't think there's any way of fully explaining them.

GB: Okay. Do you believe in God?

MG: I do, yeah. I think I have a real sense of God in an everyday way.

GB: You said you pray.

MG: Mmm.

GB: And do you think your prayers are answered ever?

MG: I think that, in the round, my prayers are answered. I know, scientifically, that if people know they're being prayed for they often feel better. If they're not feeling well and someone prays for them they feel better. I think that's probably a psychological effect. If they don't know they're being prayed for, you can pray all you like: they don't feel any better. Having said that, I think, when I pray, what I'm doing is putting my wish for goodness to happen into the universe, and I think that counts in the same way as the Buddhists believe that when you meditate you don't just change, but you change the world. Do I get everything I pray for? No, but I get *some* things. [Laughter.]

GB: So, at the end of all that, I still find you questioning.

MG: God, I hope I'm questioning until the day I die. We're all pilgrims, really.

GB: What do you think happens to you when you die?

MG: I don't know. I suppose, I hold the view that there is a mystery at the heart of life and that I don't know.

GB: Do you think you'll meet your beloved Daddy again?

MG: Not in any physical sense.

GB: No?

MG: No. But I don't ever feel that he's gone from my life, or my grandmother. I know they're dead. I'll never meet them again, but they are very much part of my life.

GB: Have you any idea of a fella standing there with a ledger . . .

MG: [Laughs.]

GB: . . . adding up your pluses and your minuses?

MG: Absolutely not, no. I think that's such a limited conception of the Deity.

GB: Having said all you've said so far, could you pithily sum up your meaning of life?

MG: "Faith, hope and love, and the greatest of these is love." That's the centre of the Christian message. And I kind of like to think that a large part of my work, really, is my own version of trying to do that. I mean, faith is trust, you know? I think a large part of everything I've ever done in my career has been about the exploration of trust and what breaches trust in relationships, and the importance of trust — the importance of hope and optimism. God knows, I'm like a broken record about that. But, most of all, the importance of love.

GB: Last question. Suppose it's all true, all that the nuns taught you, and all that the clergy taught you, and you meet him, her or it at the end of your days . . . What will you say to him, her or it?
MG: "I'm home."

GB: Okay. Thank you.

SEAN O'SULLIVAN

In the Land of the Blind . . .

The venture capitalist "Dragon" and IT engineer Sean O'Sullivan likes to think his surname means "one eye", from the Irish *súil* (eye) and *amháin* (one). In 2004, while running a charity in war-torn Iraq, he came to the conclusion that this name must be either a prophecy or a divine joke, when a medical condition left him blind in one eye. This and the skin cancer he had also developed convinced him of something that the assassination of his closest colleague and the kidnap, torture and killing of others, had failed to do: it was time to leave.

If he hadn't left then, I don't suppose we would have been sitting together talking, on a Saturday afternoon in March 2014, in Dublin's Wisdom Centre. His JumpStart operation, which employed 3,500 Iraqis in the reconstruction of their own blighted country, was being aggressively targeted by al-Qaeda, and Sean, who refused to use bodyguards or carry a gun, was a sitting duck.

The fact that his cancer proved treatable and his eye recovered fully is one of the things that persuades Sean that his life has been spared for a purpose. Quite what that purpose might be is up to him to find out, and it's a challenge he takes very seriously.

None of that was what I had expected from someone who made his fortune – the first one – from computer programming. But then, Sean O'Sullivan is full of surprises. He is a venture capitalist who definitely prefers to put the stress on "venture" rather than "capitalist", and his CV suggests he is either a latter-day Leonardo or a gadfly, since he has flitted (actually, I suppose gadflies must *gad*) from one career to another not only with remarkable abandon but with astonishing success.

By the age of twenty-seven he had coined the term – and, more importantly, the engineering principles behind – "cloud computing" and worked out ways to put maps on mobile phones and computers, at a time when most of the rest of us didn't own either of those things. He made enough money to know he would never have to worry about it again. He was loaded, which, for the youngest of nine children raised in poverty by an abandoned single mother, was quite some transformation.

However, where other people might have found such *nouveau-richesse* addictive, he saw it merely as a means to the better end of working out what life was really about.

Hardly surprisingly, he didn't necessarily get it right first time. Singing and playing in a New York rock band, Janet Speaks French, may have earned him some modest hits, but it didn't fulfil him. So, off he went to film school in L.A., during the course of which his mother, Joan, developed rapid dementia. Sean's award-winning student film *String Worms on Budd Terrace* movingly tracks the decline of this remarkable woman from diagnosis to death, through chapters of fear and faith, humour and humiliation, delusion and distress. In the process, it also reveals an awful lot about Sean himself and what makes him the way he is. You can watch it on his Vimeo site, and I thoroughly recommend that you do so.

By the time he graduated, the second Iraq war was imminent, and Sean blagged his way in. Initially he wanted to "embed" with peace activists, but then, once hostilities commenced, he found himself unable to stand by and film burning hospitals. His first instinct was to put down the camera and try to help, which made him a lousy war photographer, but a fairly exceptional human being. No wonder his future missus, the war correspondent, Tish Durkin, took such a shine to him. Ten years later, they have swapped the rebels of Tikrit for the rebels of Co. Cork, although, for reasons which will become apparent, they both still spend a lot of time on aeroplanes.

Has Sean found the meaning of life yet? I don't know. He continues to thrive in business, although, as he laughingly admits, he has lost hundreds of millions as well as made them. That's all part of the see-saw fun of venture capitalism.

He remains driven to use his talents and his wealth in ways that will improve the lives of others, in order to fulfil his own. This is not a principle he had to go to Iraq, New York or L.A. to learn. He got it from his mother, a modern-day St Joan, whose faith and inner voices told her that you don't need money to have worth. You get most out of life if you give your all: laughter, faith, hope and love. And the greatest of these . . .

Well, you know the rest.

∿

GB: Take me back to the homeland life of your mother and father, very much an Irish-American family. You were one of nine, circumstances not good, in New York. Describe that home situation for me.

SOS: Well, my biological father wasn't involved in my upbringing at all. I never had a connection with him. I don't believe he was a good person. He left the family to its own devices. The family split up. We went up to upstate New York to escape his abusive behaviour to the children, and so my mom was left to raise the kids. And he was actually a lawyer in New York. He could have, arguably, easily afforded to pay child support, but he chose not to.

To me, what matters is I had a very loving mother, who took care of us all and who raised us all, and she did a wonderful, wonderful job. She was a great role model.

I don't have any actual memories of him. The first time I actually encountered him was in a lawsuit. I was trying to get some money for my mom, who was not able to support herself in the end and didn't have any retirement income or anything to rely on. So we were trying to claim back against the child support for twenty-seven years' unpaid maintenance. He had a brownstone in midtown Manhattan and I eventually ended up wrestling that out of his control. We were able to sell that brownstone for the benefit of my mom and for the rest of the family.

GB: And you took this action?
SOS: I did. I was twenty-seven. It was actually before my first company had gone public, and I was living the life of a struggling artist, as a rock musician in New York, but I had to write all these briefs and take him through all the court systems. He had appeal after appeal after appeal, even though it was a cut-and-dried case, before we actually got justice.

GB: When you went after your father, then, for this unpaid maintenance, when you met him in the courtroom you spoke to each other, obviously. You had to . . .
SOS: No. I didn't.

GB: No?
SOS: No. Actually, I had no idea who the person was, standing next to me. And the judge started saying, "Oh, so this is just a family mis-understanding." He had no idea that I'd not seen this person since I was three.

GB: What became of your father in the end?
SOS: He had a stroke and he died after he was evicted, and so I don't think it ended well for him.

GB: Overall, in spite of that — which is a bit like saying, "Apart from that, Mrs Lincoln, did you like the play . . . ?" — do you remember having a good time as a child growing up?

SOS: Oh, yeah. You know, it was a hectic thing with nine brothers and sisters, and so you entertain yourself.

GB: You didn't go hungry?

SOS: Uh, we went hungry from time to time.

GB: Really? But you would still agree with the well-known lesson that children, if they're loved and in a loving family and a loving environment, are not aware of all those other things.

SOS: Yeah, absolutely. I actually didn't know we were poor. In the wintertime, say, all of us would be in this one room in a house which had a wood stove that we would go and cut the wood for, and we'd heat the house and we'd all sleep in this one bedroom, and it would be freezing, of course, in the mornings, when you'd wake up to re-stoke the fire. But that was just what we did. And I think, actually, humans can take a tremendous deal of hardship without actually having adverse effects. We can live on a lot less than we choose to live on.

GB: Religion? Mass regularly? Family Rosary? Any of that?

SOS: Yeah, my mom was very religious. She would have gone to Mass every day and she worked, in the end, you know, for Catholic charities, and so I would have been going to Mass every Sunday, and it was a lot of fun.

GB: So, okay, at fourteen, in school, you came across a computer, and you very quickly realised your gift for programming and design and all that sort of thing.

SOS: It would probably have been a little earlier than fourteen. I was maybe eleven or twelve. But it was just something I attacked, I loved. I didn't have very much control over my own physical environment. All the clothes I had were hand-me-downs or gifts from the Salvation Army, so just to be able to be powerful in some context, where I could actually have some control over something, was a nice thing.

GB: And one of your things came real good and you sold out for a lot of loot. So, having been as poor as you describe, what did money come to mean to you?

SOS: It just does give you quite a bit of freedom, I suppose. Actually, in some ways, I don't really feel like the money is mine. So, I don't see any joy in spending money wastefully. I mean, I don't fly first class: I sit in coach. And I have a seven-year-old Toyota Prius, because it's good on the gas, and it's got scratches on the side.

GB: But surely, you have heard the expression that if you don't turn left at the door of the aeroplane your daughter-in-law or your son-in-law will?

SOS: Yeah, yeah, yeah . . .

GB: That doesn't upset you either, does it?

SOS: Well, actually, I don't want to encumber my children with too much of this needless weight, because money taxes the soul. I'm sure I do, to some extent, but I don't a lot. I think it's a responsibility of the parents to make sure your kids have a good education and it's the responsibility of the kids to live their life beyond that. I feel good about my accomplishments in life, having started with nothing. So, I'd rather have my kids have the joy and the pride of doing something for themselves rather than having it handed to them.

GB: But there's nothing intrinsically wrong in making a lot of money . . . ?

SOS: I don't think there's anything at all wrong with making money, as long as . . . You know, there's two ways to make money: one is to *extract* value out of society and another one is to *create* value. So, you could be extracting fees out of people, say, through transactions and finance charges and all sorts of things. Or you could build things which are incredibly valuable, that benefit society at large. I only work on stuff that's on that category. You know Bob Dylan's song *Gotta Serve Somebody*, right? We all have to be of service.

GB: Just go back to the computer. Did you invent cloud computing?

SOS: Yeah, I invented some concepts behind it — certainly the framework of the concepts. And then I named it "cloud computing". With George Favaloro of Compaq Computers, we coined the phrase "cloud computing", and so that's one of those things that I guess I'm a little famous for, yeah.

But the thing that I feel more proud about is the street-mapping on computers, which, unquestionably, we were the world leader in, and we brought the whole industry forward in a massive way. As I've told numerous people, it took seven years for the first million people to use that technology, but then, twenty years later, a billion people had used the technology. And twenty-three years later two billion people had used the technology. And that's kinda cool. I'm very proud of what we did as a group and growing that company and having thousands of people working for that company and tens of thousands through associated companies.

GB: Wonderful. So then, you made a lot of money and it seems to me, you tried to catch up on a misspent youth which wasn't quite misspent enough. So, in spite of having money, you went to live in a grungy flat with the other members of your group, which was called Janet Speaks French. Then you did a course in film-making. And then, as one does, you took yourself to Iraq as a freelance war photographer, an action which many people might have thought was crazy, because it wasn't really the safest place in the world to be at that time. Why did you do that?

SOS: Well, I was a film-maker at the time and I just thought, "You can cover whatever you want to with a film. Why not cover something that's important?" So, I was able to be invited in by the Saddam regime to follow a peace-keeping activist group, and I faked up some IDs that said I was an approved photo-journalist and was able to sort of sneak past the checkpoints, to get into Iraq while the war was just starting.

GB: Then you set up JumpStart, a charity involving something like three-and-a-half thousand Iraqis in the reconstruction of Iraq. Was that why you went there in the first place?

SOS: No. When I was there, I just saw needs that frustrated the hell out of me. And I said, "Jeez!" And, you know, my mother had actually just passed, just a year or so before, and I didn't have a girlfriend or anything. There was nothing holding me back from just going in and trying to make a difference.

GB: Sean, what is this urge you seem to have for improving the lives of other people?

SOS: I think all of us have a calling to do something significant with our lives. And, as you have intimated, money isn't that important. Since the age of twenty-seven or something, I don't need to earn any more money for the rest of my life. I'm taken care of. So now, it's about the search for meaning. You know, for me it's about creating significant companies, creating significant change in the world that leads us to a better outcome. There's a wound that needs to be just cured, and that wound is all the injustice or all the wastefulness that we see all around us all the time.

GB: Tell me about Mohaymen, your Iraqi partner.

SOS: Mohaymen al-Safar was the co-founder, really, of JumpStart International, which was this humanitarian organisation we built in Iraq to help reconstruct hospitals and campuses for colleges and mostly ministry buildings. We built thousands of homes for people across a period of a few years. After the United Nations pulled out of Iraq, we were the largest humanitarian organisation in Iraq. Mohaymen was the guy I relied on as my right-hand man, and eventually he was targeted . . .

GB: What happened to him?

SOS: He was going about the work day, going from one site to another site, and a car pulled up and put nine bullets through the Hyundai that we drove around in. And he was hit and killed. Six of the bullets hit him, and he was killed instantly. The odd thing is that I was actually out of the country at that moment, which was rare. I would normally have been in the car with him, but he was by himself that day.

GB: Obviously, there is a feeling in you that you are somehow responsible for his death . . .

SOS: Well, you know, the person who is responsible for his death is the person that pulled the trigger.

GB: Sure.

SOS: I was running that organisation and I did feel responsible. And he wasn't the only person that was killed. There were a number of others that were kidnapped and tortured. And that was a difficult thing.

GB: In that context, during the time you were in Iraq, you must have had some narrow escapes yourself?

SOS: Yeah, I did. The first time I went into Iraq, actually, the car in front of me was blown up and the car behind me had the windows shot out . . . But our car was fine, so it was no problem. [Laughs ironically.] I have to say, I'm not a fan of war. In fact, I'm kind of a pacifist. I didn't carry a gun; we didn't have armed guards. We just were doing humanitarian work. I appreciate the need for soldiers, and I appreciate the need for what they do. It's an important role people have to play. It's just not a role that I choose to do myself.

GB: Did you feel at that time that there was somebody looking after you?

SOS: Yeah. I never felt so secure as to think that I was bulletproof! [Laughs.] I did feel that I was lucky not to have suffered more. There were signals eventually that said, "Okay, Sean, you should be leaving the country," and I guess, basically, I thought that those were somewhat, perhaps, divinely inspired. One was I got skin cancer and they had to cut out — you can probably see it up in the corner here — like, an inch of my skin this way, and, like, an inch or two this way. [Lifts his hair to show the scar.] Actually, it's almost the same procedure that you do if you're doing a facelift, but I only got the facelift on the one side. [Laughs.]

So, I had got skin cancer. But then, I got an infection in my left eye that made me blind in my left eye and it actually ate the skin off the surface of my eye. And I was walking around with a bandage on my head from the surgery for the skin cancer, and then I had a patch on my eye, and I was just saying, "You know what? God is probably telling me something." [Laughs.]

Remarkably, despite being blinded in that eye — and it was a loss that I thought I'd have for the rest of my life — over the next year or two it grew back, and the eye, actually, is perfectly fine now. I probably would have stayed until something bad happened.

GB: However, the good news is that, arising out of all of this, we meet Tish . . .

SOS: Yes.

GB: Patricia Durkin, the present Mrs O'Sullivan.

SOS: Yes.

GB: And she was a war correspondent. Tell me how that happened.

SOS: She was in Amman, Jordan. She had been trying to get into Iraq desperately, because she didn't want to miss the war. She was working for the *New York Times* magazine and the *Atlantic Monthly* and *Rolling Stone*. She's a fantastic writer. And we went around for several weeks together, covering the events and stories, and I think it was at that point that we sort of fell for each other.

GB: And how long were you together before you married?

SOS: We were together for a year before I proposed, and then we got married on New Year's Eve.

GB: And you have Charlotte, who's eight, and then Mathias, who is six. And Mathias is a very special child. Tell me about Mathias.

SOS: Mathias has autism. He is non-verbal at this point, although he's able to repeat sounds, and he's gaining some words. And that's been a huge progress. A year ago or so, he would have had maybe eight or ten words and now he has fifty or a hundred words. The struggle with Mathias is just in trying to maximise his potential, and that's what my wife and I are working on.

GB: How are you doing that?

SOS: We have put Mathias in a school in New Jersey for about the last nine months, where my wife and I are travelling back and forth. And so I'm in New Jersey for about a week a month and she is back over here for a week a month, so my wife and I get to spend about two weeks a month together and he gets the care he needs. And Charlotte and I are here in Ireland and Charlotte's going to a national school here.

GB: So, both children have got accustomed to being without one parent for two weeks a month?

SOS: For three weeks a month, yeah. And it's very trying for us as a family, and it's difficult for Charlotte, because she misses her brother. And yet it's the best thing for Mathias.

GB: We all talk about what somebody is "worth": "What's Sean O'Sullivan *worth*?" "What's Gay Byrne *worth*?" Has Mathias's situation made you reassess that kind of assessment of the "worth" of people?

SOS: I view the worth of people not by the money that they have but by the contribution they can make to a business or to a society, and I don't think they're in line. I look at my mother as a person who I respect tremendously as a role model. She worked for Catholic charities; she started a Home Health Aid programme. She actually had a huge impact. You don't need money to get that done.

GB: Even though Mathias can't speak to you, does he understand everything you say?

SOS: No.

GB: His frustration must be colossal.

SOS: Yes, his frustration is colossal and he has difficult moments, and he will reach out and scratch and bite and do things in moments of frustration, and we have to get him past that. And we are working on that.

GB: And when he meets Charlotte, does he welcome her with arms around her?

sos: Yeah, they love each other. He's a loving child and he's a joyful child and he's not a burden in that way.

GB: Insofar as you can, are they being brought up Catholic?

sos: Yes. Charlotte just had her First Confession on Wednesday.

GB: A delightful time.

sos: Yeah.

GB: Do you pray?

sos: Yeah. I mean, I go to church as much as I can, every Sunday, unless I'm travelling or something. I enjoy the teachings of Christ. I think he was a great philosopher. I think he was a great storyteller. I think he was a great moral guide for the world.

GB: Who do you pray to, and what form does your prayer take? And for what do you pray?

sos: I pray for help all the time. I am constantly looking for answers to problems I'm confronting. There's something about relieving yourself by handing the problems over to God and asking, "Okay, how should I solve this?" And then I actually do this remarkable trick — I think everybody should do this — I do this at night as I'm going to sleep, as I'm lying in my bed. I think about these problems. I ask the Lord to solve one of my problems, whatever it is, every night. And then I wake up in the morning and I generally have the answer. And you could say, "Okay, that's just putting the problem into the back of your mind and having your subconscious solve the problem." But to me it's more than that.

GB: It sounds vaguely to me like where you got the idea for cloud computing . . .

sos: [Laughter.] Like, yeah . . . Er, no! That's *not* how I got the idea of cloud computing, but the image of just turning it over to the clouds . . . My image of God is — I don't actually so much think of the physical face of, say, Christ or whatever. I think God is actually all of us together, in a way. I know that sounds bizarre and New Agey, but there is God in each of us, right? And there is a fabric that connects us all.

GB: Go back to Jesus. Did you suggest that, to you, he was just a very nice guy and teacher and a philosopher, or was he more than that?

sos: I think there were so many miracles present in Jesus' life that you have to just think that that was just a totally God-related person. And he was incredibly connected to God and he was incredibly connected to a spirituality, and his lessons are incredibly important to all of us. And so I don't see a need to categorise Jesus in the way that he is categorised. Do I believe that miracles could happen, that he could come back after being dead? I actually could see miracles happening like that. There are things that are completely anomalous, that have no medical explanation and no rational explanation.

I believe he came back to life. I believe there's something to that. Was it in the same body? Almost certainly not. [Laughs.] How was it done? I don't know how it was done. But I believe in the teachings of Christ. I believe he was a fabulous role model for all of our society, and I believe that just as a philosopher, that's good enough for me.

GB: What happens when you die? By which, I mean, will you see your mother again, perhaps see your father?

sos: Yeah. I was at my mother's bedside, not exactly the moment she died . . . I was there a couple of seconds before she died, and then I went to call my sister to tell her to come, and then I went back into the room — it was twenty-six seconds later — and she had died in that period of time, and her soul was no longer in her body. And everyone else around the room was still looking at her body as if she was still alive, and I said, "No, she's gone!" And that was remarkable to me, that there could be the presence of a consciousness in a person, and then you come back and it's a body, it's meat, it's not a person any longer. And that is scary and weird. Where she went, I don't know. I imagine that there's something that continues, and maybe that continuation is much more meaningful than what exists here, but I don't know how it continues. I don't know.

GB: Okay, last question. Suppose it's all true, what your mother believed, what they taught you in Catholic schools when you were growing up, and you die, your time comes, you're met at the Pearly Gates and you meet God. What will Sean O'Sullivan say to God?

sos: "Thank you. Thank you. It was a great, great experience, and thank you for giving me the opportunity to live and experience an amazing variety of life."

GB: That'll do. Thank you.

sos: Thank you.

|CHRISTINA NOBLE

Noble Is As Noble Does

I know the cliché is that what doesn't kill us makes us stronger, but life seems to have inflicted obscene and absurd degrees of hardship and suffering on Christina Noble, to test that theory.

She has passed all those tests with distinction.

Our interview lasted over two hours and for much of that time I found myself thinking, "How on earth are they going to edit this?" The *Meaning of Life* slot is a half-hour pint pot, which means that if you record a quart-sized interview like that, three-quarters of the material – in other words, three words in every four – will end up on the cutting-room floor. Is there any point in a process as wasteful as that?

Actually, yes.

Over the course of two hours, you reach a level of intimacy which simply is not possible in the sort of short-and-sweet interview I used to do for *The Late Late Show*. That was where Christina and I first met and she had told me elements of her story then. I soon realised that I hadn't heard the half of it.

A few years ago, *Angela's Ashes* prompted a whole rash of Irish "misery lit". Clearly, a lot of people read Frank McCourt's memoir and thought, "Well, we had it pretty tough in our house, too." For a couple of irony-filled years, tales of destitution seemed to become Ireland's biggest export – the bedrock of our GDP. Never mind that very few of those accounts had anything like the elegance or the pathos of *Angela's Ashes*.

Christina's two books were an exception to that rule, because they added something to the *œuvre*. The point of her very sorry tales was not to wallow in self-pity but to draw attention to what happened next. You see, Christina not only survived a childhood litany of bereavement, abandonment, rape and homelessness, topped off by a violent marriage and an overdose: she somehow also converted all that bleak experience into a philanthropic vision.

Vision is one thing, but she also had the right combination of *naïveté*, bloody-mindedness, charisma and smarts to turn her vision into a reality. As a result, she has transformed the lives of literally hundreds of thousands of Vietnamese and Mongolian street children, many of whom are now themselves transforming other lives, having qualified as teachers, architects, engineers, civil servants and more, as a result of the education and care the Christina Noble Children's

Foundation has given them. No wonder, Deirdre O'Kane has decided to make a movie about her.

I wanted to understand what sort of alchemy — what cocktail of faith, hope and charity — could turn her dreadful upbringing into such noble deeds. I also wanted to hear how her many encounters with evil — and not as an abstract but as a cruel, daily reality — could ignite so much relentless, muscular goodness. No wonder the interview took two hours.

~

GB: This little island is full of sad stories, of lives broken by alcohol and abuse and violence and poverty, but reading about your early life makes *Angela's Ashes* seem like a summer holiday. Start by telling me about your parents — where they were from, what sort of people they were.

CN: My mammy, Annie Gross, she came to Dublin to go to college and met my father and his friend at a bus stop on the way. My father was a tall handsome-looking man at that time and they fell in love and ended up getting married. But Daddy became a chronic alcoholic. He drank everything. He drank us out of house and home.

GB: So, where did you live at this stage?

CN: I lived in Marrowbone Lane Flats, C-block, and I was born at Christmas — the night before, Christmas Eve — and Mammy was very sick. She was always sick. She was always having children.

GB: Always. She died when you were ten. What do you remember about that?

CN: Her death? The actual death? I remember Dr Finnegan came, and I heard Dr Finnegan saying, "This woman is dying." I heard him say that. And I said to Our Lord, "If you don't let Mammy die, I'll be a Carmelite nun, and I won't ever, ever come out for my whole life. Just don't let Mammy die." Of course, she did die.

GB: Did you blame God for taking her in some way?

CN: I did a little bit, because I didn't understand how God could take somebody's mammy away. And because we also were very kind to God ourselves — in a sense, kind to him. We didn't neglect him: we went to church.

GB: So, after your mother died, then your father had to take care of all of you. Was he still drinking heavily at that stage? He was . . .

CN: Oh, yeah. My father drank heavily all the way through.

GB: Were you taken in somewhere?

CN: First of all, I tried to look after the children as best I could. The baby, Philomena, started calling me "Mammy", and still does. We were taken to an aunt and an uncle, because there was eviction from Marrowbone Lane, and we were taken to this aunt and uncle who were both alcoholics. Well, the uncle — I can say it to you — he would beat us, and he'd put the poker to get hot and in the fire, and then he burnt all my brothers with the poker.

GB: So you ran away. . .

CN: I just want to say: they abused us very badly, both sexually abused — not the aunt, she didn't do that — and physically, certainly. But there was a kind of mental abuse as well. And then the Irish Society for the Prevention of Cruelty — they came and we were taken to the Castle, to the Children's Court.

GB: And where did you end up? In an orphanage?

CN: Yeah, well, then they put us into the different institutions. They separated us.

GB: They split you up, yes?

CN: Split us all up. I was up in Whitehall. It's like a Magdalene laundry place. I ended up there, and I ran away from there, like, within a night of going in there. And then they caught me and put me back in there again. And then I jumped out the window — the very top window — and I broke my leg and my arms and smashed all my ribs and every-thing, and then I was taken to St Kevin's Hospital, where I spent several months. I ran away from there, you know? That's how I ended up living in the park.

GB: I know that you ended up in the Phoenix Park — living where in the Phoenix Park? In what? In a hut . . . ?

CN: No. If you walk down, there's a big hill like a dip that leads to the Conyngham Road. Now, if you go to the end of that, right where the wall ends, on the left there's some railings sort of coming up and they're connected to the wall on Conyngham, and inside of there is a real dark place. It's bushes and everything. The only problem was getting up on the railings, because they had spikes on it. But once you were in there, you were quite safe from people. You know what I'm saying?

GB: And about how long did you spend in that place? Was it a year and a half?
CN: Yeah.

GB: You were living like a smart fox.
CN: The only friend I had was the moon. I used to love it when the moon came out, because things were bright and I felt safe.

GB: And how old were you at that stage?
CN: At that stage I was about eleven.

GB: And what did you live on? How did you get food?
CN: That was very difficult. First of all, you could watch the people in the park, when they'd come to the park. So, sometimes people would stay and have picnics and things and then they'd put their food in the bin, you know? And I didn't like that, but I had to go and take the food out of the bin when they had gone, because I didn't want them to see me, and I also felt shameful. [Tearful.]

GB: . . . Was it from there you were taken and raped?
CN: I wasn't taken from the park. I was dragged from the quays in a car. I think there was three people in it. And they dragged me in there . . . Now, this is hard to talk about, okay?

GB: Well, now, only tell me what you want to tell.
CN: [Crying.] I'm sorry. I'm so sorry. [Pauses, crying.] I think there was three people in it, you know? And they dragged me in there . . . [Distressed.]

GB: That's all right. That's okay. We'll just . . .
CN: . . . They raped me. They made bad marks on my back, some of them still there. They beat me. They were making fun of me. And then they took me and threw me out of the car in — I think it was near College Green, but I'm not sure. [Crying.] I'm not sure, but I think it was there. I couldn't go into the police station, because I thought they might put me back in the institutions. You understand me? And, I remember, it started to rain and I was happy. I was glad it was raining, because the rain . . .

GB: Washed you . . .
CN: [Upset. Pauses.] Yes. And I prayed to Our Lord . . . Mammy . . . And I was very angry at that time with Our Lord. I was very angry. "Why did

you take my mammy away? Why? I have no brothers and sisters. Why? Why have they all died?" Because the institutions said they all died. Each one of us were told each one of us was dead. Why? Why? It didn't make sense that I was still alive.

GB: Well, you ended up pregnant. So, where did you have the baby?
CN: I had the baby in St Kevin's Hospital, in James's Street.

GB: Yes.
CN: And I had a lot of haemorrhaging and whatever the story is, and then I was taken to the Navan Road with the nuns with the big things on them [indicates a headdress] . . .

GB: Yes.
CN: . . . and they were okay. They were kind enough, you know? There wasn't anything bad about those nuns. They were good nuns. And Sister Catherine was in charge of the nursery and that's where my little Thomas was.

GB: And was your baby taken from you then?
CN: Yes. I went to feed Tom as normal, and Tom wasn't in the cot, and I said, "Sister Catherine, where's Thomas? Where's Thomas? Is he sick?" 'Cause you know how you get panicky. And I charged down to Sister Louise, and I said, "What's happened? He's not in his cot." And she . . . [Becoming tearful.]

GB: I know what you're going to say.
CN: She said, "He went with a good Catholic family today — this morning."

GB: He went to a "good Catholic family".
CN: That was it.

GB: Can I ask you, Christina, how old would Thomas be now?
CN: I'd say, he's about fifty-one.

GB: You never heard another thing about him? Never?
CN: I don't know if he's dead. I don't know if he's alive.

GB: No record.
CN: I could probably try with the official adoption people here or something, but would Thomas want to know [crying] how he was conceived? Do you understand me?

GB: Uhm.

CN: Would it do more damage to him? [Very upset.] What kind of an effect would it have on him? Is he a happy person and he doesn't know, and his life is happy with a family and maybe grandchildren? And, if he knows, what's it going to do to him? I don't know.

GB: Through all of this, Christina, did you hold on to your faith, and did you pray and did you still believe in God?

CN: You know, when you live alone for a very long time and are really excluded from society, and you've lost everything and everybody, and even when you leave the country and you've lost your country, the only person you have is God. I didn't quite understand why he let the bad things happen. But I love Our Lord, and Our Lord knows I love him. And I've prayed to Our Lord. I never feel alone now. I just feel he's there. And the angels. You know, people would think I'd be certified insane talking like this, but I do feel safe. I do feel love around me.

GB: Now, the next thing I want to talk to you about is you went to London. You fell for Mario, the Greek, and you had three children. Now, was that a happy time for you? Was that a liberating time?

CN: [Shakes her head.]

GB: No? Why?

CN: Because he was beating me up. But I had to marry him, because I was afraid of him. He'd beat me unconscious and he'd kick me and everything. And he battered me to the point where I just went down, and then he kicked me.

GB: Was he a drinker?

CN: He used to drink whiskey. He used to put whiskey on his cornflakes. And I had the children as well. When the children were born, I had to marry him, because he was afraid I was going to leave him. Do you understand me? And he told me if I left him, he'd kill me. I left a few times and he'd catch me and he'd beat me up again — put me through this wardrobe with a mirror once, when I ran away with the children and he got me. But, do you know, he's dead now. He died a few years ago.

GB: Through all of this, can I ask you, were you a good mother to the children?

CN: I was a brilliant mammy.

GB: Were you? [Smiles.]

CN: Yeah . . . I just became worn down and everything. I ran away. And I'd saved up any tablets . . . didn't even know what they were . . . I suppose a mixture of everything. And I took them with this gin. It was in New Street, in Birmingham. I wanted to go under the train, because then you never wake up, you know? I didn't think about my children at this point. It was all gone. It was all dead. It was like a dead feeling inside. And the train was late. And I collapsed on that platform, and I was in intensive care for quite some time. I nearly didn't make it at all, apparently. And after that, they put me into a mental hospital.

GB: Can I skip ahead now from that blackness and darkness of that story to . . . Where did the idea of the Foundation come from? And why Vietnam and, later on, Mongolia? What gave rise to that?

CN: I just dreamed about Vietnam. And that would have been in 1971. Yeah, I had a dream about Vietnam where I saw these kids running, and I saw the sky was just red, crimson, blazing, black — everything. I saw all these kids running, and I could see the faces . . . and I saw this girl . . .

GB: War, napalm, bombs, guns . . .

CN: Her hands were out and I was trying to catch her . . . I could see all this ground opening up . . .

GB: The great photograph . . .

CN: And I always said, "I have to go to Vietnam." So, I think it was in '87. Again it started, that I had to go — I *had* to go. My own children grown up — I waited until then, until they went into their universities and that. And then, in '89, I got in.

GB: But what did you want to do, Christina?

CN: What is it I wanted in my life? I wanted love, I wanted education, I wanted protection. I wanted a house over my head. And I wanted to be happy and free. Happy. And how could I make this happen for the children? I started with the first two that I met, Huong and Hang. And we made a contract by hand. [Indicates a handshake.] And they lived on the street: they hadn't got a dime. On the streets of Saigon, at that time, there was hundreds of thousands of people. So, I said, "Okay, I need to build a medical and social centre to help the poor to have a place to come to with dignity — to be able to feed the children, to get them back to their health."

GB: You just went ahead and did it.

CN: I did it. I did. And I worked very hard, and I begged like you could never imagine anybody begging. And there was a lot of suspicion about me, and who can blame them, you know? "Who's this mad yoke coming in with nothing, really?" [Laughs.] For some reason, they grew to love me, with time. The President of Vietnam, he was giving me this big award — like, just a few years ago, really. It'd be like getting a Nobel Peace Prize at the time, in Vietnam. And, coming down the stairs, he said — the President said to me, "Mama Tina, you no sing *Athenry*?"

GB: [Laughter.] And you did.

CN: I said, "You like I sing *Athenry*?" He said, "I like." So, I went back up and I gave it full blast with everything in my body, like. Truth and what it stands for, you know? And how important freedom is, you know? And he said, when I came down, "Mama Tina, you make me emotional."

GB: Now, can you give me any idea of how many children have benefited from your Foundation and your help and your guidance in Vietnam and around that area?

CN: Well, Vietnam and Mongolia are over 700,000. And that's official. That's official.

GB: And those children have ended up as what?

CN: Well, they end up educated. And then some of them go to college, university. They'd do anything, like — could be an architect, graphic art, design, engineering . . . We have about a hundred projects in Vietnam, all across the whole country.

You know, our Foundation, somebody stole in our Foundation. You don't mind me telling you that? Quite a few years ago, okay? A person stole.

GB: Embezzled, yes.

CN: Yeah. That's a very bad thing to do. I don't need to hurt that person by talking about them now, because I think they're sorry and everything, and we got all the money back. But I'm saying, from everything bad comes good. That's what I'm trying to say. Because then I met the Fraud Squad, do you understand me? And then Paschal Walsh was the sergeant, and Liam, they investigated the case — all these people for quite a long time. I don't know how long. And then, when it's all finished, done with and over, then they said, "We want to raise money for you." And guess what? They cycled to Paris, and they raised — I think it was €92,000.

GB: [Whistles.]

CN: We got this huge, big beautiful building . . . and a big sign: *By the Garda Síochána, Ireland.*

GB: [Laughter.] Well done. Now, can I ask you, then, out of all of this — and you've described this wonderful achievement on your part — is this God-driven?

CN: No, it's not God-driven.

GB: What is it then? What drives it in you?

CN: Just my love for humanity . . . and to try to give choices to children, choices I never had — to try to make it possible, instead of a child's life being wasted and either sold or used in prostitution or brothels. There is no way that a child is born from the womb to the street, to just die, to be used and abused, to suffer from diseases and starvation and just die. It doesn't make any sense.

Our Lord, yes, is a player, in the sense that sometimes it's so difficult: you're so exhausted and worn out or you see such horrific things — horrific! And you just sometimes scream it out of your body — you know, scream the anger, about what other people do, humans do to humans. And that's the thought to Our Lord . . . and you say, "I need your help." But I don't do it for Our Lord, because that's silly, to say, "Oh, I'm doing that because of Our Lord . . ." Oh, big deal! And you think you'll get a place in Heaven? No way!

GB: [Laughter.]

CN: Now, I don't want to be giving you the impression I'm a big, religious freaky character. I'm not.

GB: So, as far as you're concerned, Christina, who and what was Jesus?

CN: Our Lord was a very good man: the Son of God, we were told — the Holy Trinity, really. I believe that Our Lord does exist and Jesus does exist, and I have seen something which I'm hesitant to tell you about, because I don't want people to think I should be certified insane.

GB: Try me.

CN: Well, when I was very sick there, a few years ago — I had a cancer, you know — and I went to Maynooth — you know, Maynooth College — and there's a very special man up there called Holy Joe. And that's his name, Joe. He used to be police and he retired. And he was a holy man. And I asked him, "How can I deal with all of this?" And he never said much to me. He just used to listen to me. And he'd go and pray in Latin behind me. And there was a little altar on the left, in this room, and I saw this amazing, big, huge — I don't know how to express it — it was as if the sun was coming in to me. There was no sun there, but it was as if the sun itself had come inside the room and was coming towards me. And through it was the face of Our Lord. It was Our Lord's face.

GB: And what did this face say to you?
CN: Nothing.

GB: And what did it convey to you?
CN: That it was okay.

GB: Okay.
CN: It's okay . . . And that peace, you can never explain it. It's just something — no matter how peaceful you are in life, you cannot explain this . . . Oh, it was just beautiful.

But then Holy Joe came . . . And he was sweating and shaking, and shaking and sweating, and crying. And then he said to me, "You've seen him too, haven't you? You've seen him, Christina. You've seen him!" I said, "Yes."

GB: You have great faith in Our Lord, that's quite clear. Do you think the Lord is responsible for all the evil things that have happened to you, all the bad things that have happened to you?
CN: No.

GB: No. If not, then what? How do you account for that?
CN: I don't think that Our Lord is — how could he be? — responsible for what the human beings do. He gave everybody brains, didn't he? — gave everyone intellect. It's what we do with it.

People can do evil acts. I'm not saying they're born evil: I don't think people are born evil. But there's something about *some* people — that there's no conscience, there's no sensitivity, there's nothing. And I've seen what they do: nine-year-old, pregnant, stolen, raped, abused.

GB: Do you think there's a come-uppance time for the sort of people you're talking about?

CN: I think there is a pay-back time. I think there has to be. Even if it's only their conscience comes back alive again and they remember all those horrific things they have done.

GB: You've been on the wrong end of a lot of bad things people have done to you. Do you forgive them now?
CN: I have always forgiven, because it's part of who I am and everything that I am. If I didn't forgive, Gay, how could I go and do the work I do? I couldn't. Because I'd still be this bitter, twisted human being. I wouldn't be free. You know what I have? Freedom. And I love every-thing that I am. I will never change.

GB: Final question. You're a great believer in the Lord, you've said so. You're regularly in contact with him. When you die — which I trust and pray will not be soon, Christina — but *when* you do and you're up at the Pearly Gates, and you finally come face to face with him, what will you say?
CN: I'll just look at Our Lord and I'll say, "It's grand to meet you again." Now, that's if it was Our Lord that I met. And I'll say to him, "I could be wrong, but I thought it was you." And then I'll say, "Will you let me do this before I go in the Pearly Gates?" And I'll do it for you now. I'll do this [singing: *The Fields of Athenry*]: "By a lonely prison wall . . ."

GB: [Laughter.]
CN: [Singing.] ". . . I heard a young girl calling . . ."

GB: You'll be turned away!
CN: [Singing.] "Michael, they are taking you away . . . For you stole Trevelyan's corn so your young might see the morn. The prison ship lies waiting . . ."

GB: [Singing.] ". . . in the bay."
CN: Everyone!
GB & CN: [Singing.] "Low lie the fields of Athenry" etc. . . .

GB: You'll be turned away. I can assure you, you'll be turned away.
CN: God bless!

MICHEÁL
Ó MUIRCHEARTAIGH

Mise Éire

A few days after Micheál Ó Muircheartaigh agreed to our interview in 2010, he announced his retirement as an RTÉ commentator after an astonishing sixty-one years in the job. I trust that our request was not the final straw that convinced him he'd had enough. That fluke of timing meant that we were suddenly, by sheer good fortune, at the front of a very long queue of people wanting to interview him about his life and career. Not that anyone tired of hearing and reading about him. He was always, by a country mile, the most loved person on the RTÉ Montrose campus and probably in the country at large.

He was eighty at the time of our conversation. You wouldn't have guessed it: his hair is still sandy, his posture upright, his handshake firm and his face largely unlined. He had recently led his children and grandchildren on a yomp up Mount Brandon. And I mean *led*.

A clue to the secret of his rude good health is the Pioneer pin he wears on his lapel, although he does not shout about his commitment to total abstinence. That is probably why people in the sporting world – who are not generally noted for their restraint when it comes to alcohol – have always listened respectfully to what he has to say on the subject.

Don't delude yourself into thinking that Micheál's teetotal life made him in any way boring or stay-at-home. In fact, listening to him, it is a wonder that he and his lovely wife, Helena, ever found the time or opportunity to have eight children. He seems to have been out, day and night, bouncing like a pinball between greyhound race meets and GAA matches in all parts of the country.

No wonder he is as happy as he is: he has had a life of doing what he likes and liking what he does. Mind you, I suspect that this sort of fulfilment has as much to do with mindset as it has with one's choice of activities.

Church has been an important bedrock throughout his life, and it remains that way. I was not surprised to see him, at the close of the 2012 International Eucharistic Congress, reciting *Ag Críost an Síol* in front of a crowd of seventy thousand and a global audience of millions. It brought together three of the things he holds dearest: the Irish language, Christianity and Croker. He looked like the cat who had got the cream and the international audience, many of whom had never heard of him, lapped him up.

That famous voice and the cadences of west Kerry should be recorded and placed in a time capsule, or transmitted into the vast voids of space, as a representation of what Ireland sounds like at its very best. I heard him once reading from his memoirs about preparing, as a child, the family home in Dún Síon for Christmas and then walking through the night, in convoy with neighbours, to attend midnight Mass in Dingle. It was unspeakably beautiful and moving, without even a scintilla of sentimentality or wallowing nostalgia. He did what he has always done best: he told it as he saw it. He does not need rose-tinted glasses, because he already sees the world — indeed, sees life itself — as a golden thing. He knows how to live.

❧

GB: Anois, Dingle, Dingle, Dingle . . . abair liom mar gheall ar do shaol san áit sin . . . Your childhood in Dingle?
MOM: Well, it was An Daingean to me or Daingean Uí Chúis, we always wrote in letters or school records. It was a lovely place. It was a small town. I lived three miles outside of it, to the east, near the sea — went to the local convent until I reached maybe First Communion stage.

GB: And there were eight of you in the family, I know.
MOM: Eight. That would be a common number for a family at the time.

GB: And you were about fourteen when your mother died.
MOM: Exactly, yes.

GB: And do you remember the last conversation you had with her?
MOM: I do, indeed — dropped up after school. I don't know whether she had a premonition that she wouldn't last long. She said, "Well, look after the books, anyhow" or "Don't neglect the books, and I will do what I can for you from the other side" — an taobh eile, what the philosophers call "the other world". So, that's where she is since 4th February, '44.

GB: And you remember those words clearly from her?
MOM: Well, they were strong words, in a way, and they were reassuring words. "I will do what I can for you."

GB: So, there were eight of you, then. How did your father cope?
MOM: We had an aunt, a sister of my father's, who had spent her life in America. She returned . . .

GB: This is Auntie May?

MOM: She was Auntie May to the whole parish, or to the whole county, really. And, you know, she was a strong-minded lady — great interest in education as well — and wanted all of us to keep going to school. So, she came home, early in '47.

GB: So Auntie May became a second mother to you?

MOM: Exactly, yes.

GB: In just a spirit of self-sacrifice, was it?

MOM: 'Twas indeed. Yes, she had lived her life in America, came home I think once — maybe in the early 1930s, maybe the late '20s — and then lived in New York. She had three brothers there: she had Mike and Dan and John. So I'd say she was a sort of a mother to everyone there as well.

GB: Go back to your father now. Even with Auntie May there, did he have to be strict with eight of you around the place?

MOM: Well, I don't recall him being strict. We were working as a team, like all families and farms did at the time. For instance, in the morning, now, before going to school, one of my jobs maybe was to light the fire and then go and bring home the horse, to bring the milk to the creamery, because the creamery was a vital part of life on a farm, that time, and it brought a monthly income. And it was heaven on earth to me, that type of work.

GB: And do you remember it, as you grew older, as a particularly religious household?

MOM: Well, I think every house, in a way, was a religious type of house at the time. There'd be the Rosary at night — not every night, but pretty often. And then there was what I'd call the religion of the people. People believed strongly, you know, in, if you like, the goodness of God, that there was goodness in people.

GB: Tell me about the Stations.

MOM: The Stations . . . sort of a group of maybe ten families. So, with ten or eleven houses, you'd have it [Mass in the house] roughly once every five years. And then the house would be done up as if there was a wedding of the High King to take place in your house: preparations all over.

GB: Repainted, re-whitewashed . . . ?

MOM: Up very early in the morning, repainted, whitewashed, everything in order, and then the arrival of the Parish Priest and the Curate and the Clerk. It was great pageantry, if you like. They'd get down to work quickly. One of them would go down to the sitting-room, hearing Confessions. And if it was a winter Station you'd be seated on a chair like this and a neat fire next to him. The penitent would come in and sit in another chair — no box or anything — and exchange, you know, the sins and the forgiveness. And while that's going on, with people in turn coming in, there'd be a Mass in the kitchen by the Parish Priest. And then they'd reverse roles. And then, of course, when the whole thing was over, there'd be food for everyone — never drink in my days.

GB: Oh!

MOM: Food, and plenty of food as well. Especially, maybe, a big bucket-ful of boiled eggs. And it was a test of you how many eggs could you eat. It was a tremendous occasion. And it still is carried on, and I hope carries on for ever.

GB: After that, then, you went off to boarding school, I know. And how long were you in boarding school, do you reckon, altogether?

MOM: Well, I was three years in Coláiste Íosagáin, Baile Bhuirne.

GB: Coming from a big family, how did you react to boarding school? Were you lonely or sad . . . ?

MOM: I wasn't, and I wasn't lonely leaving, because I was always, if you like, inquisitive. I had never been on a bus in my life at this stage and that bus journey into Tralee, if you like, was the equivalent of going to Disneyland nowadays.

GB: And what age were you, now?

MOM: Going fifteen. And then getting a train to Cork. I had never been on a train in my life. It was a completely new experience.

GB: Now, there would have been a very strong religious thing in Baile Bhuirne?

MOM: Oh, there would, indeed.

GB: Yes.

MOM: And I think it was the thing of the time, that everybody took the Pledge at Confirmation. Now, religion was strong in the people's hearts at the time, but, as I mentioned earlier, the religion of the people was there as well.

GB: Now, the Retreat . . .

MOM: The Retreat, yes. A Mission at home in Dingle, but at school a Retreat, and three days of silence. It was a pity it wasn't videoed. You'd see people with sorrowful faces walking around the football pitch, brooding on the evils of their life. According to the priests, the missioners, we were all damned, and the whole world with us. And it would make you think, really. [Laughter.] But then it was an experience, the Mission or the Retreat — three days.

GB: All right. Leaving that behind now, you came to Dublin . . .
MOM: Yes.

GB: . . . and the teacher training college, St Patrick's . . .
MOM: Drumcondra . . .

GB: . . . another strong religious ethos.
MOM: It was. The Vincentian Fathers. If you were there in the morning when the Dean would come around — and again, the religion was there — the morning call, big dormitory — he'd come in the door, you'd hear the door swinging if you were awake. *"Benedicamus Dominum."* And if you didn't answer with the *"Deo Gratias"*, he'd stop outside your unit. *"Benedicamus Dominum."* It would be getting louder and louder until a disgruntled *"Deo Gratias"* came as a response.

GB: [Laughs.] Now, tell me about your teaching career. Were you a born teacher, do you think?
MOM: Well, I liked it. And I was possibly fairly good. And why I liked it more than anything: when you're in the company of young people — and young people are usually outgoing; they're happy, they're optimistic — I think it helps to keep *yourself* that way. And one of the pupils was Luke Kelly.

GB: Ahhh.
MOM: Luke lived in East Wall, but Luke Kelly — I still remember the fuzzy head — he was small when he was big, and he was small when he was small. But he was great gas, you know? He was always cheerful. And if he had a good manager, I think, he'd have made the Dublin team.

GB: Really!
MOM: I think he would. You know, he was gifted with his feet, but he mightn't have been that interested in it. He was music-mad.

GB: What about corporal punishment? In those years, corporal punish-ment was perfectly acceptable and routine?

MOM: Oh, it was, indeed. And when you got a job in a school, you were presented with a leather. That's as important as the chalks are.

GB: And what would have been your judgement?

MOM: Well, I thought that it didn't feel right, because when I was going to school I got away with a lot. I didn't get as much of the punishment as others did. And I saw people getting punishment that they didn't deserve and, very often, that they didn't know what it was for. But then it was part of the thing and nobody complained. But, for that reason, I always thought there is something wrong about it and I was delighted when it was gone.

GB: Okay. Now, somewhere around there, 1950, you saw an ad, did you, for Raidió Éireann?

MOM: Yes, it was 1949. I was still in Drumcondra.

GB: So, they wanted a commentator for football matches.

MOM: Well, it wasn't an ad so much as a notice. Seán Ó Síocháin, whom you'd have known . . .

GB: Indeed.

MOM: . . . operated a lot of the radio as a singer. He broadcast an occasional game through the medium of Irish, but by then he was the Assistant General Secretary of the GAA and he was concentrating on his singing. He decided to stop commentating on games. So, Raidió Éireann, as it was at the time, they needed somebody who would do games through the medium of Irish. There was a notice in Drumcondra, there was a notice in UCD and other places: *Anyone interested invited to come to Croke Park* on a certain day — come in and you'd get a trial. And about ten of us, we spoke about this. We said it would be great gas.

GB: Agus bhí an Ghaeilge go flúirseach agat?

MOM: Bhí an Ghaeilge, bhí an Ghaeilge againn go léir, agus raghaimid ann. Get into Croke Park free — that was an attraction on its own. Get into Micheál O'Hehir's box was sort of a Christmas present beyond all presents. So, we went along in the spirit of adventure. We'd have fun. And when the adventure was over for me, I was asked, would I broadcast the Railway Cup football final on the following Thursday week. And I said, "Why not?" And that's how it started, if you like: pure chance.

GB: When you finally gave up teaching, thirty years later, to concentrate on your broadcasting, did you miss it?

MOM: I missed the teaching. I always found the Christian Brothers — they were great people. They were very, very devoted to education. They were devoted to the welfare of the pupils. And I enjoyed my term as a teacher and thought a lot before I walked away from it.

GB: It is true to say that, without them, there are so many of us who would never have had an education of any kind . . .

MOM: Throughout the country. And, to me, no amount of money spent on education is wasted, in any part of the world.

GB: Are you sorry at their demise, the Christian Brothers?

MOM: Well, I think the need for them no longer exists. They were there when there was not an educated laity that could perform the job of teachers. But then, by degrees, as the standard of education among the ordinary people rose, they had fulfilled their role. By the time that they died out, it was unfortunate that it got mixed up with other issues, you know, that were a regrettable minority, no doubt. But, as often happens, the whole lot would be tainted by the sins of a few.

GB: Now, we move on, and I want to hear about Helena and where you met and how, and how long did the courtship last?

MOM: I was always a free spirit.

GB: You were!

MOM: I always looked upon myself as a free spirit.

GB: As a bachelor . . .

MOM: Yes, sort of. Now, when I was in Dublin, you know, going into O'Connell Street, whether I turned left or right — did it matter, really? — or went straight on and enjoyed it and knew where I was going and all that . . .

GB: This is building up to Helena . . .

MOM: Exactly. And then, I remember, some time in the mid '60s — it might have been around 1966 or thereabouts — in school the first day, and Gerry O'Donoghue, one of the fellow-teachers, he said, "Where are you going to be staying this year?"

I said, "I have no place yet. I stayed in a hotel last night. Do you know of any place?"

"Well," he said, "there's a cousin of mine around in Templemore Avenue, and they have an apartment to let at the moment."

I said, "Book that for me."

And that's where Helena lived with her mother and three sisters. Her mother was a widow at the time, Mrs McDowell. So, four McDowell daughters and one man upstairs that was seldom there, really, because when I went out in the morning, God only knew when I came home. She was there, practical and sensible, like she is today. So that's how it started. We finished up getting married in the Rathgar church, in 1970, and we're together since. Buíochas mór le Dia.

GB: And this must have curtailed your rambling considerably?
MOM: I don't think it did.

GB: Well, how could it not?
MOM: Well, I had the excuse that, with the job I had, I had to be moving. I had to be going somewhere, and I was going to matches and going to dogs and going to horses and going playing golf. And that never changed much, really. And she was sensible enough to realise that was part of the life that I needed. So, very considerate of her, I must say.

GB: But that's a life we all dream of . . . and none of us ever attain it . . .
MOM: Exactly.

GB: . . . And you did!
MOM: Well, I attained it, yes. But, still and all, I suppose, when it really came down to big decisions, she was the boss.

GB: Now, you have eight children, God bless you both.
MOM: Yes, indeed.

GB: And they're all university graduates, and that's wonderful.
MOM: Well, that's the sign of the modern times.

GB: Nonetheless, with eight of them, there must have been a fair stretch on the finances?
MOM: There was, indeed. My betting, you know, had to be curtailed a little bit. [Laughter.] You know, that was a big sacrifice, because you always imagined the next bet is going to be the one that will solve all problems. But it had to be curtailed. And I had, I think, a good philosophy on betting: bet what you can afford to lose.

GB: Were you a strict father?

MOM: Not really. I was always a believer, again, mar is eol duit. I'm very fond of the Irish sayings: Beatha duine a thoil — that a person's life is really what *they* want, not what *you* want. So, as far as possible, I let them decide what they wanted to study and how they did it and so on. So, I'd be the very opposite to being strict.

GB: Now, through your life, of course, you have had the extraordinary advantage of never drinking. Did you ever taste alcohol?

MOM: Only with a very bad flu one time . . .

GB: Medicinal?

MOM: Yes, and that was the only time. And it was a great advantage, I think. I never had any desire to drink. It's not something I miss, or it's not some benefit that other people have that I see myself sort of deprived or lacking in not having it. I never had a desire to drink and I've spent a fair bit of time in pubs, in company, at occasions and banquets and festivals.

GB: Well, this is what I want to ask you. You've been at functions and banquets and festivals and parties and ceremonies and so on. Agus tú féin ag seasamh ann agus gach aon duine eile sa seomra ar meisce.

MOM: Bhuel, ag ól.

GB: Ar meisce.

MOM: Ar meisce.

GB: How did you cope with that?

MOM: Well, I never felt that I missed out on anything by not drinking. That's a point I often made in visiting schools, because a lot of young people would tell me they drink, because it's expected of them. Everybody does it. And I'd say to them, "If you don't think it suits you, you should have the courage to say, 'Well, it's okay for others, but maybe not for me.'" You don't do something because a lot of people do it. But there is a new attitude towards drink, I think, especially among athletes and players.

GB: Oh, yes.

MOM: Players now that go on tour, they go on tour to preserve their fitness. And they'll train while they're on tour. They'll limit and control their drink. There was a time when a tour meant non-stop drinking until you got home. Thanks be to God, that day is over, and it's the players that saw it themselves. And that's very positive, I think.

GB: You never worried about the children, when they were growing up . . . ?

MOM: Well, I think if you have what I call the basic faith, I think faith teaches you that you shouldn't worry, really: that if you have faith, as we say in Kerry, in the Man Above — I suppose nowadays we should be saying the Man or Woman Above — that eliminates a lot of worry. Worry doesn't solve a lot of things.

GB: It is appropriate for a man of your age to think about death. Do you?

MOM: Not really.

GB: No?

MOM: I think most people don't think about death.

GB: Well, you must think that it's closer than it was when you started . . .

MOM: Well, you know, you look towards the end of the rainbow. It's out there somewhere, and the somewhere could be nearer; it could be further away! And it was a great consolation to read recently that the first person to live to be 130 years, in Ireland, has already been born. There's nothing wrong with saying that person could be me. But I haven't actually thought about it yet. Maybe now I'll do a little bit of thinking about it, but I'd be hoping that it's far off.

GB: And would you be scared at the thought of it?

MOM: I don't think that it's something to be scared of. And I think that's one of the things that religion teaches you. I remember, now, when my father died, he died suddenly. I wasn't there. But, it might be a year or two before he died, I remember buying him a walking-stick for Christmas — a walking-stick was a very acceptable present in old Ireland — gave him the stick and he had a look at it and he apparently liked it, and he said, "Now, I won't use that, but will you make sure to put it into the coffin with me, because I'll need that when I'm walking around at night." There was this belief that souls were released at night. That was believed in Kerry, anyhow. And it's not unknown in the folklore in Kerry for groups of people that are dead to come back to play matches at night against current teams. And the final whistle was the first — we used to call it "an chéad léas den mhaidin, nuair a tháinig breacadh an lae" — and the minute breacadh an lae, that was the full time, and they had to be gone — they had to disappear, gone — they had to disappear.

GB: Dawn.

MOM: It was in the tradition. So, I'd be hoping, definitely, that there is something after death.

GB: Yes?

MOM: And that something could be exciting, like playing matches or whatever it is. We're led to believe that it's a state of happiness.

GB: And do you think, in that state of happiness, you will see your loved ones again? Your mother . . . ?

MOM: Well, yes. That would be the wish. But I have never met anybody that said for certain. I'll see . . . But you'd be hoping to meet all the people you knew, of course.

GB: You do a fair amount of charity work, Micheál, with GOAL and Niall Mellon and the hospices . . .

MOM: Lots, yes, for GOAL . . .

GB: What gives rise to that commitment in you?

MOM: I think most people, especially if somebody approaches you and asks you, people are only too delighted to help. Like, the causes you mention there now, or Special Olympics, or going out to Calcutta with John O'Shea, which I did once. I went with Self Help to Malawi, to see how the other side lives, the side that have no wealth, and to appreciate through that what you have. And I think that cultivates in you the wish and the will to give something.

GB: Incidentally, you've said that the GAA is much more to you than a sports organisation. What is it to you?

MOM: Well, it is, because I saw it as I travelled from one end of the country to the other or travelled outside of Ireland, really. It's a social vehicle, where all the people of a community can have something in common. It gives a spirit to a place. And community spirit, I think, is much, much greater than financial wealth for the community to have. If they have a spirit, they'll overcome a lot. The GAA supplies that in huge amounts, wherever the GAA is.

GB: What do you think the Old Scripture, the Old Testament, was?

MOM: Well, I often thought it didn't apply to the practicalities of Ireland. You know, it was a wonderful story and all that, but I always thought that the Old Testament was a little bit detached, that it never made the connection.

GB: Well, we Catholics were never particularly encouraged to read it anyway.

MOM: No.

GB: But what, do you think, is the New Testament, then? Matthew, Mark, Luke, John?

MOM: Well, that's more understandable. You see, it deals with a person that we associate with. You know, Críost. But you could relate to the characters of the New Testament, and you see them in modern life.

GB: And who do you think Jesus was?

MOM: I believe that he was what they say he was: the Son of God, who has also lived on Earth, served his apprenticeship on Earth, to see the type of beings that are on Earth. And, as he found out to his cost in the end, there were many types there, the good and bad.

GB: And do you believe he rose from the dead, physically?

MOM: Yes, indeed. And Easter is very much in the Irish folklore: An Cháisc. It was the finale to something that was being preached, that he did rise. We all learned the Catechism off by heart, and I think there's nothing wrong in believing that.

GB: Do you think that you would have the faith that you have, were it not for the Irish language?

MOM: Well, it is true that there is something in the Irish language: the language and the religion, they're all the one. And I think the best example of that — I don't think it happened anywhere else in the world — in certain parts of the Gaeltacht they never referred to the church as "an séipéal" or "an teampall": it was "teach an phobail" — the people's house, *our* house — where they were free to go in, where they'd be listened to, where they felt at ease — an teach pobail. And I think that's how a church should be seen by most people. I always thought that it had some little extra dimension, no matter what you were dealing with.

GB: Do you believe in Hell?

MOM: I don't, really.

GB: Why do you recoil from that?

MOM: It's too extreme. And we were led to believe that you went to Hell if you committed one mortal sin that was not forgiven. Now, didn't Christ say the just man falls — is it five or seven times a day? It is almost impossible not to fall. So, I don't believe that a God who is the essence of goodness could destine anybody to what Hell was. And I believe, in the end of the day, the Good Lord forgives everything.

GB: Did you ever think of being a member of any other faith?
MOM: Not really. I think that's the case with most people. I know it's a strange way: we were born into that. Loyalty is a very strong force in the human being. Sometimes you're loyal to things that maybe you shouldn't be loyal to, without questioning them. But I have never questioned it, because I always try to see the good side of it. And, rather than see the people who transgressed as representing it, to see the thousands who did not, and the goodness in those. And that is still there. And, with the help of God, it will come back again.

GB: Last question, and it's the standard final question on this programme: when the day comes and there you are at the Pearly Gates, and you've got past Peter in one way or the other, and you confront the Lord himself, or herself — as Gaeilge nó as Béarla, what will you say?
MOM: Well, I'll listen for a while, and I'd hope that the Lord, at some stage in his life, that he heard the song *Are You There, Moriarity?* and that he'll say — as that famous one by Jimmy O'Dea, he used to finish off: "Flap your wings, Moriarity" — and that he'll . . . [gestures being waved in]. Now, it's only a wish, and you'll never know: a lot of wishes come true. That would be it.

FIONNULA FLANAGAN

A Rose by Any Other Name

May I offer a small tip to all aspiring interviewers? It does not matter how famous the person to whom you are talking is: whether they are a president, a pop star, a movie icon or royalty, write their damned name, in bold capitals, across the top of your crib sheet. If you do this, you might stand a chance of avoiding the humiliation I experienced at the start of my interview with Fionnula Flanagan.

"Hello and welcome again, and our guest this time is Fionnula O'Shanahan. And welcome, Fionnula, and thank you for you visiting us."

"It's actually Fionnula Flanagan . . ."

She was right. It actually was. Fortunately, we weren't live, and such fluffs can be edited out. But, still, not the best start.

Fionnula is an Emmy- and IFTA-winning actor, as comfortable working in Irish as in English, on screen or on stage, and on either side of the Atlantic. She is also the daughter of a hard-drinking revolutionary, who fought in the Spanish Civil War and then brought all his idealism and rage back to Dublin with him. The influence of drink and revolution has been strong in Fionnula's life, although the former has now been transformed into something very positive by her sober decades and her marriage to Garrett O'Connor, Medical Director of the Betty Ford Clinic.

The revolutionary element is still there. She is as happy to be called an activist as she is an actor, and as willing to share a stage with Messrs McGuinness and Adams as she is with fellow-thesps.

The voice and delivery, which made her a leading interpreter of Joyce from even her earliest days, are still mesmeric. And she has all the poetical eloquence and turns of phrase of a lifelong bilinguist. Unusually, though, for an actor, she also has an aura of ease, by which I mean she is at ease with herself. I wanted to know the secret.

❧

GB: Now, I have to tell you that you and I were born in the same hospital, the Coombe, and probably baptised in the same church, St Nicholas of Myra.

FF: Yes, St Nicholas of Myra.

GB: And I gather from reading about you that your mother was okay about the Church, but your father was belligerently anti-Church. Is that so?

FF: Yes, he was. He was actually anti-cleric, very much so, and he didn't trust the Catholic Church. And no priest was ever allowed across our door. My mother was quite devout and never pushed religion upon us, but we all went to Catholic schools.

GB: Where did the anti-Church, anti-cleric thing come from with your father? Do you know?

FF: Well, I think it was based on many things. When he was a young man he joined Saor Éire, and it was a socialist movement. And then, of course, he went to Spain to fight against Franco and to uphold the Spanish Republic.

When he came back from Spain, I remember all the men and women who came back from Spain were immediately excommunicated. And to be excommunicated in Ireland of the late '30s and early '40s was horrendous. It narrowed your ability to get a job, for sure, and certainly to advance in whatever you were doing. Well, he took that on board, and that fed the bitterness and fed the resentment and the anti-Church, anti-institutional feeling. And, of course, the Government at the time here was very interlocked with both the Archbishop of Dublin and the Catholic Church, in my memory.

GB: Then, afterwards, the family settled into a reasonable standard of living, did they?

FF: Oh, no, our fortunes fluctuated. My father drank, and sometimes we were okay, and then sometimes we literally did not know where the next meal was coming from. And my mother was a terribly genteel Irish county person, and it really offended her . . . We lived in a Corporation house, on the north side of Dublin, and she hated it.

GB: And, in spite of the attitude to the Catholic Church, you went to Catholic schools. How was that?

FF: Well, there wasn't anywhere else to go. I went to Scoil Mhuire, and my brother went to Scoil Cholmcille, in Marlborough Street. And then, after that, I went on to Sandymount High School. And then I went to Scoil Chaitríona, in Eccles Street.

GB: So, how much of all of that religious upbringing is left, if any?

FF: Those Dominican women were wonderful, and they knew the key to freedom was education. And I admire them for that and I am grateful to them. And I think that there were a lot of really wonderful things about compassion and thinking of helping the poor: that was a consciousness in Ireland of the time that was part and parcel of the Church, as I knew it.

GB: From your point of view now, were they misled or misguided people, do you think, in their belief and in their vocation and in their dedication to a higher power?

FF: No, I don't think they were misguided. I think that they were women who were passionate about teaching. And we had, teaching us mathematics, someone who was a world-class mathematician. We had a teacher of Irish, Sister Aquinas, who was a brilliant, absolutely brilliant, woman. And the fire inside them, to pass on knowledge and to make sure that we would be able to use it, was great. It blazed in them. So, if they believed that they were doing it for the glory of God, well, fine. There are wonderful buildings all over the world and great symphonies written for the glory of God, and they were doing their bit, and I'm glad I had them as teachers.

GB: They would have seen the Church as the Body of Christ.

FF: Yes.

GB: How do you see it?

FF: Well, I don't see it as the Body of Christ. I see it as an institution, whose first job is to keep itself in office and to keep itself going, at all costs. It's a very wealthy institution. It's an institution that has done a great deal of good all over the world, and it's an institution, like all others, whose aims and goals have been politicised by its very leaders, to its cost and the cost of the people who are its followers — its flock, if you will.

GB: Well, what do you think Jesus was, is?

FF: Oh, I think he was a revolutionary. And to have the brilliant idea that love is what will make a difference in the world, not savagery . . . I thought that that was a marvellous message. I still do.

GB: So, nothing divine about him, then, as far as you're concerned?

FF: No, I tend to think of him as a prophet. I don't think of him as divine. I don't know what that is, either.

GB: Was there a moment that you can recollect that you decided that you didn't want to be part of this any more, the Catholic Church?

FF: I'm not sure that there was a specific moment, but it did happen when I was in my early teens. I began to understand that, because I was a female, I would never qualify for even the middle-management job, never mind the top job, in the Catholic Church. I thought that that kind of inequality was wrong. I still think it's wrong. And I'm thinking now of the Catholicism of the '50s.

GB: It was all dark, sinful and forbidding . . .

FF: Dark, sinful and terrifying. Family planning didn't exist. And that, to me, was outrageous. I mean, I do remember the beginnings of it. I remember the fight, even before you get to the abortion question, even before that: family planning. Look at the fight it took to get it in here. And we were told that it was a plot by Northern Protestants to limit the Catholic population. I mean, give me a break! [Laughter.]

So, when you consider that those were the kinds of rules you were being given to shape your moral compass, it's amazing that more of us didn't go mad.

GB: We did.

FF: And then the ones who didn't left.

GB: That's why you're still sane!

FF: Well, I wouldn't make that claim so fast . . .

GB: If your moral compass doesn't come from religion, where does it come from?

FF: I think it comes from my parents. Nobody was ever turned away from the door, even though we didn't have anything. The Travellers would come to the door, and my mother always gave them something: food, money, clothes.

My father once gave a pair of good shoes to a man who came to the door, and the man said, "I can't take these. They're too good, and if the Guards see me with them, they'll think I stole them." And my father wrote down his address — and at the time we had a telephone — and the phone number, and he said, "If that happens, have them phone me and I'll tell them."

GB: That's extraordinary.

FF: That was magnificent. Who'd want a moral compass better than that? You don't need an institution to give you better than that. And I'm glad.

GB: Go back to your father. You say he drank a lot. Do you mean *a lot*?
FF: Yes.

GB: He was an alcoholic?
FF: Well, I would say he was, yes. Certainly, his drinking was a cause of great grief and pain to his family.

GB: How did that affect you?
FF: When I was a teenager, I was very alienated from my father. I loved him, I adored him, and I know he loved me. But as I grew older, I blamed him for the unhappiness it caused my mother and I had contempt for that. It was many, many years of living before I could come to realise that he was, you know, terribly isolated.

GB: Isolated?
FF: Yes.

GB: Why?
FF: My father knew a lot of people, but I don't think he had very many close friends. And he was subject to terrible panic attacks, which we called temper tantrums. You know, he used to lose his temper in public and my mother would die of embarrassment when he would shout and carry on. But, actually, I now know that they were panic attacks.

I remember, as a child, feeling that I wanted to protect him from ridicule. And, of course, as a child, you shouldn't feel that you have to protect your father. His job is to protect you. So, I remember being fiercely protective of him — that my school mates wouldn't make fun of him or feel sorry for him. So, it was that kind of precarious feeling and, of course, you resent that too, and it's frightening.

GB: Did it turn you against drink?
FF: What it did was, I said, "I will never drink the way my father does." My father would have a hangover in the morning and would be throwing up in the bathroom. That never happened to me. So, I thought, "Oh, well, it doesn't bother me. I'm fine."

So, in my early twenties and on into my thirties, I had my own experimentation with wine and with drugs, and at first, it was great, it was wonderful. You know, it was social, it was parties, it was great. And then, bit by bit, I began to realise that this was not really helping me. In fact, it wasn't that I couldn't remember where I parked the car: I couldn't remember that I *had* a car, you know? And I'd go home in a taxi and say, "Somebody stole my car. Where's the car gone?"

So, I did begin to realise that it was time that I left that alone. It was beginning to interfere with my life. And I'm sure, although I never showed up drunk on the set or on stage or at an interview, I certainly showed up resentful and angry, and probably hungover. But my father never got sober and I did, thank God.

GB: Why did you get into acting in the first place?
FF: We didn't have any money, and I'm the eldest of five, and my father would be away — oftentimes he didn't come home for days. And I would put on little plays in our kitchen for my mother. She was our audience.

Then she used to take me to the Gate on a Saturday afternoon, later on, and we'd sit in the one-and-sixpenny seats. And I knew — I don't know how I knew this, but I knew — that up there on the stage, in the light, they were having a lot more fun than I was, sitting in the dark. You know, there was something wonderful about that.

And as time went by, of course, as a young actress, you know, you have feelings about . . . you know, it's all about you, and it's about the play and things like that. But as you grow older, you come to realise the deeper significance of how you can actually touch people's lives, and that there's somebody sitting out there in their living room, all alone, watching you on telly, or in a cinema, or in the audience, if it's live, who might be in total despair at that moment in time. They might think they're the most awful person, that they have terrible griefs or terrible crimes committed, terrible things they've done, and there's that moment in time when you can touch them and they know that you're just like them: "It's all right. It's okay. You're not alone." I think that's what it's about. So, when you get the opportunity to do that, it's wonderful.

GB: But you knew that America was the place for you, fairly soon, as distinct from Ireland? You knew your opportunities were there?
FF: Well, I suspected that they were, because several things combined. I was a divorcee. I was not welcomed with open arms by many people here at the time, to come back and live here. And then I met the man I'm married to, Garrett O'Connor. He was on the faculty of Johns Hopkins University, in Baltimore, and I met him when I was on tour. And we decided to live together, and then we decided to get married. And that's how it happened. It was a combination of events.

GB: So, this programme is called *The Meaning of Life.* As far as you're concerned, what is the meaning of life? What are we all doing here? And what are you doing here?

FF: I really do believe that life is about service — being of service and making the world a little better place than it was ten minutes ago. Own, really *own*, who you are. There was a time in my life when I lied like I breathed. It came so easily to me.

GB: Lied?

FF: Lied . . . To fabricate . . .

GB: To yourself or to other people?

FF: Oh, to other people . . . and to oneself, of course. Fabricate reality the way you wanted it to be. And I don't do that any more. And when you don't do that any more, you're not tyrannised by it. And so there's a freedom in that. And I think that owning the shadow part, or the dark side of ourselves, where the things that we're ashamed of . . . There's an expression in the Twelve-Step programmes that says, "You're only as sick as your secrets." So, once you have owned your secrets and given them to someone else and said, "You know, I don't like this part of me" or "I wasted this" or "I did that," "This is a bad habit of mine . . ." then it can no longer tyrannise you. And then you can begin to catch it when it comes at you, and change it.

GB: But what did you lie about, and to whom?

FF: Oh, everything! I mean, I lied about who I was, I lied about my attitudes. I was very concerned with having people *like* me. Now, I'm not so concerned about that. You know, I think courage matters. I think there are times when you have to risk that people are *not* going to like you. And now, I really just want people to *believe* me. And it's up to them whether they like me or not. That's not something I can control. But I can control, to a certain extent, whether they'll believe me.

GB: You obviously went through the Twelve Steps, then?

FF: Well, let me put it this way, that the Twelve Step programmes have been enormously enriching in my life, yes. And they have given me a way to look at my background and where I come from, and where I hope I'm going.

GB: When you are going through a bad time — or, indeed, if you could imagine one of the grandchildren being desperately, desperately ill —

do you think you would revert to some kind of prayer at that time?

FF: Oh, yes. At one point, one of my grandchildren ran away from home — seems to be a very popular thing to do! And she was fifteen and missing for about four months.

GB: Oh!

FF: Yes. And, of course, immediately we thought she must be dead or trapped in some cellar by some terrible killer or some awful torturer — or, you know, horrible things happen. So, at that time I did a very basic sort of prayer, which was "Let it not be. Just let some kind of courage and goodness prevail and touch her and protect her" — the courage and the goodness of the world, which I do believe in. And that I did ask for. I did ask for her protection. And she showed up, unscathed.

GB: As a matter of interest, what excuse did she give for this sudden dash for freedom?

FF: I don't believe she ever gave an excuse. When she was found — when she was caught, actually — she and some other kids, a group of them, were on their way to Humboldt County, because the marijuana crop was about to come in. And they were going up there to help reap it — and smoke it, of course. So she didn't have an excuse. She wanted to live her own life. Of course, at fifteen, you know everything.

GB: Of course. Do you believe in good and evil?

FF: I believe in good and I believe in beauty, and I believe — yes, I do believe in evil. I think it's totally much more banal than we think, as Hannah Arendt said.

GB: Banal?

FF: Banal, yes. Totally banal, evil.

GB: What do you mean by that?

FF: Well, you know, people say, "Well, look at the Nazis and Hitler. They were evil." Well, yes, but they all went home to their families and played music and read stories to their children and made supper, and they led ordinary lives. They made their evil — they made everything they did — just part of their job. And that's how they got away with it. [Laughs.] That's how they propagated it.

GB: And do you believe there is a come-uppance for people who do these evil things?

FF: You mean an afterlife?

GB: I mean, in plain, simple terms, do the Hitlers of the world and the Stalins of the world and the Mugabes of the world get away with it?

FF: Unfortunately, I think they do. Look around you. You don't have to go to Hitler or Stalin. We've the reports that came out . . .

GB: Sure.

FF: . . . You know, the evil, the cruelty, perpetrated against children. It's in the papers every day. And I think people do get away with it.

GB: So, why be good?

FF: Oh! [Laughs.] Well, I think the impulse is to be good. The impulse is towards the light and towards helping people. Well, that's if you believe in civilisation at all. You see someone hurting, you want to help them, you want to give them a Band-Aid, or just speak to them.

I believe in beauty, and I believe in fostering beauty . . . and gifts — gifts that people have. So, how can you do that, if you're only interested in yourself, or in destruction?

GB: Go back to your father. Do you think you'll see him and your mother again?

FF: Well, I carry them around in my heart all the time, and I remember them when they were younger, when I was a child. And a memory of my father is of a day when the black swans were given as a present to the Dublin Zoo, and the snow was on the ground, and he met some photographer from the *Irish Press* who was going up to photograph them. And he said, "Oh, oh, let me go and get my little girl. She's in school here in Marlborough Street, and we'll bring her up too." And so, there was a photograph in the paper of a very frightened girl in pigtails holding out a piece of bread to a very savage-looking black swan who was approaching.

And what I know: the photograph I got then was one that didn't contain my father. In the paper he's standing to one side and he's looking very shabby. And he didn't have an overcoat, and the snow was on the ground, and it was wintertime, and he had his hat on, sort of "to the Kildare side", as he always said. But he didn't have an overcoat and had a shabby suit on. And yet he brought me up to see the black swan. And I think that kind of courage, in the face of misfortune and poverty, is wonderful.

GB: But I'm asking you, what do you think happens when you die?

.FF: Oh.

GB: Do you think you'll see him and your mother again?

FF: Oh, yes, you did, you asked me that . . . I don't know that I will. I don't know that I believe that. I don't know that I believe in that kind of afterlife.

GB: The soul, Fionnula. You have a soul. What do you think it is? And is it immortal?

FF: Well, it had better be, I tell you [laughter], because after all the ways we were told to save it, and all the time we spent trying to save it, and still do, it had bloody better be immortal. [Laughter.]

GB: All right. Do you think about death?

FF: I think about it more in terms of being either left alone or leaving my husband alone. In the partnership that we have now, that's long-term, I think about death in terms of what happens if I die first. And then I think about it: if he went first, what on earth would I do? And neither picture is very happy to contemplate. I haven't got further than that.

GB: You don't fear it?

FF: No, I fear being alone and I fear *him* being alone more than I fear *it*. But I don't know what *it* is. With my mother, it was a gentle sort of exhale, and she was gone. Her spirit was gone elsewhere. I don't fear it in that way, no.

GB: Last question. Suppose, when you get there, that what the nuns told you was all true, and he is waiting there for you. What will you say to God?

FF: Well, like any well-brought-up child of my time, I'd wait to be spoken to first before I'd speak to him or her, whichever it is. So, I'll wait and see what God has to say to me. And then I'll answer the questions as best I can, if there are any. Yes, I hope I'll be able to account for myself and I hope that I will be given either the benefit of the doubt or shown some compassion. If it's the God of '50s Catholic Ireland I don't want to meet him or her. I'll go with whatever there is. I'm not interested in that God, who is punishing, male-only and had extremely narrow views. So I'll go for any of the other household gods who are hanging around. I'll take my chances.

COLM TÓIBÍN

The Complete Heretic

Soon after I interviewed Colm Tóibín for *The Meaning of Life*, his play *The Testament of Mary* opened on Broadway. On paper, it was a formidable combination: one of Ireland's finest actors, Fiona Shaw, speaking the words and ideas of one of Ireland's most talented writers. It attracted rave reviews, but also angry Christian pickets, whose refusal to see the play did not prevent them expressing outraged opinions about it. Perhaps because of their boycott, the production failed to sell enough tickets to cover its relatively modest costs and its producers were forced to pull the plug.

This year, the same production has opened in the Barbican Centre in London. Again, rave reviews, but, so far, no pickets, although perhaps that is because the Barbican Centre is so hard to find.

What the conflicting reactions show is not only the theological and cultural gulf that exists between London, Ireland and America, but also the extremes of positive and negative reaction you can inspire if you mix secular imagination with sacred beliefs.

Tóibín used a similar, highly imaginative treatment of scriptural subjects and characters in his novella of the same name, which tackles the same themes through prose instead of drama. It was described by the *Irish Times* as "completely heretical", and it was clear from the reviewer's own gushy prose that this was a good thing. The implication was that heresy is not what Holy Mother Church has always told us it is: a belief in, or promotion of, religious untruth. No, heresy is a sign of intellectual and moral liberation from the shackles and delusions of traditional dogma. Discuss.

Actually, having read Colm's book and discussed it with him, I do not think that strident heresy is his aim. It is true that he is not afraid to voice thoughts and ideas that might shock and offend some — for instance that Jesus' disciples were a bunch of misogynist misfits, who spun Christianity out of the disaster of their founder's death, and that Jesus' mother ended her days bitter and disillusioned. However, in creating this alternative "testament", Colm is not simply treading on religious corns for the sake of it. He has a serious point to make.

Read the Gospels as he reads them, as works of carefully constructed propaganda by writers like himself, and you too will probably start to question whether the religion and faith to which those Gospels gave rise are houses built on sand. That is what Colm decided his own faith was, many years ago, while at UCD. Far from this making him put that faith in a skip and forget about it, however, he keeps returning to the subject. I wonder why.

An early book of his was called *The Sign of the Cross*. It was a series of travelogues in Catholic and post-Catholic Europe, but it was much more subtle than some of the anti-religious grenade-throwing that was going on at the time. Colm was genuinely interested in what religion could do *for* people, as well as *to* them. So, he had no problem expressing awe at the inspirational effect Pope John Paul II had on a group of pilgrims in Poland; but, equally, he had no problem pointing out the contradictions between the passionate Easter displays of piety in a Spanish city and the brutal record of its (until recently) Fascist populace.

Given that Colm went to school in Enniscorthy, at a junior seminary school now notorious for clerical abuse, you might expect him to be more cynical and angry about the Catholic Church. Instead, he remembers that one of the abusers, in particular, was a brilliant teacher.

I was intrigued to learn that Tóibín's gently eloquent speaking voice was something he had to construct himself through sheer power of will, during those school years, in order to master the stammer he acquired after the very early loss of his father to cancer. Back then, writing was the natural recourse of a boy with much to say, but with no confidence in his own ability to get through a sentence. Now, though, he has long since found his voice and I am all ears.

GB: Enniscorthy. Your childhood. Were you a happy lad?
CT: Oh, I don't think so, but there was nothing particularly to be unhappy about. There was a lot of regimentation: you were always being told what to do. And I've always found that very difficult. Once I learned to read, which was quite late, that gave me enormous freedom.

GB: You were an altar boy?
CT: I was an altar boy. Actually, quite liked it, because you were left alone as an altar boy. Your job was to ring the bell at a certain moment. You know, genuflecting, doing all the things across the altar.

GB: Tell me about your parents, Patrick and Bríd.
CT: Well, my mother wrote poetry. And some of the poetry she wrote, before she married, was published in the *Irish Press*. In other words, she

actually could do it. My father had won a university scholarship and he got a job as a teacher, a secondary teacher in the town. And they married in their twenties and had five children.

They were very, I suppose, ordinary, conservative people, living in a small town, very happily, I think. The problem was that, when I was eight, he became sick, and so that changed everything.

GB: How sick?
CT: He needed a brain operation. I think it was a six-hour operation, in an unfortunate ward — I never forgot the name of it. Honestly, the ward for brain surgery in Vincent's was called Mother Mary Aikenhead, which, of course, we thought was desperately funny.

GB: So, what effect did that have on you, then?
CT: I think it changed the house And it was never discussed. What happened was my mother had to make a decision. She just went up to Dublin and stayed with him all the time. The house simply didn't have either of them then. So, we moved to an aunt and went to stay with her. And they were very nice to us. It wasn't as though they did anything wrong, but, of course, we didn't know what had happened. And I don't think anyone ever explained to us.

GB: Do you remember getting the message that he was dead, finally?
CT: Well, I remember Aunt coming into the bedroom and waking up my older brother, and him going out and not coming back in; and lying there, realising that only means one thing now . . . And at what point are they going to come in looking for me?

GB: Before all that unfortunate thing happened, was it a religious household, apart from you being the altar boy and ringing the bell in the church and all of that? Was there family Rosary and Mass?
CT: Yes, again, this is sort of shrouded in a sort of comedy. My mother was in charge of the Rosary, which I think was quite common. So, the Rosary happened at a certain time and my father, for whatever reason I don't know, would start what we called in our house "a fit of laughing". He found the solemnity, the whole business of the family kneeling down, and all the children . . . whatever way it struck him, he would laugh. Maybe he only did it once, but, whatever it was, it was very memorable, and it was lovely. And my mother had to put a stop to that. So she would take a very dim view of it.

GB: Now, did you write about your sessions with [the psychiatrist] Ivor Browne, in later life, with [his wife] June Levine, that you had not grieved properly for your father's death?

CT: Yes, I became very friendly with June Levine, because she worked for *Magill*. Ivor, her husband, has no small talk, and it's a bit of a disaster if you're trying to have dinner, because Ivor can't do just general chat about things. And sometimes, if Ivor was sitting beside you, he would look at you. We used to call him "the Doctor" or "the Professor".

The Doctor, one evening, said to me, "Are your parents still alive?"

I said, "Oh, no, my father is dead. He died when I was twelve."

And he said, "Oh, right. And how did that affect you?"

I said, "Ah, it wasn't too bad, because, you see, I was going into secondary school, and he was teaching there, and I was so worried about it that when he died, it was really a great relief." And I said it like that.

And Ivor looked at me and said, "You know, I thought that about you from the very beginning. You haven't grieved. You've never dealt with that, have you?"

And I said, "No, Ivor, I'm all right."

Ivor keeps looking at me and says, "No, I'm saying it to you. Did you hear what I said? You're going to have to do something about that."

And, anyway, he kept at me, and he started getting June to keep at me. And eventually, June said, "Look, I need your help, because Ivor is running this sort of seminar session in the disused church in Grangegorman. Would you come?"

And it was really tough. You went in on a Friday morning and you left on a Sunday afternoon or Sunday evening, and you slept there. He used the system a lot for people who had, say, been abused, just simply so that you would have the experience again, so that you would get it out of you — it would not be in you, locked in you, any more. You simply went into another state of feeling or mind, which I didn't know you could do. And I went back straight into the morning that I heard that my father had died.

GB: Was this tough on you. Did you cry?

CT: Oh, yeah. Oh, no, no, it was very almost violent. It was hitting me, like something inside me was trying to get out of me.

GB: And did you feel better when you came out?

CT: It wasn't as though you woke up on Monday morning and said, "I'm a new guy, and I'm really ready for things, and I'm going to become

Head of the Bank of Ireland now or run for politics." [Laughter.] It was that you had a knowledge that you didn't have before of how hard this had been. You never tried that shrug again in your life. You never tried that "It was all right. I was just a kid. It's a long time ago." You realised, this was actually, probably, the worst thing that had happened, and it was really severe, and I should recognise that, rather than have it as something hidden, unconscious, damaging and poisonous.

GB: Who do you speak like, your mother or your father?

CT: Well, I have to go on about speech just a bit, because when that thing happened where we went, at age eight, to the aunt, when I came back I had a stammer or a stutter. So much so, that I couldn't even say my own name. My own name was the worst part, because it has two hard [consonants]. . . [stuttering C-c-c-c-c . . . T-t-t-t-t . . .] So, I had to learn almost a sort of softening of my own voice.

GB: And who taught you?

CT: I did it on my own. But it meant, of course, that writing was wonderful, because you could do it without any worry.

GB: So, you went to your daddy's school?

CT: No, I went to my father's school for three years, which actually was very hard, because I was in the very corridors . . . All his colleagues were teaching me. I was the boy being looked at by everyone. "He's the one. He's the son . . ." And, also, the fact that I was really no good. And, eventually, after three years, my auntie Kathleen, whom I was very close to, said that maybe I should go to a boarding school, St Peter's, because they got very good results.

GB: They figured rather largely in the Ferns Report, so you must have known some of the victims as well as the perpetrators. Or did you . . . ? Was there any semblance of that with you?

CT: I certainly knew the perpetrators, because there was a seminary attached. It was a diocesan school. And some of them, of course, were very nice as well. One of the priests who got into terrible trouble and served a jail sentence was also, I have to say, an extremely good teacher.

We were so shocked — I mean *so* shocked — about certainly one of the other priests. I remember a sermon he gave about a thing called "The Paradox of Faith", and it was a brilliant sermon. It hit a spot with me. And I was reading T. S. Eliot. I was being serious about this. And *he* got into trouble.

And, on the other hand, there were priests there who lived their priestly life to the full. In other words, they were a serious inspiration. There was one priest, Father Larkin, who was my English teacher, who helped me enormously in every way, gave me confidence. You know, he would just write things at the bottom of my essay . . .

GB: Were you coaxed at any stage, since it was a seminary, to join the priesthood? Did they ever say, "Colm, would you ever consider . . . ?"
CT: No, they never did that, but what they said was "We're doing a vocations workshop, and we're bringing in very good people, and anyone who is interested can stay on," just not go home. And a few of us did. And I did.

GB: You did.
CT: I did, yeah. And, again, it was terribly interesting. And I had been publishing poems by that time in a Capuchin magazine, and the Editor of that was a Capuchin priest called Father Donal O'Mahony, and he came to talk to us. And, of course, he was terribly interesting. He had read widely, and he had a glow, an inner light in him. And I noticed, one night — as everyone else was getting ready to do something, to go down to have tea — I just noticed him slipping away on his own. And I thought of where he was going back to, a bare room, and I thought he was going back to read and pray. And that interested me.

GB: But, in the final analysis, it wasn't for Colm. Was that the decision that was made?
CT: It wasn't even made. It just dropped away.

GB: We'll come back to all of that later on. First of all, university: History and English, and then off you went to Spain. What was this thing about Spain you had?
CT: My friend, Gerry Fanning, said to me that you could get a job just by turning up in Barcelona as an English teacher — that the whole city wanted to learn English, which actually was true. And it just sounded glamorous and exciting.

GB: I thought it all had to do with Hemingway and your ambition to be another one?
CT: Yeah, there was a big Hemingway thing. I got a job, one of the summers, working in the Grand Hotel in Tramore as a barman. And I remember going down to the beach in Tramore on my own with a

book called *The Essential Hemingway* and reading it and thinking, "If only I could get this glamour, this Spain, going off and being with people who are friends . . ." And I loved the sentences, the glamour, the crispness of the style. Yeah, so when Barcelona was mentioned, all that came to me. I could be moving into a novel. I could be having the time of my life somewhere wonderful.

GB: But during your time in Spain, you went to France and Poland and Lourdes . . . Am I right in saying you went on pilgrimages?
CT: No — did that later, for a book.

GB: Yes . . . *Sign of the Cross.*
CT: But, you see, how it started was there were a few ways you could get home cheaply. One was to get a train over to Lourdes and go back on the JWT pilgrimage.

GB: Yes.
CT: And one of those nights, I must have turned up a day early, and I went down into the grotto, maybe that night when I arrived. And, of course, it was very, very powerful in a way that I hadn't expected.

GB: Were you a believer at this stage?
CT: No. Oh, no.

GB: So, you got into the waters.
CT: But it was the ritual that interested me. And that hit me emotionally. And I must have got into the waters next day. If they'd only known!

GB: But were you searching, Colm?
CT: No. I was curious about the ritual. I wasn't searching for a belief. But, look, it was almost as though someone said, "There's a bullfight on" or "There's a big demonstration on." No matter what was on, I would go to it. I'm still like that. So, if there's a procession on and you're in Lourdes, for God's sake don't be sitting around your hotel reading more Hemingway. You've read enough. Go and look at it, for God's sake.

GB: At what stage did you discover you were gay? Was that a slowly dawning thing . . . ?
CT: Yeah, in one way it was slowly dawning, and in another way I think people are really skilled — certainly I am — at separating two things: knowledge from some other thing. So, while you could know some-thing — really *know* it — on the other hand you could pretend you

didn't know it, and you could function as though you weren't. And I think this is a very common thing for people who are gay, that they spend some years of their lives denying it, hoping it will go away, or maybe just not understanding the full consequences of it . . . Certainly not seeing it as a gift . . . and doing everything possible to hide it from people you didn't think should know.

GB: Did your gayness have an effect on your attitude to the Church, or had your faith gone completely by then?

CT: I think it had gone by then. The Churches simply didn't speak to me about anything much. I mean, the issues for me would have been more serious, in a way. They would have been to do with the afterlife, eternal life and faith, and I had simply stopped believing that. So, the Church's teaching on homosexuality just seemed like another thing the Church did. I mean, the Church at the time was against — I think it still is against — contraception. I mean, all of the Church's teaching seemed really not worth much of our respect at that time.

GB: So, who did you tell about your gayness? Did your mother know?

CT: I think people suspected without knowing, and it was never discussed. But going around flaunting the fact wasn't my style.

GB: Now, getting to your book *The Testimony of Mary*, in which you depict Mary as an old woman, rather disgruntled, rather unhappy, and she is confronted by these people — i.e. the remainder of the disciples — who want to get her to say certain things about her son and the life he led, which she knows are untrue, and they're trying to concoct a good story. And, obviously, this would be offensive to a great number of people — horrifying to a great number of people. What are you trying to achieve in that?

CT: I suppose, the first thing I was thinking about was the idea of trauma, the idea of unresolved experience. I mean, the issue of people's faith didn't bother me. I didn't think about that. I thought only about her. I mean, twenty years after the Crucifixion, had she lived and had she been through that experience, what it would have been like for her to think about it. And to think about the idea of it being her son. For everybody else, it was their Saviour, but for her it was the baby, it was the boy. And all you had to do was to think about the extraordinary, dramatic cruelty of crucifixion. Now, if she was there and if she lived on, would she have always said, "Of course, it was really wonderful, because we needed to sacrifice someone, and wasn't it marvellous . . . ? I'm proud it was my son." Would she ever have said that? Would she ever have thought it?

GB: And what put it in your mind that she thought that her son was always a misfit and off the wall and that he surrounded himself with this gang of weirdos and misfits?
CT: Well, sometimes the words come first, so I didn't use "weirdo", because obviously I'm trying to find a sort of language she will use. I did use "misfit".

GB: Misfit.
CT: I used stammers, because here I was going back inwards. I was looking at my own sort of not-having-my-feet-on-the-ground business: how worried a mother becomes watching a son who seems hopeless or seems filled with a sort of courage that the mother knows he doesn't really have.

GB: And so, do you think the fellas who knock at her door to come and get her to say things about her son and the lifestyle he led — do you think they're just like you: they're fellas trying to concoct a good story and keep people's interest?
CT: Yes. Matthew, Mark, Luke and John really, nowadays, would be sitting in my seat. They were writers. The interesting part is that John was much better than the other three. He really was. I mean, if you read them, you think John would win the Booker Prize. The other three would not. And it's John who puts Mary at the foot of the Cross. And John, of course, had lived in Greece. John had probably seen Greek theatre. So you can imagine John is in the audience watching these wonderful actresses come out, grief-stricken figures holding an entire 2,000-seater, like the O2 or Bord Gáis, like, *holding* them, and realising: I *need* a woman; I need a grieving woman. Can someone get me one?

And, of course, what they did was they put shape on the story. And for Mary herself, the story has no shape: it's chaotic, it's awful. She can barely think about it. But they're already working out ways of not only telling it, but spreading the news of it.

GB: You know that Salman Rushdie got himself a *fatwa* for doing far less than you're doing in this book?
CT: Yes, Salman is a friend of mine.

GB: Does that trouble you?

CT: No, no it doesn't. I really wanted people to believe that I was serious, that I wasn't involved in a mockery of their most basic religion.

GB: It's interesting that, although she's very cynical and sceptical about the miracles, including Lazarus, she doesn't say they never happened.

CT: No.

GB: Do you, Colm Tóibín, believe the miracles happened?

CT: No.

GB: Do you believe he was God, the Son of . . . ?

CT: No.

GB: Well, do you believe in God?

CT: No. The idea that God intervened in history two thousand years ago, once, and sent his son down . . . I'm afraid I can't see that as being true. But I can see it as being immensely significant in our history, in the way we live, in the way we've been brought up, in our literature, in our music. I mean, you can't listen to Bach, for example — and I love Bach — without realising this mattered enormously, once.

GB: Well, then, when you look back at your parents, for example, and all the people worldwide who do believe and who sacrifice themselves in the service of others for this faith, do you think your mother and father were simple sort of people, who were a bit wanting, in this belief . . . ?

CT: I think it's terribly important to have absolute respect for other people's beliefs, especially their religious beliefs, because you're talking about something so private, a space that's so empty in all of us, that some people fill in this way. If you said, "I think the way you fill your space is in some way wrong, simple-minded, foolish," I think that would be a great arrogance, a very great arrogance, to go around saying, "I'm sure I'm right, and not only that, but I'm sure you're a fool." Because you often go into this beautiful space within yourself or this beautiful architectural space and utter these prayers and enter into a sort of spiritual state that not only satisfies you, but may be something we all need inside, in some guise or other, and for you it's this.

GB: And are you sad that you haven't got it?

CT: I think it's a melancholic business, when you have been brought up with it, with the certainty of it. But I also have learned to deal with it. So, yes, if you're asking me, "Is there a sadness attached to living in the world, knowing that when you end, it will end?" I think that is very frightening, actually. That "Thou art dust and to dust thou shalt return" hits me hard, when I hear it.

GB: So when you die, the switch goes off: end, finish, darkness, nothing.

CT: Yes. Isn't it appalling?

GB: Were you ever attracted to any other faith, like Buddhism or Islam or Hinduism?

CT: No, although recently I had a puncture on the N11 — and I don't know if you can imagine me with a puncture, but I can't mend a puncture — and a man came up like an angel behind me — did the whole thing for me. And I said, "Is there anything I can do for you?" He said, "No, I'm a Muslim" — he was an Irish guy, he was from Wicklow — he said, "No, I'm a Muslim and we always stop for anybody who's in trouble."

GB: Get away!

CT: And I looked at him and he looked at me, and I got from him that absolute religious sense of something, a glow from him, that I'm talking about having got in childhood. And I do think that there is something we can get from certain people who have that, which is very powerful and not to be in any way dismissed.

GB: Just go back to the book again and Mary and these fellas. If indeed they were just a bunch of chancers and misfits and long-haired, off-the-wall people, the argument must have occurred to you that, within a month at the most after his death, they would have disappeared and they would have gone and been forgotten about, instead of the fact that their story has endured for two thousand years.

CT: Yes, I thought about that. I suppose, what I'm thinking about is the idea that it was a very strange time. It was a time when the Romans were moving in everywhere. So there was a vacuum going on within Jewishness, and this religion came and had something very beautiful about it. There are a number of things that are very important, for example, the Sermon on the Mount. Also the whole idea of "Do unto others as you would have done unto you," of helping the poor — all of those matters. But it still is a mystery to me. So, therefore, I have to be open to the idea that there's something I don't know. You know, I'm a great know-all, and I don't know this: how this spread in this way. This single figure from a village, crucified in this way, as many others were crucified . . . that it's slowly becoming faith and spreading.

GB: Well, what does Colm Tóibín believe? What do you think he was?

CT: Oh, I think that he was somebody with enormous spiritual grace. Around him, people felt this extraordinary glow from him, this extraordinary ease in themselves.

GB: A sort of JFK charisma?

CT: Yes, that's something we have seen in politics. But I've seen it, more interestingly, with religious people: an extraordinary sense of selfless-ness, of giving up on the self in order for the self to have something else, which is a glow, which is a way of inspiring others. I saw John Paul II in Poland with his hands over his face for about half an hour, with an audience of a million people, at night in Częstochowa, and it was the most powerful thing I saw in all those travels.

GB: Why did he have his hands over his face?

CT: He just wanted to give these kids some idea of what the religious life might be like. He didn't mention sex. He didn't mention anything to do with rules. He just gave them the inspiration of his silence and his prayer. And it was astonishing to see.

GB: Standard last question. Suppose all that you were taught in school by the Christian Brothers, and your parents believed in — suppose, now, all that's true. You arrive at the Pearly Gates, and you are met by God. What will you say to him?

CT: Oh, I'd ask had he passed the book on to Mary, *The Testament of Mary*, and had she read it, and what did she think of it? Because I'd love to know.

MARY BYRNE

The Why? Factor

"I shouldn't be here. I've got pneumonia."

As entrances go, it was certainly dramatic, but Mary Byrne meant it. She had been nursing a serious chest infection all week, but, mindful that RTÉ would cop it for cancellation charges for the crew if she pulled out on the day of recording, she got up off her sickbed and honoured her commitment. I am very pleased she did.

You can take the girl out of Ballyfermot, but you can't take Ballyfermot out of the girl. Actually, you can't *even* take the girl out of Ballyfermot: she refuses to leave. Even after her record deal earned her enough to buy a better house, she was adamant that she couldn't buy better neighbours. And why would she want to move away from Tesco, once they'd promised to keep her old job open for her? "I'd take it, too, Gay. No problem."

Recently, that has seemed more likely, with Mary admitting that the ticket and record sales which flared up after her *X Factor* adventure have now fizzled. The people who wanted to dream her dream with her have now turned their reveries elsewhere. That is the nature and the curse of the talent show. *X Factories*, like any abattoir, need new blood, and all too soon the person with the X factor becomes the person with the *ex*-factor.

Was she silly to fall for it? I don't think so. She didn't stand on stage and sing because she wanted immortality: she did it because she knew she could. And not everyone can, certainly not like Mary. Moreover, she showed everyone else she could, too. That is the giant leap from potential to fulfilment that so few people manage. It's the difference between a hairbrush diva and a star.

Of course, the other thing Mary quickly realised was that people were not just voting for the woman from Ballyfermot: they were voting for themselves. In her triumph and fulfilment, they saw their own, which is why they will carry on shouting out to her in the street, even if she never sings another note.

So much for fame, but our interview is not about that. It's about life, and Mary's life has been largely shaped by women.

She idolised her dad, but it was her easily led mammy who ensured that she grew up knowing the knock of the bailiffs and the chink of the pawnbroker's shilling. It was she, too, who allowed Mary to mitch off school, from the age of twelve, because she hadn't the heart to make her go. She'd done all right herself without an education, hadn't she?

Then there were the very sensible religious women who, twice in her life, listened respectfully to Mary's attempts to articulate her sense of vocation and then steered her kindly into what they could see would be a more fulfilling life for her.

Finally, there is her daughter, Deborah, a young woman who is both her rock and her *raison d'être*, sustaining her through the lows of abandonment and single motherhood and the highs of *X Factor* fame.

Mary is a survivor, and it is clear that her faith has, from time to time, been a lifebelt. But it is more than that. It is the heart of a relationship with a God in whom, to paraphrase Einstein, she doesn't just believe: she knows. She loves God, as the Good Book tells her she should, like her neighbour and herself, quite certain that the feeling is mutual.

∾

GB: I want to start with your book. "We are the kind of family where people make mistakes, take wrong turns and end up in places they never expected. It makes for some great stories and for sad endings."
MB: Uh-huh.

GB: Sounds a bit bleak, Mary.
MB: It's not, really. We're just like most families out there who've had their ups and downs, had their happiness and had sad times as well. My life hasn't been bad. I used to love, Monday morning, getting on the 79 bus and heading to the pawn [broker] in Queen Street. I used to love coming home when the electricity was gone, sitting on my daddy's knee, having my dinner by firelight and him telling us stories. So if that's bleak, well, then I want bleak, because that was a happy time for me.

GB: Tell me about your mother and father — your mother, first of all. I know that she couldn't read or write, and she left school very young and married young.
MB: She was a very strong woman. And I don't think she realised how strong she was. She was very foolish with money. That was her downfall. She was very generous: she would give you her last penny. And she had the ability to overspend, or over-help, and leave herself with nothing and leave the family with nothing.

GB: Tell me about your dad.

MB: Dad was a very hard-working man.

GB: You said he was a saint.

MB: Oh, an absolute saint on this Earth. He put up with so much. He put up with my mother getting herself into more debt. And he worked every hour God sent him. And every penny he got he would give to my mother — biggest mistake of the man's life, because Daddy earned some money, but Mammy just squandered it.

GB: Did they love each other?

MB: Ahhhh!

GB: Did they, really?

MB: You know, Mammy — she couldn't understand why he stayed with her, why he still loved her. She didn't feel a lot of worth about herself, either. So that's where I get that low self-esteem from.

GB: So, you never knew anything else but love from them both?

MB: No, never did. She'd go to Mass every Sunday and some Sundays she'd take me with her. And if I didn't want to go, she wouldn't force me. And I appreciate that so much, because she left me with my own thoughts and my own way of living.

GB: So, you do remember going to Mass on occasions?

MB: Oh, yeah, most Sundays I would go.

GB: And would your parents go together?

MB: Dad wasn't a church-goer. He had his faith, but he wasn't a church-goer.

GB: You must have encountered Father Mick Cleary and Tony Walsh in Ballyer?

MB: Father Mick Cleary I met, and I adored him and I applaud him. Father Tony Walsh I fell in love with, like everybody else in the parish.

GB: Why?

MB: Because he was . . . Well, now we know, he was a player. He used to get up and sing. He used to do Elvis. We thought he was brilliant.

GB: What is extraordinary is that in a place like Ballyfermot, which would be a fairly close-knit community, that the two boys — Father Mick Cleary, his rather unorthodox domestic arrangement, to say the

least, and Father Tony Walsh, doing something much more serious —
did you never get any inkling or rumours or stories?

MB: Yeah, about Father Cleary we did.

GB: Did you?

MB: A lot of women used to talk, and you'd hear them saying, "Ah, we
know that's his son, and that's his girlfriend." Ah, yeah, people knew. But
people respected him. I mean, he was with a woman. And he should
have been *allowed* be with a woman. He shouldn't have had to hide that.
That's a natural, beautiful love. He should not have had to hide that.

GB: But the hypocrisy of doing that and then preaching something else . . .

MB: Yes, that was wrong.

GB: And Father Walsh?

MB: I have no opinion on that man any more: I just have disgust. He
was so trusted in that community. Children trusted him, their parents
trusted them, I trusted him. But he's a monster. There's no other word
for the man: an absolute monster.

GB: Your mother had a fairly relaxed attitude to your attendance at
school . . .

MB: Yes, definitely. My first couple of years were wonderful, because we
went from Low Babies to High Babies to First Class with Miss Doherty,
who was an absolute angel. After that, I lost interest in school and I
wanted to stay at home. Mammy wouldn't let me until I was at least
twelve.

GB: [Laughs.]

MB: She just didn't have a hard bone in her body, to push me into school.

GB: Just as you're talking about her now, it strikes me, you never saw
her reading a book, clearly. Did she read the newspaper? Did she read a
magazine?

MB: No.

GB: No?

MB: She used to colour. I'm getting very upset now . . . She used to sit
with us, and she'd buy colouring books. And, Gay, I swear to God, she'd
colour. And we'd have a page each, and we'd put our initials on the top,
and whoever coloured the best she'd, like, give a little prize. And, I
think, God love her, she didn't realise how much of a lesson she was

teaching us through her own downfalls. I mean, I don't get into debt. I hate bills. I would pay them the minute they come in the door. She didn't. I will sit and read a book as often as I possibly can, to keep my reading going.

GB: She couldn't.

MB: She couldn't. She was a great singer. She didn't have the ability to get out there, or the confidence to get out there, and it took me years to do it, but I eventually said, "No, I'm not going to waste what she wasted." So, I've done everything that she should have done, and I've done it for me and her.

GB: Now, Mary wants to be a nun. Where did that come from?

MB: Oh, God, I don't know. I had a stand-in nun. Our teacher was out sick. And she was a little novice, and she used to come in and she'd sit with us, and she was reading the book *Heidi* to us. And I just fell head-over-heels. And that's when the first notion of being a nun came into my head.

GB: So, you went to speak to them.

MB: I went to Father Tony Wall — I think I was about fourteen — and he said, "I would like to send you down to the Sisters in the Seven Oaks" — which is down in Ballyfermot — "and see what they have to say. Just talk to them."

I can't remember the name of the nun I was speaking to down there, but she was very nice, and she gave me loads of advice and said, "You're only fourteen. You haven't seen anything. You haven't experienced life." So, off I went and experienced life.

GB: Take me, then, to the fella that you got engaged to . . .

MB: Brian.

GB: . . . And a short time before the marriage, you called the whole thing off.

MB: Yeah, Brian. I met Brian when I worked in CB Packaging. I think I was sixteen. I was only there about three months when Brian took a shine to me. Brian was seven years older than me, and I remember him saying, "Ah, the best-looking girl I've seen in a long time." And, of course, I was chuffed, you know?

We won a Datsun 120, four-door, at a raffle in Tallaght village, in the Priory. But we couldn't drive it, and we didn't want to drive it. So, we sold the Datsun — we got two thousand and something for it — and we bought a house in Springfield.

Before we moved into the house, Brian proposed to me. And, of course, I didn't hesitate. I said I'd love to, and we got engaged. We were together for a year. We planned the wedding, we done everything.

But, just coming up near it, I knew it wasn't right. I just knew . . . I loved Brian, and I still do care a lot for Brian. Brian was another chapter in my life that I'm very grateful for. He taught me an awful lot about who I am and how to be the woman that I became. And I will always be grateful to him for that. But I just didn't love him that way any more. And I don't think he loved me that way either. And he was right. I outgrew him.

GB: Okay. So then, there was a lesbian relationship. Was she a local girl?
MB: She was.

GB: Lorna.
MB: Yes, she was a good friend of mine. We worked together. And she became my best friend and I could tell her anything. And she was there at the time of me leaving Brian and we travelled away. I didn't know she was gay at first, and I *definitely* wasn't gay, but I fell in love with her as a friend before anything else. She was attractive, she was my friend, she was kind and she was there. And things just happened. I'd never had that experience before, and neither had she. But all I know is, at the time when it happened, I needed it. She needed it. It was a wonderful experience. And I don't regret it today.

GB: Did you think you were committing sin?
MB: Oh, yeah, definitely. I mean, I was brought up in that religion — that, you know, two of the same sex is wrong: you shouldn't do this. No more should you have intercourse with a man outside marriage. Because it was embedded into me, my subconscious used to be all over the place, because I was committing sin. I still had this faith, but I still wanted to do this. I wanted to experience this. And I didn't see any wrong in it.

My belief, I suppose, is that we have a God who gives us all this love. I know man and woman were made for each other. It's obvious. But I also believe that everybody deserves love, and it doesn't matter whether it's the same sex or the opposite sex. You cannot help who you fall in love with. And we shouldn't be condemned because we're drawn to the same sex. We all deserve happiness and if I had stayed — just say, I had said, "Right, I am gay, and I'm going to stay with Lorna" — I think that God would have said, "Well, that's your happiness."

GB: So, you went off to Majorca together.
MB: We did.

GB: And then off to Israel and the kibbutz. How did you end up knowing about Israel and the kibbutz?
MB: It was just after my Uncle Willie died. Lorna had been speaking about Israel prior to this. She had seen this thing called Project 67, which was in England, and it was a chance to go and work in a kibbutz in Israel, and she would love to do it. And I kept saying, "No, I'm not sure." But it just took me Uncle Willie to pass to give me the push: "Yeah, I want to get out of here."

GB: And what did you do in the kibbutz?
MB: I would work in the factory doing the drilling — like, we'd make nuts for machinery — or I would be out picking grapefruits, or they would have me in the kitchen helping the staff, which were all Israelis, in the kitchen. I got on well with them all.

GB: And Lorna was still going on at that stage?
MB: It was still going on . . . kind of . . . It was ending at this stage.

GB: Ending? Why?
MB: Well, I had met a gorgeous man.

GB: Ah! That tends to concentrate the mind a little bit . . .
MB: Yes.

GB: Okay. While you were in Israel, you visited all the holy places: Bethlehem and Jerusalem. Did that do anything for your spiritual life or your religion?
MB: Mmmm. I remember going down into where they said Christ was born. And everybody was singing *Silent Night* in different languages. It was one of the most moving experiences I'd had in a long time. Everybody was crying. There wasn't a dry eye underneath that cave where this little area had been set out. I just got the same feeling I always got: I just know Christ is there and that he's always been with me. I just kept turning away all the time and going on different paths. So, down in that little room, all I felt was the beautiful warmth that I felt every time I was in a situation like that, when it came to Christ or religion.

GB: Did anything else affect you spiritually while you were there in the area?

MB: Up on the Mount of Olives . . . Again, the nun thing came in then. They were all around me, there was loads around me — we were doing a tour — and I just had this feeling. Everybody was pushed aside and I was standing there on this particular place where they said Christ had walked with his Apostles. And I was looking out over Jerusalem and I just felt, I belong somewhere in this religion, in this moment, with Christ. So, to me, it was the nun thing again. It started hitting me again then.

GB: Okay. You're back in Dublin, and now you go back to the convent again to try . . .

MB: Yes, I do.

GB: And by now you're singing . . .

MB: By now, I'm back into the pubs and I'm doing a bit of singing.

GB: So, you're going to be a *singing* nun! I have this mental image of you, suddenly, being a white Whoopi Goldberg in your wimple and your veil and your Rosary . . .

MB: [Laughs.] That's probably the only nun now that I will play, if I ever get the chance. [Laughs.] So, I go back to Clondalkin . . .

GB: . . . and you've seen life, and you've experience. So what does the nun say to you this time?

MB: I go to Sister Nuala, and I'm sitting there, and I think she knew there was confusion, because I think at this stage she would have taken me in, if she knew that I knew exactly what I wanted. But being the very clever lady that she is, she started asking me questions: how did I feel I had the calling?

So, I told her about the experience of sitting in the church three weeks prior to this. It was in Ballyfermot, it was in the Assumption church. There was about three or four other people in the church. It was in the middle of the day. And I said, "Christ, I don't know what to do." I said, "I'm literally lost. Do you want me to be a nun? If you want me to be a nun, let me know. Or if you want me to do something else, let me know." I started to cry and I said, "I'm very confused, God. I've had so much in my life: I've had a lesbian relationship, I've had a relationship with a lovely man that I lived with for four years, I've had a lovely relationship with Dave from Israel. I'm sitting here now, and I'm lost."

And I put my head down — swear this on any Bible you want me to swear on: I felt somebody come in beside me. There was no one there. I felt a very unusual warmth that didn't just go around my arm but went right through my body. And I felt I could hear someone saying, "Everything's going to be fine." And that lasted — to me it felt like about ten minutes. I never looked up. I just sat with that beautiful feeling and my eyes closed. And when I opened my eyes, the tears were rolling down my face. I didn't even know I was crying. The other three people that had been there had left the church and there was nobody there. But I felt that feeling all the way home. And I decided, I'm going to have to do something about this.

And she said, "Well, it sounds like you may have got the calling, but you still sound confused to me." Now, she did say out straight to me, "I'd like you to just take a while to think about it, a couple of months, and if you still feel the same, come back to me and we'll start to talk about it."

GB: Smart, bright woman.

MB: I've met so many. They didn't just grab at people: they wanted people to be sure they were coming in to do this for the right reasons.

GB: So, you withdrew from the convent, you're going away to think about it, and then, of course . . .

MB: That fateful night in Ballyfermot, in the Lawns . . .

GB: Robbie.

MB: . . . when I seen this fine piece of stuff standing against the bar.

GB: Bingo. And that's how Mary became pregnant.

MB: Exactly. He'd long hair and he had a beautiful face and the most divine eyes I've ever seen in my life. And I just fell madly in love with him. I actually said to him, "You're walking me home tonight," and he goes, "Okay." So that's how it started, the love of my life.

GB: But then, when the pregnancy happened and the baby happened, Robbie . . .

MB: He walked, yeah. He had told me before I became pregnant that he was seeing somebody. I mean, we were having a bit of . . .

GB: Ambivalence, it's called.

MB: Yeah. And I got pregnant in the meantime. And then, when I went to tell him about it, he wasn't interested. Obviously, he had decided he wanted to be with the other lady.

GB: In your book, however, you never, ever suggest that Deborah was a mistake . . .

MB: No, no.

GB: . . . that you regret it. Anything but.

MB: No. On the night that we made love — and I specifically say, "We made love", because, to me, it was love — when she was conceived, she was conceived in my heart, with all the love that God had given me to give to anybody. So, she was no mistake. And, if you see her today, she is a lovely kid. She is intelligent, she is bright . . .

GB: You speak so lovingly of the relationship, it is astonishing. But having said that, did you rail against God, did you rail against Robbie, did you rail against circumstances, did you rail against life?

MB: No. I remember going to Confession. I said, "Bless me, Father, for I have sinned . . ." I said, "I have a child outside marriage and I feel so guilty that I haven't given her a great start in life."

And the priest said, "That's not a sin, in my eyes. And I definitely don't think it's a sin in God's eyes." And I think he was going against the Church by saying this, but he didn't care. He looked at me and he said, "I don't think you should be worrying about this, chicken. The love you have for that child is all God asks you to do for now."

And I walked out of that church again renewed in my faith — in Christ and in that priest — and went home and took my little baby and hugged her to death and said, "I'll do the best I can for you, sweetheart."

GB: Did you eventually forgive Robbie?

MB: I don't forgive him for what he did on Deborah.

GB: No.

MB: I mean, me, it's fine. He didn't have to stay with me. We were adults. We knew what we were doing. But he should have had time in his daughter's life. She's his eldest daughter. But he's missed out on one hell of a girl. That's all I can say.

GB: Okay, let's move on to more cheerful things. Now, you say in your book that at that time when you were entering *The X Factor* you thought of Cliff Richard and what he said about the presence of Christ in his life, that you hand over completely and say, "This is it. This is what I want to do." Did you do that?

MB: Yeah. I did it about three years before I went for *The X Factor*. I was in Tesco and sitting on the till. You know, I was saying, "There has to be more to life than this . . . Every path I've taken has taken me on the wrong thing. I don't feel I've done what you wanted me to do." And I know everybody has something that God wants them to do in their life . . .

That's when the Cliff Richard thing came into my head. He said, "I just opened up my heart and I opened up my spirit to Christ, and I allowed him to take me on whatever path he took me on." And so I said, I'm doing exactly that: I opened myself up. For some strange reason, everything started to come in. It was like there was doors being opened in every direction. I had no intentions of going for *The X Factor*, even though everybody was persuading me. I said, "If it comes to Dublin, then I'll know it's meant," because Simon Cowell had said it'd never go back to Ireland. And what does he do a year and a half later . . . ?

GB: Dublin.

MB: They announced it's coming to Dublin. So, straight away . . .

GB: This is a pointer.

MB: . . . Christ has given me this, in my opinion. This is him saying, "Okay, you said you'd go, if it came here. I have it here now. The rest is up to you."

GB: You didn't win, but everybody thought you *should* have won, and you had all of that adulation, and you're sitting there enjoying all of this. And suddenly the self-esteem goes "Voooommmm . . ." [Upward hand gesture.]

MB: It hasn't gone "Voooommmm"!

GB: It hasn't . . . ?

MB: No. I still have low self-esteem. I still look in the mirror sometimes and don't like the person I see.

The most beautifulest thing that any one human being can get out of life is an ordinary person who you don't know walks up to you and says, "You've changed my life, and you're an inspiration." And that's been said to me by hundreds of people.

GB: Were you sucked in by the fame thing? It's a very seductive thing.

MB: I don't think I'm famous.

GB: So why do you think you had that effect on so many people?

MB: I think, just because the age I was, for starters. A lot of people out there, across the water and here, kind of were living a little bit of their dreams through me, being the woman that I was, the age I was, on the stage, and they were saying, "Well, if Mary Byrne from a checkout in Ballyfermot, at fifty years of age, can get up on this big stage that was so international, and get to fifth place . . ."

. . . That's what it's about. I think people looked at me and said, "She just keeps experiencing, and she's still learning. And we all can do that. We all should just get off our bums and get out there and keep learning." So I think people just love me and remember me for that.

GB: Was the Queen a memorable night for you [the gala concert during Queen Elizabeth's visit in 2011]? . . . And she was delighted to meet you too, let me tell you. Not many people know this, but she actually said, "You're the reason I came over here . . ."

MB: [Laughs.] I can well believe it, Gay.

GB: So, what effect did she have on you?

MB: The first thing she said to me was "Your life must have changed now, has it?"

And I kind of looked at her, and I said, "It has a little bit, ma'am, yeah." And then I said to her, "Do you watch *The X Factor*?"

"No, not on a Saturday night. It's too late. But I would get to see it on a Sunday." And she actually said to me, "I loved your voice," and said to me, "I wish you all the luck in the world. And I hope the singing keeps up for you until you're ready to stop." And she walked away.

GB: Well done.

MB: Smiled back at me and gave me a wink.

GB: So, you have now mixed with kings and queens and yet kept the common touch. You're still staying in Ballyfermot?

MB: Yes.

GB: You say that very definitely to me, "Yes." Why?

MB: Because, first of all, I love the house I'm in. I love the neighbours I have. People look out for me in Ballyfermot. And they're very proud of me, bringing Ballyfermot to the headlines. So, apart from that, it's where I was born and reared. I love the area. Why would I want to go anywhere where I don't know anybody and sit in a house and look out the window and say, "Well, I don't know him and I don't know him"? And I have no intentions of leaving.

GB: And if this all ended tomorrow, you will still be Mary Byrne, and you'd still be in Ballyfermot, and you'll still sing for people . . . ?

MB: I would like to keep singing for people. If that didn't work out, then I would definitely go back to Tesco's for my job.

GB: And no problem?

MB: No. And I swear that on a stack of Bibles for you, Gay: I would go back to Tesco's, no problem.

GB: So, what about the little would-be nun then? How much of that is left? Are you a Catholic?

MB: Yes.

GB: Do you go to Mass regularly?

MB: The odd time I will go to Mass.

GB: Why only the odd time?

MB: Well, first of all, there's a lot of *busyness* going on with my work. But, even when it's not busy, at times I would prefer to sit and watch Mass on the television — just get my little bit of prayer from there. Or what I do like to do is I have a beautiful statue of Christ and Our Lady, and I have a little kind of thing made in my press, and I would sit and light a candle there and just say a few prayers for all who have passed. And I would do that every Sunday.

GB: And what do you pray for?

MB: I pray for my family, I pray for the homeless, I pray for the sick, I pray for my daughter and myself, I pray for our homes. I pray for all those I know who need God to touch them.

GB: And when you were on *The X Factor*, did you pray for success there?

MB: Every single day, though I never prayed for success . . . I would say, "Jesus, if this is what you want me to do, then please walk on to the stage with me." And I used to ask my mam and dad to walk on to the stage with me as well. But I do believe that, when I prayed, Christ was with me. And that's how I got through, because this is what he wanted me to do.

GB: What do you think Jesus was, or who do you think he was?

MB: I think he was a wonderful prophet. I believe he was the Son of God. I believe he suffered for us. I believe he was kind. And I believe the God he thought he spoke about was a kind and forgiving God — not what we were taught many years ago, *fire and brimstone*. I believe he was a wonderful man who I'm very much in love with. I don't think I'll ever love any man the way I love this spiritual man that's in my life. I think he is a way of hope, peace and, most of all, what we all need, love and kindness. That's what I believe Christ is.

GB: And, obviously, from what you've said, you believe that your mum and dad are in a nice place?
MB: I believe they're in Heaven.

GB: And they're together?
MB: They're together.

GB: And they're looking after you.
MB: They're there 24/7 with me and with everybody else that needs them — the family, always. And I know I'll see them again. And I'm looking forward to it.

GB: One last question. Suppose, Mary, it's all true — and you believe that it *is* all true — what the nuns taught you, what you learned in school . . . and you finally arrive at the Gates, and God is waiting there, in whatever form he or she takes. What will you say to him or her?
MB: Well, I think I'd say, first of all, "Thanks for an adventurous life," because it was. My life has been very colourful. And I would say, "If I'm coming in, thanks for forgiving me for the few sins that I did commit . . . And where's the party . . . ?" That's what I'd say.

GB: You're great, Mary Byrne. Thank you very much indeed.

COLM WILKINSON

Bring Him Home

"Where the heart is." A simple phrase, but a complicated notion. These days, Colm "C. T." Wilkinson's heart is presumably where his wife and family are, and where they have been for a number of years, in Toronto.

Ah, but is it home?

A few days before I interviewed Colm, during a riotously successful Irish tour, I watched him getting quite overcome on RTÉ's *Nationwide* programme, when Anne Cassin took him back to his early childhood home in Dublin. That modest house in Mangerton Road, Drimnagh, where the ten Wilkinson children were raised until the success of their dad's asphalting company made them upwardly mobile, is clearly the Eden from which Colm feels he was forever banished as a child.

Except Colm doesn't believe in Original Sin. And who can blame him? Very few sins are original these days. And this was a sin of the father.

Like his dad, Colm is a self-made man. Perhaps *too* like his dad. They didn't see eye to eye and Colm still craves the approval and encourage-ment of the dour Belfast man who was seldom, even in life, capable of giving it. Imagine the old fella's disappointment: he gave young Colm the opportunity to pave, or tarmac, his way to riches. And what did the lad do? Joined a rock band and then pursued a ne'er-do-well career as an itinerant singer. What a catastrophe.

Of course, that's not quite how Colm sees it. Perched on top of his Toronto hill and a small mountain of gold discs and musical awards, he quite rightly regards his voice as his treasure – certainly his livelihood – and he guards it jealously. He often wears gloves in public, not out of Michael Jackson-esque affectation, but in case one of the many fans who want to shake his hand might pass on germs that would keep him off stage. A quick "selfie" for you might mean weeks of unemployment to him and the self-employed Irishman never loses his fear of being out of work. No offence, but of course he doesn't want to touch you.

He quite freely admits that he is a man of contradictions. His most famous part – written for him, I'll have you know – is that of Jean Valjean in *Les Misérables*. It is an unashamedly evangelistic Christian parable. The only redeeming thing in revolutionary France, it seems to say, was the power of faith. Except that Colm, the man who has put that faith into words and song for twenty-nine years, doesn't actually believe a word of it. He admires good deeds. He sees the Bishop, whom he played magnificently in the recent *Les Miz* movie, as a model of humanity. But, still, it's the humanity Colm believes in, not the Bishop's underlying faith.

Here's another apparent contradiction: while most Irish actors and singers struggled to stay off the dole in the 1970s and 80s, Colm took to the road and the West End stage to put bread on his family's table back in Bray. For a devoted husband and family man to spend so many nights in dank dressing-rooms on the Charing Cross Road, or playing half-empty showband clubs in rural Ireland, is a true sign of his love for home. Some homes are lived in, some are made. And Colm's every vocal sinew was stretched to put a roof over his family's heads — no matter how rarely he shared it with them.

He loves coming back to Dublin, but it clearly unsettles him, not least because he no longer has a home here, outside the comfort and obsequies of luxury hotels.

It's not home. It's not Mangerton Road.

∾

GB: Colm, you were born in 1944, in Mangerton Road, an ordinary terraced house. There were eventually ten of you: six girls and four boys. Would you describe that household for me?

CW: It was mad. But I remember my mum, as a kid, she managed. We didn't have all the comforts of life, but I see photographs of us now, and we were always well dressed and well fed. And my mum was a fantastic manager.

GB: Was it a religious household, as you recall it? I'm talking about holy pictures and Novenas, First Fridays, Mass, all of that?

CW: Yes, my mum was very, very religious. My dad, I would say, was what Brendan Behan would call "a sick Catholic". When things were going bad, he started praying. [Laughter.] She had strong belief. And, at times, I wish I had that belief, because she'd a core and a central belief that she had happiness from.

GB: Okay, I pick up from you, then, that the wonderful religious training which you got at home — and you were through the Christian Brothers like the rest of us . . .

CW: Tough, tough, tough.

GB: . . . whose stated aim was to get you through the Inter Cert and Leaving Cert and get you a good job in the Civil Service, but whose real purpose was to instil the tenets of Holy Mother Church in you . . .

CW: The fear of God . . . !

GB: . . . failed in your case?

CW: Absolutely, totally! Failed.

GB: Even when you were in school.

CW: I was questioning all this thing about "God made the world in seven days" and all that stuff. It didn't add up. I remember, in school, this guy is giving what you would call a "Religious Doctrine" class, and he said, "Any questions?"

And I stood up and I said — I remember this, because he bawled me out — I said, "Look, if God knows all things past, present and to come, how come there's so much death, carnage and poverty in the world? If he knows, why doesn't he prevent this? Why does he allow this to happen?"

And he says, "You're getting very close to Calvinism there. Be very careful."

GB: [Laughs.]

CW: [Laughs.] But he never answered my bloody question! And that's one of the sticking-points for me. Even to this day, I don't understand suffering. If there's supposed to be some sort of a God up there, a God that understands and helps people, I don't understand why I've seen so many people suffer.

GB: Your father was in his own business. Was it the building business or asphalt . . . ?

CW: He worked for a firm and as an asphalt contractor. He worked as a spreader and then he eventually went out on his own. And I worked with him for about five or six years. But I couldn't hack it: he was too much of a self-made man — wouldn't let the reins go. Very contentious stuff going on there between him and me — didn't have a good relationship. So eventually I just up and left.

GB: Was he a happy man?

CW: I don't know. He was a very quiet guy and said very little. And I would say, within himself, had a lot of emotional turmoil. I was very resentful of his attitude and his quietness and his reticence to talk to us, as kids, because we wanted to interact with him, and he wasn't the "Let's have a hug . . ." type. And that generation wasn't, as you know.

GB: They weren't. No touchy-touchy, feely-feely.

CW: No. He actually came to see me. I was doing *Superstar* for three-and-a-half years in the West End. He came to see me on my last night. And all through to that he was saying to my sisters, "When is that fella going to get a real bloody job?" And I was in the West End, playing Judas, in one of the biggest hits of all time. [Laughter.]

When I did *Les Mis*, he came over to see one of the shows in the Barbican. His only comment was "That show would be nothing without our Colm." And nothing else — said nothing to me. And I resented that, I have to say. I resented that a lot, because he's your father. You expected him to say, "Well done."

GB: You needed him to say that.

CW: That's exactly it. I needed that kind of response, but we didn't get it. But maybe that's what made me try a little harder. My dad had a very, very hard time trying to express himself, but there were times when I didn't talk to my father for years. And I'm not great at that either. And I'm learning to try to do that. And I'm learning, trying to say to my kids, "I love you. I love you. I love you."

GB: I want to talk to you about talent. The biblical interpretation is a gift, presumably from God.

CW: Yeah.

GB: Do you regard your talent as a gift from God, or do you regard it as something that's in your DNA from your ma and pa?

CW: I regard it as both, because when we grew up there was so much music in the house and so much singing going on. And my dad had a very good voice, and he had that falsetto thing. As regards your question, I also think, possibly, there is something that comes with your emotional baggage as well, that's in your voice. I don't know what it is, but seemingly, I have an ability to tell a story and tell emotional stories very well and get to the core of them. And they pay me money to do that. They pay me to make people cry, in other words.

GB: But you don't see it as something directly given to you?

CW: I'm not sure. I do believe there's a force out there. I don't believe it's Jesus Christ of Nazareth. But I do believe that I've had experiences — very few, and actors will tell you also that they've had the same experience. I remember doing *Les Misérables* one night in New York, and everything seemed to align: everything seemed to fall into place. It was like a spiritual experience. And I was like a third eye. I was like a channel, and it was as if I wasn't there: I was standing in the wings, watching myself doing it. It was a very strange and a very wonderful experience, at the same time.

GB: It wasn't threatening or sinister or anything like that?

CW: No, it wasn't at all. It was very comforting; it was a beautiful experience.

GB: And what do you now think it was?

CW: I thought afterwards: the energy, the orchestra, the interaction with the actors on stage that night — everything was perfect. Everything aligned. All the stars aligned. But there was something else that made that happen to me. Something outside. That has happened about twice or three times to me in my life.

I believe in another thing too. There is a saying, and it's a bit clichéd, but that we're not physical beings having a spiritual experience: we're spiritual beings having a physical experience. I do believe that we don't really know who we are. And we are arrogant and presumptuous enough to think, on this small piece of dirt that we're flying around in, that we understand everything, that we know the beginning and the end of things. It's too big. It's vast. But, as Einstein said, "I don't want to know God: I want to know his thoughts." And that's what I'd want to know. I would love to be able to live for hundreds of years, to see the way this is going to evolve. I would love to see exactly how this happened. I would love to see how, but I don't have that time. I've so many other songs to sing, and I don't have the time. But, you know, I have to be very, very grateful. I was very fortunate and very blessed with my life, the way it progressed and the people I met, and my family.

GB: And so much of it random.

CW: Random. Going from place to place just to do the work, but being supported by a wonderful woman.

GB: Ah! Now, you see, I was just working up to that . . . because the story is that you met Deirdre, and you were set up to meet Deirdre by your sister, who was already a star on Irish television in *The Riordans*. Is that so, or is it not? It was a set-up?

CW: Denied! Denied by all of them, except me. [Laughs.]

GB: Was it "click" at first sight? And was she instantly the only one for you, or do you even believe in that concept?

CW: I do.

GB: You do?

CW: I do believe that you see something in a person that does resonate and connects with you. But I was afraid — very fearful. I was in contention with my old man at the time. I was leaving that firm. I wanted to be a musician. I thought, "What will I do?" I didn't have anything to offer a girl like Deirdre. No financial future, if you know what I mean. So, I backed off. And Deirdre, of course, thought this was me trying to be arrogant or whatever. And, of course, that made her more interested. But it was insecurity and *is* an insecurity, I think, that is built into most Irish people.

GB: Are you generally a pessimistic person or an optimistic person?

CW: I would say pessimistic. I'd say glass half empty rather than glass half full.

GB: Even now?

CW: I fear even now, yeah. I have this thing that they're all going to wake up and say, "Who's he?" You know, they're going to find out. But there's an insecurity built into the Irish, where they don't think they are as good as they are.

GB: Is it a money insecurity or is it something else?

CW: It could be both. I realised, when I was financially stable, that it wasn't about the money. And fame, that doesn't really matter.

GB: By the way, why were you never a drinker?

CW: I saw so much carnage around me, Gay, due to alcohol . . .

GB: Even from a young age.

CW: Yes. I saw so much carnage, and I saw also that people in pubs did a lot of talking, and it wasn't a lot of action. I also saw a lot of money being wasted on alcohol that could have gone elsewhere.

GB: But in the musical company you were keeping, if I may say so, that made you stick out . . .

CW: It did. But I got off the booze . . . Now, I'm not saying I didn't drink. I had my "wey-hey!" days, during the early days of *Superstar* here. [Laughs.] And I had great friends who knew how to drink very, very well. And I enjoyed their company, don't get me wrong. But I realised, when I went to *Superstar* I'd stay out to maybe three in the morning, and I'd have a matinée the next day. The minute you hit the stage the barometer kicks in and the energy level is always down. You talked a lot, your voice level was down. And I decided, "I have to get rid of this. I have to stop. I have to get out of this." It was too dangerous, if I wanted to sing eight shows a week and do them at a level I wanted to do them at. Because consistency is the word in my business.

GB: I want to come back to that in a minute. But, first of all, you got your breakthrough as Judas in *Jesus Christ Superstar*. How controversial was that show at the time? We tend to forget about this aspect.
CW: Unbelievable! I mean, we were all told we were going to burn in Hell. And my mother didn't talk to me for six months . . .

GB: Because . . .?
CW: Because I played Judas. She kept on saying, "Colm, you know what that man did to Our Lord." And I said, "That's only a musical, Mother, and it's based on history . . ."

GB: And were there placards outside? Campaigns?
CW: Absolutely!

GB: You did four-and-a-half years of *Phantom* in Canada . . .
CW: Yeah.

GB: Take me through your daily routine of doing that for four-and-a-half years.
CW: You live like a monk, basically.

GB: Eight shows a week?
CW: I did eight shows a week for the first two-and-a-half years, and then they wanted me to stay. I was only supposed to be there for six months. I had a Green Card; I was on my way into America. They asked me to stay, and they said, "Okay, we'll put it back to seven shows." And eventually, in the last year, I got it back to six.

GB: And how, during a run like that, do you make yourself brilliant every night?
CW: Again, lots of sleep, lots of discipline, in terms of looking after yourself; the best support team in the world, Deirdre; and just looking after yourself. People don't realise the size of the muscle that they're

dealing with is like the top of your fingernail. That white part of your fingernail is the tissue in your throat. That's what you're working with. And I keep on saying this to the kids: if the body is not right — if you're not right — this [indicating his throat] is not right. So, it's a physical thing. You have to exercise it, you have to keep it going. So, I'd say, you have to have sleep, no booze, no cigarettes, no drugs. You just have to live a very clean life.

GB: And were there nights when you felt you were less than brilliant, that you were ho-hum?

CW: Absolutely. And there were nights, then, when you felt, "That was very good." But as long as it was consistent. Consistency is the word.

GB: Why consistent?

CW: Because people would come a year later and expect you to sound like you did the year before. Like, *Les Misérables*, singing *Bring Him Home* twenty-eight years later, they expect me to sound like that now. [Laughs.] They take the piss out of the song in the States, singing [he sings], "It's too high, God, it's high. The song's too high. Pity me, change the key. Bring it down, bring it down, bring it down . . ."

GB: [Laughs.] So, Jean Valjean sings "God above . . ." which is a prayer . . .

CW: Yeah, a prayer.

GB: . . . 'Cause the story is of Christian redemption.

CW: Yes.

GB: How do you, not believing in . . . ?

CW: . . . In Jesus Christ of Nazareth, which is a different God . . .

GB: You're making a prayer . . .

CW: I'm making a prayer to what they would consider to be Jesus Christ . . .

GB: Yes.

CW: Now, twenty-eight years ago I think I had more of a belief in the JC feature than I have now. I also was so taken with the book and with the characters that Hugo described in that book. The Bishop, for me, was the nearest thing to a saint I have ever read — absolutely perfect man, perfect life. And if you honestly believe in the lyrics and you believe in that person, you don't act: you are. And that's what I would try to attain. This was this man's beliefs. Maybe I have doubts, but this man believed in it. It's not my story. This is his story.

GB: Insofar as you've spent your life performing for other people, do you have any sense of the effect that that has on them, the audiences?

CW: Yes, I do: a very strong effect. And it's a bit of an ego-trip to say, "I get a lot of mail." When I was doing *Les Misérables*, I would get probably six or seven letters a day, because it meant so much to people, that song *Bring Him Home*. Unbelievable. The gay community adopted *Bring Him Home* and *Empty Chairs* as their anthem. And I remember singing in New York at a gay club. I'd never been to a gay club before, and it was one of the most emotional experiences of my life.

I got letters from convicts to say, "I identify with this man, overcoming adversity." This guy approached me when I was signing an autograph, one time when I was in the States. And he said, "I was a junkie. I was watching a television show, and you came on and you sang *Bring Him Home*." And he said, "It just changed me." I swear to God. I'm looking at this guy — he said, "I went and I got help," and he said, "I had to come here today to tell you that."

Those kind of things happened all the time. The music affected millions of people. And still does — very positive stuff. And it makes me gratified, because I was in musicals that changed other people's lives.

GB: Do you pray? I presume you don't.

CW: I pray. I've more a Buddhist sort of philosophy now in my life, but my prayers are usually "May all beings be happy, content and fulfilled. May all beings be healed and whole. May all beings have whatever they want and need. May all beings have inner peace and ease." And I pray for my family.

GB: But to whom are the prayers addressed?

CW: The prayers are directed to the people that I love and directed to a force, hopefully, that will help them. My father said something [smiles]: "Those who are afraid to look around, look up." And there is a lot of sense in that. I am trying to find out who I am. I'm trying to get back to the silence. I'm trying to get back to the quietness and just look at what I am doing in relation to other people's lives. And I believe the power of prayer can be very strong.

GB: And Deirdre is a practising Catholic. Do you talk about religion or faith together?

CW: Yeah, yeah. She doesn't really interfere, because she knows I'm a stubborn bastard.

GB: [Laughter.] Does she try to convert you?

cw: No. She will say, the odd time, "Yeah, that's a bit of Thích Nhât Hanh that you're practising right there," when I'm going mental over something. [Laughs.] She's great at that!

GB: But there is no argument about faith or religion or anything like that?

cw: No, no . . . I go down to Mass sometimes. I'm not totally disillusioned with the Catholic Church. I've always said to my kids, "Look, pick what's the best there. Like, the Commandments are a great way to live your life, if you can. But take what you want and leave the rest behind."

GB: A couple of years ago, Deirdre was very ill: brain tumour . . .

cw: Yes.

GB: Was there a temptation to go down on your knees and pray at that time?

cw: I don't remember praying. I just remember thinking that, if I got out of this situation, with Deirdre, that I would never, ever be afraid again, because this was the most fearful thing that ever happened to me, that I could lose Deirdre. It was such a stressful and frantic time. What I was concentrating on more was letting her know that we were there and letting her know that there was love there all the time and that we were holding on, and for her to hold on.

GB: And it all came right. Maybe that was the prayer . . .

cw: [Laughs.] [Sings, "God on high . . ."] Yes, maybe that's what it was. You know, I'm not trying to get out of your question. Did I pray? I absolutely could have. I would have done anything — *anything* — to get her back.

GB: Tell me the story your son told about you and the book on anger management . . . And is it true?

cw: Yeah, it is. I saw this book on anger management and I thought, "I could do with that" . . . because people think I possibly have a short fuse. So, I ordered a book, in Indigo. Indigo phoned back and said, "Mr Wilkinson, your book is in." I went down to collect my book and they had given it to somebody else. So I threw a looper! I went mental in the shop. [Laughs.]

GB: You lost it! [Laughs.]

cw: I lost it in the shop. Now, I'd forgotten all about that, and then the kids brought it up and said, "He's the only person I know who got in a fight over an anger management book."

GB: "Mr Wilkinson, it's about anger management."

CW: I said, "You've got me all the way down from my house and you've given the book to someone . . . What sort of a shower of idiots are you?" Yeah, that was pretty good, all right.

GB: On the other hand: Buddhism, you don't drink, you don't smoke, you don't use dairy products . . .

CW: It's all to do with keeping this thing going. [Indicates his throat.] I'm going to try and pull back now. My family have said, "You have to sort of wind down." I'm sixty-nine. It's time to sort of smell the roses. You've only got a certain amount of time left and I'd like to be able to go around with my family and spend time with the kids and be able to carry the suitcases.

GB: Do you think about death? And does it concern you?

CW: I hate it. I hate the thought of all mortality. I am afraid of the un-known. I don't like the idea of dying and I don't know where I'm going to be.

GB: That was my next question: What do you think happens after?

CW: I know for a fact I feel certain presences — well, maybe I ask for them — when I go on stage. And I usually suffer a lot from stage fright and nerves . . .

GB: Do you?

CW: Oh, absolutely — big time. Always have, always will. Like, an opening night is like going through a brick wall — throwing up, don't eat for days, unbelievable stuff. But you manage to get through that and you settle down after a while. But when I'm going on to the stage, I'm thinking of my mam, dad, and my sister and my brother. And I'm thinking, "Be with me tonight."

GB: They're there.

CW: Yeah. Well, I'm asking them to be there.

GB: Do you think you'll see them again?

CW: I hope I will, but I'm not too sure about that. I'm sort of a Born Again Agnostic. You know, there is a big question mark. I don't know, but I wish, I hope.

GB: Final question, which will bring a sigh of relief to you.

CW: No, I've loved this. I could talk all day. "Me, me, me, me, me . . ." Singers, that's the way they warm up. Ego-trippers, for God's sake! You know, "Enough talk about me. Let's talk about you. What do *you* think of me?"

GB: [Laughter.] Okay, suppose what Deirdre believes in, suppose what your mum believed in, suppose what the Christian Brothers believed in — suppose it's all true, and you finally pop your clogs and you meet *Him* at the Pearly Gates. What will you say to him, it or her?
CW: Would it be Jesus Christ of Nazareth? It would be.

GB: I don't know. How would I know?
CW: Yeah, okay. I would say, "Right, guys, you were right, I was wrong. Okay. But I know there's going to be a great band in there. Could I put my name down as singer?"

GB: [Laughter.] I bet that wins him over.
CW: I hope so.

|CELINE BYRNE

Praying Twice

"*Qui bene cantat bis orat.*" Whoever sings well, prays twice. St Augustine's famous saying perfectly captures the way in which beautiful music can be an amplifier for the soul, moving both singer and listener in ways that mere words could never do.

You understand the phrase perfectly when you hear Celine Byrne sing. Words like "transcendent" are often used glibly, but in her case, it is appropriate. Her voice lifts and transports you – I am not entirely sure where, but you return to Earth with a pretty good idea of what Heaven sounds like.

And to think it was all a big, happy accident!

Had Celine not been taken to La Scala by her hosts during a summer she spent *au pair*-ing as a teenager in Italy, and had she not been prevented from pursuing other career ambitions by her first pregnancy and enrolled instead for singing lessons, I might never have got to hear what Heaven sounds like.

Celine and I had met before this interview and I suspect that, somewhere, I have one or two very smug-looking Punchestown selfies to prove it. But, of course, there's meeting and there's *meeting*. Guests on *The Meaning of Life* now know to expect the kind of searching questions that would never feature in other chat shows. Where most shows survive on a well-established exchange of celebrity stardust for product promotion, *The Meaning of Life* is as good as useless for plugging.

Thankfully, when Celine agreed to appear on *The Meaning of Life*, she had no particular "product" to promote. True, she was half way through a sell-out tour with José Carreras and was preparing for a major role at Covent Garden, but she was much more interested in self-exploration than self-promotion.

It is not fashionable for thirty-something women to express deep, devout faith, as Celine well knows, having been mercilessly ribbed about her religion by her girlfriends on many a night out. Not that this has silenced her: her Catholic faith and her family are the only things that enable her to make sense of her life and talent, and so she would much rather be talking about them than about the Callas Prize or her next role.

It is always upsetting to hear – and, sadly, it happens all too often – that a brilliant and well-loved star is tormented by depression in the way that, I discovered, Celine has frequently been. It takes great courage for them to name their demons publicly, and I know it is something from which fellow-sufferers take great solace. I am therefore pleased to report that, through a combination of belief and sheer bloody-mindedness — not to mention a husband who sounds like a cross between a saint and Superman — Celine's demons have been, if not exactly exorcised, at least kept in check.

Hence, I suspect, that heavenly voice. Hence the world at her feet.

GB: Take me back to Caragh, outside Naas, in Co. Kildare, and the house into which you were born. Tell me a bit about what that was like.
CB: Well, it's a little village between Naas and Newbridge.

GB: It wouldn't have seemed to me to be a home pulsating with opera and classical music . . .
CB: Absolutely not. There would be music on the radio and music playing in the house, so music was something that I loved, but it was never something that I thought that I would be doing when I get older.

GB: You had three brothers, one sister?
CB: Yeah.

GB: Was it a happy existence?
CB: I suppose, Gay, it was like any house. I mean, there was ups and downs, there was rows, there was killings, and, yeah, I suppose it was normal.

GB: And was it very religious?
CB: We were Mass-goers, and we all were Catholics, like the typical family, I suppose.

GB: Now, at what stage did you start to sing?
CB: Well, I always went around the place singing, and I suppose every girl wants to be a pop star. When I was growing up, if there was any fights or anything, I would go outside and just sing away, and I'd sit on the swing, to a point that, actually, the swing became my favourite place. I loved singing and I suppose it was just a hobby that developed into a career.

GB: Now, what I found out about you is that when you were a youngster you were dyslexic, which is cumbersome, but it can be overcome. But also you were depressed. In fact, you were paralysed with depression, to the extent that you developed symptoms similar to epilepsy, and you had little seizures. Tell me about that.

CB: Well, the dyslexia never really hindered me from a learning point of view, because I have a very good ear, and that's the way I learned. I knew that I'd always pick up things from an aural point of view. Moving on from that . . .

GB: Depression.

CB: Yeah.

GB: How does a child know that she's depressed?

CB: I didn't know I was depressed, Gay. I was very frustrated growing up, and there was an awful lot of things going on, and I couldn't, as a child, understand what was going on. I went to hospital after an epileptic seizure, or what seemed to be an epileptic seizure. My mam brought me in. I had to get an ECG. And I wasn't epileptic at all: that was the diagnosis. And what it was was the anxiety side of depression had got the better of me. And the first time that happened was coming up to my Junior Cert, and I started to just have these fits.

GB: Extraordinary.

CB: But, I mean, I got over that fairly quickly.

GB: Okay, thank you for telling me about that. Now, let's go back . . . You did your Leaving Cert and then you went as an *au pair* to Milan, and there the great discovery was made of opera. Is that the way it happened?

CB: Well, it sounds like a *eureka* moment, but, of course, there was an awful lot building up to that. When I was in school, I did my first stage performance. I was chosen as Eliza Doolittle in *My Fair Lady*, and I really enjoyed that.

GB: No, what you mean is you got a round of applause!

CB: Oh, no. I just felt good, because I think, when I was younger, I was always searching. I was so insecure, and because of things that happened in primary school, I didn't want to be picked on in secondary school, so I was always kind of brash and "If you come near me I'll kill you" kind of thing. You know, the real bogger. But when I was on stage, it was great, because I could be somebody else and not feel that people were criticising me. And I just loved to be on stage. And I knew then that's what I wanted to do.

So, when I went to Italy as an *au pair* for a year, after I left school, they gave me tickets to La Scala, because I told them I loved singing. And they said, "Have you ever been to an opera?"

And I said, "No, no, I wouldn't be into that highfalutin stuff."

And they were like, "Right, you should go. It's very famous."

So, I went along and, yeah, I was taken in by the whole thing — very shocked by it, in a good way, because I loved it. And I remember looking at this soprano, which I didn't then identify as being soprano, thinking, "That's the kind of singing I want to do. That's the kind of stage I want to be on."

GB: "That's what I want!"

CB: Yeah, "That's what I want to do."

GB: Okay, so then you come home with your head ringing with arias from Milan . . .

CB: Well, at eighteen, when I came back from Milan . . . I'll start again, because this is a big story . . . I had been with somebody, so actually my eldest son is from another man. So, we'll talk about that. Not that that's anybody's business, but it's relevant.

GB: Not all that relevant, but it doesn't matter. If you want to talk about it, by all means, talk about it . . .

CB: I shouldn't disown the father of my first child, should I, really?

GB: You became pregnant?

CB: Yes.

GB: So, we now have a situation, because normally a teenage, unwed pregnancy would be, in a place like Caragh, or indeed anywhere else, for that matter, in Ireland at that time . . .

CB: I wasn't the first, and I won't be the last, Gay . . .

GB: Not the first, not the last . . . But it would have been the cause of major scandal and outrage and gossip and all of these kind of things.

CB: Of course.

GB: But, in fact, all of your crowd rallied round, it seems to me, and they all took charge of you, as it were, because they wanted you to have the baby, and *you* wanted to have the baby. But you wanted to do this studying of music at the same time. Is that a good reading of the situation?

CB: Yeah, it is, absolutely, because I didn't want to go to college at that stage because I was pregnant, and I didn't want to sit at home and watch my belly grow. So, I decided, "Okay, what did I ever want to do?" And I said, "Well, I'd love to do some singing lessons, proper singing lessons."

So, that's what I did. And I started my studies in the Leinster School of Music. And then after that, when Noël was born, which was the most amazing thing that ever happened to me, my mam used to drive us up, and I'd go in for my hour lesson, and she'd sit in the car with the baby. And then I decided I wanted to really pursue this, this world of singing, because it seemed to be something that was very natural, and it seemed to be something that I was good at. So I enrolled in the DIT Conservatory of Music and Drama to do a degree in music performance.

GB: And so now you knew that was what you wanted to do?

CB: Absolutely. But it was only new to me, so I didn't really understand. Because when I went to DIT, when I auditioned, they said, "And who do you admire most . . . ?" I suppose they were waiting for the answer "Maria Callas" or something. Sure, I hadn't got a clue at the time who she was! And I remember turning around and saying, "Oh, I'd love to sing like Barbra Streisand . . ." and they kind of went, "Okay . . . !" [Laughter.] "That's interesting." But then, more and more, as I studied the classical art of singing, I enjoyed it more and more.

GB: And the pregnancy, was it a chore for you, an obstacle, or was it a joy? What was it?

CB: You know, it wasn't a planned pregnancy. But, in saying that, he changed my life. I never knew what real love was until I gave birth. It wasn't until I had him that I decided, "Right, okay, now I have a baby. What am I going to do? Am I going to stay at home with this baby or am I going to follow my dreams?" And I said, "Well, why can't I have both? Why can't I have my family and my dream combined?"

But I remember, when I was studying for my degree in the Conservatory of Music and Drama, I fell pregnant on my second child, Ciana. And I knew there was a few people kind of talking, going, "Does she want a career at all? She has this second baby, and she's still studying . . .!" And they should have waited and seen, because then, when I went to do my Masters, I was pregnant on my third child. [Laughter.] I thought I'd get the family and the study out of the way, you know!

GB: [Laughs.] Yes, but you didn't have to do it at the same time, Celine. This was the problem . . .
CB: [Laughs.] Oh, I know . . . But it was good that I did.

GB: Yes, indeed. So, the thing is that, although you are hell-bent on your career as a singer, nonetheless your real career is as a mother. Is that how you see it?
CB: Yeah. I think my vocation in life, bestowed on me by God, is to be a mother, first and foremost.

GB: Why?
CB: Because I just think that, with the birth of my first child, it changed my life and made me see life in a different way. And I knew I always wanted to have more children. Unfortunately, I can't afford to have loads of children . . . ! [Laughs.]

GB: Now, intro Mr Thomas Deans.
CB: Yeah.

GB: Do I understand him to have been a boyfriend before, and then you separated and you rediscovered him . . . ?
CB: My husband . . .

GB: Yes.
CB: He was my first kiss, when I was fourteen. We had been friends and we'd also known each other. And we are ten years married this year, actually.

GB: Ten years, I see. And I'm trying to follow through this whole labyrinth . . . You decided to get married when many people don't bother to get married. Why was getting married so important for you?
CB: I don't know any girl that doesn't envisage themselves married and in a white dress and happily ever after, and they're going to marry Prince Charming. I think everybody wants that. I always wanted to be married. And, incidentally, it wasn't in a white dress: it was in a red and gold dress! Unfortunately for us, the timing of getting married was an issue, because any time we had money saved for a wedding, there was always, like, a baby or a deposit on a house or something like that . . .

GB: But you did have a big splash?

CB: Yeah, there was 250 at the wedding, seated for the dinner and everything.

GB: A small, discreet wedding.

CB: It was the full whammy! [Laughter.] You know, we did it, and we had a great day.

GB: Since you mentioned Prince Charming, tell me a little about Thomas Deans.

CB: Ah, he's great.

GB: Yeah, that's not enough.

CB: I call him "Mr Perfect". No, he is, he's great.

GB: You call him "Mr Perfect"?

CB: I do.

GB: After ten years of marriage? Must be some guy.

CB: Without him I wouldn't be able to do what I do. And that's honest to God. Like, everybody would say, "Oh, he's the backbone." He really is.

GB: And does he know a great deal about opera and what you do?

CB: Oh, he does *now*. [Laughter.] And he knows an awful lot about steaming dresses and putting on make-up and fixing hair. And he always makes sure that, before I go out, if there's a hair missing he's following me with a clip.

GB: But he doesn't go to all your concerts or anything like that?

CB: No, he doesn't. And what's good as well, Gay, is a little secret: that we're not under each other's feet 24/7.

GB: Absence makes the heart grow fonder . . .

CB: It's the chemistry.

GB: So, in the midst of all of this, all of that dreary depression just disappeared . . . ?

CB: No.

GB: Oh. Do you want to give me more about that, or not?

CB: I don't know.

GB: Please yourself.

CB: Isn't it a contradiction to say I'm happy to talk about the fact that I'm depressed? I mean, the idea that people have of depression is that somebody is in bed and they don't feel like getting up, they don't feel like getting dressed, don't feel like going out, and they're down and moody all the time. Okay, that's one element of manic depression. But there are also different elements of depression. Mine was anxiety. And there are good times and there are bad times. I mean, what I'm happy to say now is that I actually went off my medication in June, so I'm now not on Prozac, but I was before then. I just found it very difficult between last December and June. I just needed a help, because I just felt really down.

GB: For no particular reason? Nothing you could point to . . . ?

CB: No. I mean, there are things that happened in the past that I could say may have triggered depression, but the fact of the matter is it doesn't matter what triggered it: I have to try to cope with it. What's good is that my family keep me going, my husband and my children.

GB: Now, this had nothing to do with what happened at the Ronnie Dunne competition in '07?

CB: Oh, I was depressed then, obviously.

GB: But you were sick as well.

CB: Yeah, I had pneumonia.

GB: Pneumonia. Well, that wouldn't help.

CB: Yeah. In 2007, I entered the Veronica Dunne Competition, and when it came to the semi-final, I was feeling horrible. I knew there was something wrong with my voice, but I was singing over it. But I knew it was going. And I found it very hard to breathe. And it was my first big competition and I thought that if I'd sung in the final, I'd be known as a finalist and that would look good on the CV. But, in saying that now, it probably wasn't a wise decision, because two days later I was brought to hospital with pneumonia, so I was very sick.

GB: Ah, but tell me about Athens and the Maria Callas Competition . . .

CB: Ah, you see, my life is like a depressed story. It's full of up and downs, because after that, I got out of the hospital, I got better, and two months later I went to Athens, and I got into the final of the Maria Callas. And I was delighted.

GB: I'm going to say it before you say it . . . Not only did you win it, but you won the gold medal as well.

CB: Yeah, they presented me with a gold medal because of the high scoring and the way I had presented myself throughout the competition.

And I'm delighted, because, to date, I still hold the crown, because no other Irish person has won it to date. So . . . !

GB: Wow! I just have this image in mind of you amidst all the adulation of a win like that. You still have to come back to Naas and wash the dirty togs of the lads and the socks and the jerseys . . .

CB: And clean the toilets! Because I don't have a cleaner. I have to do it myself.

GB: You're still the busy mum, after all of that.

CB: You know, people think it might be a glamorous life. What people don't understand is I can be singing in front of thousands of people and people will applaud you, and it's great. And you have that elation and the adrenalin is pumping. But then you have to go back to a hotel room, and sometimes you're on your own, and it can be tough. I know some people might say, "Oh, pity about ya . . ." But it can be tough, you know? And then, when I come home, it's a kind of a juxtaposed feeling, because I'm delighted to be home — because I'm delighted to be with my family — but I'm also slightly depressed, because you're in a slump, so to speak . . .

GB: Well, that's show business . . .

CB: Yeah.

GB: So, you were born and raised a Catholic, you probably slid away a little bit, and then you came back to the Catholic Church. What was the occasion of you coming back to the Church? How did that happen?

CB: It took me a long time to come back to it. I never kind of turned my back on it, but I felt in some way I never had Jesus in my life, because I never knew him. I never felt close to the Holy Spirit. Like, when I went to Mass on a Sunday, I listened to the Gospel, but, to me, they were stories. I listened, and then I went and got my Communion, and I went home. But I didn't really understand *anything* about it.

GB: So?

CB: So, yeah, I suppose it was maybe after Ciana was born. I had a little bit of post-natal depression, and I'd been struggling with mental-health issues since I was a teenager. And I remember just praying to God. You know, when you're at your wits' end. And then I met somebody on the street the next day, when I was on my way to college, getting off the bus on O'Connell Street. There was a group, and they said, "Do you want to know about God?" And I passed it by, but every day they were there. So, one day, I said, "And what are you going to tell me?"

And he goes, "Come to my meetings."

So, I went to the meetings every Friday after I finished college, before I went home, for two hours. And they talked about the Bible. But they were very Charismatic. It was the first time I was introduced to Charismatic Christians. So, meeting these people, I got to know God. But I still felt there was something missing.

So then, what brought me back to Catholicism was I was singing the *Messiah* in Halle, where Handel was born. And I was just feeling really down, the whole two weeks leading in to it. And I was sitting in my hotel room and I just started to cry, thinking about things from the past that were just coming back at me. And I was crying and crying and crying, to such a point that I was in a heap on the floor, and I literally — honest to God — couldn't move my arms. I just lost all power in my limbs. I was in a horrible place and saying, "Please, God, if you're there, help me, because I can't cope any more."

There was times where I thought I was schizophrenic. Yeah, I thought I was going mad, saying, "Please, God, what's happening? Where are you? I need you, because I need something." And I don't know what happened, but an hour had passed and then I got a call to ask me, would I go to Rome to sing for the Pope, to sing the Divine Mercy Chaplet. And I thought, "Wow!" And then, all of a sudden, I kind of felt this numbness, but it's warmth . . . I really felt at peace with myself. And I thought, "Well, is this God? Is this a sign?" I questioned it. And then I just accepted it. And one thing led to another.

When I did go to Rome, I sang the Divine Mercy Chaplet and then I sang *Ave Maria* as the Madonna was being processed in Piazza Navona. And I remember looking at the statue . . . and most people would just look at a statue and go, "It's a statue." But I really felt, "Wow, this person is coming at me . . ."

And then, after that, there was Confession on the street, and I said, "Well, you know, I feel really religious. I'd love to go to Confession." And it was an Italian Confession and after Confession, he said, "Did you sing *Ave Maria*?" And he had broken English, and I had broken Italian, so trying to have a conversation was a bit difficult. And I said, "Yes." And he said, "Can you meet tomorrow, at one?" I said, "Okay."

GB: You wouldn't often do that, would you? It wouldn't be sort of recommended . . .

CB: No, when a gentleman normally says, "Meet me here tomorrow," I wouldn't. But the fact that he had a collar on and he was a priest, I trusted him. Especially when you're in Rome. I think you're safe enough.

GB: Oh, this girl is a fool!

CB: Ah, stop! And then I met him at one, and he had brought another gentleman with him. He was in his robes also, and they were from the Legionaries of Christ. And I did ask him: I said, "Why did you want to meet me?"

And he said, "Well, you sang so beautifully. I think your voice is anointed and I wanted to talk to you about God."

And I said, "Well, that's interesting, because I'm always searching for Jesus. I want to know him as a friend." And I said, "Does that sound stupid?" And he said, "No, absolutely not. Jesus should be your friend. God is your father. Jesus should be your brother."

GB: And what do the Legionaries of Christ do that's different from what the rest of Catholics do?

CB: They don't do anything different. They just brought me back to Catholicism in a way where I understood the Church better than I ever did before. Ever.

GB: I know that you're familiar with the ex-leader, Father Maciel . . .

CB: Oh, yes . . .

GB: Well, I have to put it to you that he was the poster boy for John Paul II and got away with what he got away with for years through neglect of the Vatican and so on, but he was an embezzler and a drug addict and the father of at least two children by two different women. He was a serial abuser. He was a dreadful, dreadful person. I'm not saying that you knew anything about this . . .

CB: No, he wasn't a good person.

GB: . . .but it seems to me that, because of that, the Legionaries of Christ would be an organisation you don't want anything to do with, good, bad or indifferent.

CB: That's a difficult one, because, at the end of the day, I believe in God, I believe in Heaven. And if I believe in Heaven, I have to believe in

Hell. And if I believe in good, I have to believe in bad. And I don't think that priests become paedophiles: I think that paedophiles become priests. And the Devil works in this world just as much and just as strongly as God would. He can trick anybody.

GB: Go back to the Legionaries of Christ. Did you enrol in some sort of organisation?

CB: Oh, no, absolutely not. Like, I never got a stamp: "Legionaries of Christ". Nothing like that. There was questions I wanted to ask them about religion. Why is it that when I go to Mass on Sunday that I'm not stirred in any way when the wine becomes the blood and the bread becomes the body of Christ? For me, I think it's starting to be too symbolic. There's not enough emphasis put on it. I almost think the priests should say to everybody, "Okay, now, everybody, this is a really important part of the Mass . . ." It's just kind of reamed off. But I know it's important, because I know I need my nourishment. I know I need to receive. But I go to Mass as well for my children.

GB: So, you're bringing them up the way you were brought up . . . ?

CB: I would say a bit more.

GB: A bit more?

CB: Yeah, a bit more, because my parents never sat me down and talked to me about my religion. My mother and father went to Mass every Sunday, but I remember I started going to Knock when I was eleven, and I always loved going to Knock. And I go to Lourdes as well . . .

GB: Why do you go to these places?

CB: Because I feel at peace there, Gay. And most of the time it's for healing. Things from the past always need to be healed. And I love it. I mean, Mary means a lot to me in my life. She's very good. Like, she is the Mother of Christ . . .

GB: Are Mary and Jesus historical figures to you, or are they a real presence in your life?

CB: Oh, a real presence. But they weren't before. I have a better relationship with Jesus and with Mary than I did before

GB: This brings you a measure of peace and serenity, does it?

CB: Yes, it does. Look, I'm out with my friends, and they joke about it sometimes, because I'm also a Pioneer. And I'm not saying I'm a Holy Joe: I don't bring out my Bible and hit them over the head with it . . .

GB: It's kind of uncool, as you well know, for a young woman like you to admit that you're a member of the Catholic Church and you practise your faith and all that kind of thing. So that makes you unusual . . .

CB: Well, that's a fair statement.

GB: Coming back to the Pioneer thing, I would think you don't drink because it's bad for the voice, Celine . . .

CB: [Laughs.] I made my pledge when I was twelve, at my Confirmation, and then, obviously, became eighteen, and that was it: then it was vodkas and the whole lot. So it's not that I've never drunk . . .

GB: Right.

CB: Well, that was the time, actually, that I was talking about earlier, when I was in Halle and when I was at my wits' end. And I really felt that the Holy Spirit had come for me. And I said, "I will keep Lent for ever, in thanksgiving." I just wanted to show my discipline. So I became a Pioneer — Pioneer now for nine years.

GB: Okay, last question. And I usually preface this by saying, "Suppose it's all true, what you were taught . . ." I don't have to say that in your case, because you *know* it's all true . . . When you get to the Pearly Gates and you meet God himself, what will Celine Byrne say to him?

CB: The fact that there is an afterlife and that my soul will hopefully go to Heaven, that makes me feel good on this Earth.

GB: But what will you say?

CB: I'll say, "I'm sorry for any hurt that I've ever caused in anybody that I don't know about." If I don't realise that I've hurt them, then I can't say sorry. So I'd ask for forgiveness.

EDNA O'BRIEN

Another Country

66 "The past is a foreign country: they do things differently there." L. P. Hartley's famous opening line from *The Go-Between* could almost be a motto for Edna O'Brien. How else could she explain to a contemporary audience how she came to be so pilloried after the publication of *The Country Girls*? It was banned by the censor, condemned from the pulpit and so widely vilified that her own mother wrapped her copy of the book in sacking and buried it in an out-building of their home in Tuamgraney, Co. Clare, as if its very presence in the house might corrupt the family.

Edna has been asked to recount that story so often that, with only the slightest prompting from me, she did so in a five-minute monologue at the beginning of our interview, in 2010, barely stopping for breath, let alone questions. It was like the rote-learned First Confession of an eight-year-old, at the end of which, like a seasoned school chaplain, I felt I could finally begin a real conversation.

Edna moved to London at the height of her infamy, a literary asylum-seeker. Many mistook that for a rejection of her homeland and resented her all the more for it: unwelcome here, but even more unwelcome when she chose *not* to be here.

In fact, she insists, she always loved Ireland. It was just that the love was conditional. Unconditional love, as she discovered in her ten-year marriage to the writer Ernest Gébler, can all too quickly become a charter for abuse. She divorced Gébler, but was only ever separated from Ireland. She visits regularly and, over time, the country has fallen back in love with her.

The "coercive and stifling religion" of her youth has evolved since she left, its hubris replaced by humility, now that curtain after curtain has been lifted on Oz after Oz, back here in the Emerald Isle. Edna herself has also grown more conciliatory. She still describes herself as Catholic, although her tone suggests that she half expects to be escorted from the pews for saying so.

She won't be.

∾

GB: Let me start by asking you to tell me about your early beginnings, your childhood, your parents and your family in Tuamgraney.

EOB: Well, that would take a book in itself. [Laughs.] My childhood was in a very lovely house, a stone house in the middle of a field with beautiful old trees, and there was also a very, very pervasive sense of religion. Religion was everywhere. It wasn't a house of harmony, but it was perhaps a house where I learned something about the necessity to write. I thought then, and I still think it, that literature is spiritual — that literature is a way, if you like, of making ordinary life more bearable.

My father was unlucky in that he was one of those people who shouldn't drink. He was a great storyteller, but he was a man with a high, volatile temper. My mother, in contrast to my father, was a much more hard-working woman. I never saw my mother not working — feeding hens, feeding calves, pounding meal, making cakes, making the house spick and span.

GB: I get the impression that you loved your mother; you were wary of your father. Would that be right?

EOB: That would be very accurate.

GB: But was it a happy childhood for you?

EOB: No. No. No. No, it wasn't, because I was full of fear and where there is fear, there isn't happiness.

GB: Jumping way ahead, did you eventually forgive your father for this?

EOB: I do forgive him. I do forgive him.

GB: Before he died?

EOB: Absolutely! I just didn't want to be in that place. I wanted to escape.

GB: And your mother — you loved your mother, did you?

EOB: I loved my mother and she was a wonderful woman, a very intelligent woman. I was her last child and beholden. People think of me as a rebel. Well, God help us, I was very biddable, and anything my mother wanted, I did. If I thought I should fast and drink salted water as a penance, I was full of, you know, penance and religion. I know you're laughing, but it's the truth. I associated my mother with the Virgin Mary and with divinity and with purity and all those words, so I was obedient to the point of cravenness.

When I began to feel that I might like to kiss a man or a boy or go to a dance, her possessiveness of me — her stranglehold on me — became more and more apparent. So I had a lot of strictness in my life. I had the judgement of my mother . . . Oddly enough, my father did not judge me. But my mother did, and, of course, the Church, the nuns, priests, everyone.

It is only later that I came to truly distinguish between religion and spirituality. Religion is very often coercive in any faith — Muslim, Jewish or Catholic — and Irish Catholicism excelled at it. You know, most of the enjoinders were — are — not love of God, but fear of God.

GB: What about books? Was it a reading house in any way?

EOB: No, there weren't any books. There was, as I've often said, this copy of *Rebecca* that circulated in the village. Some woman had bought *Rebecca*.

GB: In the village?

EOB: In the village. And the book was loaned by the page, but not consecutive, so you got page 104 and then you got page 2. Well, everyone wanted to read it, or whatever: it wasn't like 1, 2, 3 . . . The suspense was awful.

I longed for books. In an anthology, I read extracts of great writers, not our greatest Irish writers, but great English writers: Dickens, Hardy, Shakespeare, the Gospels and some myths. I would write other girls' compositions: you know, a day at the seaside — not having been to the seaside — or a day in the life . . . [laughs] and so on. And my own mother, from a very early age, was deeply suspicious of this vocation — because I call it a vocation— that I had for writing.

GB: Let's move on then to the Sisters of Mercy in Loughrea. Was that a happy time for you?

EOB: It was punitive, but in some ways it was more peaceful. I missed my mother terribly. Later, when I wrote *The Country Girls* — chapters of which are really, of course, not based on, but stimulated by, the actual backdrop of the convent I was in — the Head Nun, Sister Theresa, wrote to me and said, "We hear you have written a novel. We give credence an open mind." Well, I was shaking, 'cause I knew that she wasn't giving credence an open mind. They were very upset by my book. Well, everyone was incensed.

GB: "*I was not sorry to be leaving the old village. It was dead and tired and old and crumbling and falling down. The shops needed paint and there seem to be fewer geraniums in the upstairs windows than there had been when I was a child.*" Now, only a girl born and reared in a small Irish town could have written that. And it was from the heart, and you had determined "I'm getting out of here."

EOB: Out, yes. And there's rebellion in it. There's an anger also, and that's part of youth, of breaking out. I wouldn't write that now, not because I wish to placate people, but at that point in time — and I don't know when I wrote it, which book's it from? — it's how I saw things.

GB: It's *The Country Girls*.

EOB: It's *The Country Girls*. That's what I felt. I saw this world as pensive, worn, dead, imaginatively dead, and I wanted out. Now, it wasn't imaginatively dead, 'cause there were people, unknown to me, living, suffering, dreaming, cursing, hating, praying, their inner lives a secret.

GB: Now, let's move on to *The Country Girls* and when it was published, and is it true that the parish priest burned a copy of it?

EOB: They did that, but it was in Scarriff.

GB: In Scarriff.

EOB: There were two villages, Tuamgraney and Scarriff.

GB: Does that make a difference? [Laughs.]

EOB: Oh, yes [laughs], from the point of view of accuracy. But the burning did happen, and we have to remember, in those times — it was 1960 — Co. Clare, or any other county, wasn't the most culturally enlightened: nowhere was. Nowhere was. I mean, Charlie Haughey, who later claimed to like me, with the Archbishop of Dublin, had an exchange of letters about *The Country Girls* — laughable — saying that it shouldn't be let into any decent homestead, that it was filth and so on. They all thought that I was "a smear" — the same phrase that once had been said about J. M. Synge, apparently; it's in the vernacular — "a smear on Irish womanhood". So there was the little burning. A couple of women who had bought *The Country Girls* — shows you what big sales I had, Gay! — and the priest asked that the books be brought in, and the two women brought them in, and there was the burning. My mother didn't attend the burning, but naturally she told me. And I was quaking. I thought, "Oh, God!"

GB: Where were you at this stage?

EOB: I was in England.

GB: You did a runner?

EOB: I'd gone. I had scooted. Again, fear and self-preservation, both. I was thought by many — by *many* — to have done something treacherous to my own people and my own country. Whereas, within me, what I was trying to do — not something pretty or prettifying, or appeasing — I was trying to render in the best language that I could search for in my mind the reality and the comedy and the sorrow, as I saw it — and, much more importantly, as I *felt* it — around me. So, between what *I* felt I was doing and what was perceived as what I was doing, there was a great gulf.

GB: Were you conscious of people staring at you or pointing the finger or "That's the one who wrote this book . . ."?

EOB: I was. Ah, yes, of course, and more.

GB: And what did you do about that? How did you cope with it?

EOB: I don't think I was that brave. My only bravery was to write the next book. And I remember getting anonymous letters: "drowning in your own sewage", and so on.

GB: Go back to your mother again. How did she cope with this? What did she do with the book . . . ?

EOB: Well, she buried it. She buried it in a bolster case.

GB: You mean *physically* buried it?

EOB: Yes, out in a turf house. I dedicated the book to my mother. My mother went through the book with black ink. I only found this after she was dead, and, honestly, I could have killed her. She went through it, you know: Baba is given to the expletives, and I can't bear to think how my mother felt about Mr Gentleman's semi-nakedness. She must have had a seizure at that moment. So, in black ink, she'd gone through any offensive words.

So, after my mother's death, I found *The Country Girls* outside in a turf house, and it was in a bolster case, wrapped up.

GB: Secret?

EOB: Secret and sinful!

GB: Where were you spiritually at this stage, in relation to the Catholic Church? You were now married to a divorced man . . .

EOB: Oh, exactly. Well, I had erred and fallen, if you like, having become married to a divorced man. I had a very grim little wedding. It was in the sacristy of a Catholic church in Blanchardstown, and the witnesses were the two builders.

GB: Well, this must have been love?

EOB: I'm not sure, Gay. I had burned my boats by going with the man I later married. My own family pursued us and were violent, actually, towards my future husband. And I knew — I wasn't married then, I was just living with him — I knew that evening, when he had wounds and was livid with me . . . that I had burnt my boats with my own family.

GB: What do you mean "he had wounds"?

EOB: Well, there was a fight.

GB: Ah!

EOB: So, he was hit or kicked by . . .

GB: By whom?

EOB: Well, my father and men who came with him, including a priest.

GB: Ah!

EOB: It was like something out of the Middle Ages, as if I were a witch, but instead of being a witch, I was a fallen woman. But, anyhow, there was fisticuffs with Ernest Gébler, which naturally I was very ashamed of. I had no power over or no ability to redress it. I knew that I had cast my lot, and there was no going back.

GB: He must have loved you?

EOB: I think he did. I think he did love me, but he also determined to completely control me.

GB: Right. Now, in Eleanora, in *The Light of Evening* , you described finishing your book in the jotters on the window-ledge. You've done it, you've finished that . . . and he comes in, and you describe a most horrendous scene of hatred, resentment . . .

EOB: Jealousy.

GB: Jealousy of your writing ability?

EOB: Yes.

GB: Is that as it was?

EOB: Yes, absolutely.

GB: He could not bear the thought that you had written a book, and a good book?

EOB: It undermined him. It undermined his own sense of himself, his own gifts. He's dead, but — this is very sad, but that is the truth — he said, "You can do it" — meaning write — "and I will never forgive you."

GB: Did he influence your spiritual beliefs or values or theology in any way, your husband?

EOB: Well, he was very opposed to them . . . He said I came from ignorant peasants. I did come from peasants, and they had some ignorance, but they also had great stock, and they had great determination, which, thank God, I have some of. He didn't put me off God. If anything he put me slightly more *on* God, because I hate people telling you how you must think, how you must feel, even though I have, if you like, been subservient to it.

GB: Where do you stand now in relation to the Catholic Church?

EOB: I shall now do my Joan of Arc. [Laughs.] I saw some of the blatant hypocrisy of the Catholic Church, its cruelty, its untruth, its monology. That's not religion, that's not spirituality. The power of the Catholic Church in the '40s, '50s, '60s in Ireland, and maybe long after, was overwhelming. It is less so now, because people have become, if you like, a little more enlightened. They're asking questions and they're more angry, because they feel the Catholic Church has let them down. I don't feel the Catholic Church has let me down, because it was never intending to build me up. So, what I feel is that whatever relationship — including my fears and my hopes — are, if you like, between my maker and myself.

I know a nun in the Mater Hospital, who gave me so much help with *The Light of Evening*, who nursed my mother in her final and most troubled moments. That nun has — not like some of the nuns who taught me — that nun has given her life to God and is filled with compassion towards others.

GB: Do you pray?

EOB: I do pray, of course.

GB: To whom do you pray?

EOB: I pray to God the Divinity. I pray, in my little venal ways, to St Anthony. But the prayers one says must come — the way writing must come — from the soul and from the heart. They can't be mindless. The world is too troubled and troubling for any insincerity.

GB: What vision do you have in your mind when you're praying to him?
EOB: The figure seen through cloud, as I once did. I become something of a child. It's between me and the person to whom I am appealing, who I am not even sure exists. So, in there lies, if you like, a paradox.

GB: Do you think prayers are answered?
EOB: Sometimes in extremes I think prayer is answered. I would like to own a house in London or Dublin. But I doubt if that will happen, before nightfall.

GB: You have not been lucky with the men in your life: your dad and your husband . . . Is that a fair statement?
EOB: Yes, fair statement and one that we'll address for a moment or two. I have not been lucky. Certainly, in the case of Ernest Gébler, I chose a judgemental or punishing figure; not, obviously, religious — in fact, irreligious — but with the same strictures. Some people call it masochism. I object to the word. I think, in me, religion had been so instilled that I did not think or feel that earthly love should be anything but, in some form, punishing. I didn't feel it should be a romp. And now I am seventy-eight years of age. I haven't met the man with whom my whole being — heart, soul and body — would be miraculously entwined. I didn't. My prayer has not been answered in that, nor is it likely to be.

GB: Do you believe you'll see your parents again?
EOB: I am frightened to. Now, I would love to be able to say to you, "I would love to see my parents," because when I die, I hope my children will not only not be afraid, but will be longing to see me [laughs]. There were things left unfinished and, in my understanding of it, those unfinished things would have to be thrashed out, and I would be nervous of that.

GB: Do you not think the Communion of Saints theology of the Catholic Church is a very nice, comforting kind of theology?
EOB: It certainly is, so long as one can totally believe it. You see, again, it's a question of faith. Let's say a hundred per cent faith, like the nun in the Mater Hospital, who has the great name of Reparata. She has *total* faith. I do not have total faith.

GB: And do you envy her that faith?

EOB: No, I still want to be me. The feeling of the love of God, the absolute love of God, at whatever age or years I felt it, is something I am glad to have felt, but where it got lost was through fear of Hell, as opposed to Heaven. Hell and Purgatory took precedence.

GB: Do you fear death?

EOB: I fear death, and I fear the journey both towards death and after it. Everybody baulks at the word "nothingness", and I baulk too, but I don't know whether it's nothingness. And those who tell us — Richard Dawkins and many people — they don't know either. Shakespeare's great line "From whose bourn no traveller returns" to tell us of the way haunts me.

GB: Were you ever attracted to another faith — Muslim, Hindu, Protestant, Jew?

EOB: There is something about the best of Buddhist faith that is also the best about humanity. But as regards crossing over [laughs], or "taking the soup", as it used to be called [laughs], I don't think I could do that, because the other is so ingrained in me.

GB: What do you think the Old Testament is?

EOB: Well, I think it's great literature. I read the King James version frequently and am enthralled by its language and its narrative.

GB: And what do you think Matthew, Mark, Luke and John is . . . are?

EOB: The evangelists, the disciples of Christ, are the principal testament we have in which a man called Jesus lived and was crucified and rose from the dead.

GB: Do you think he was God, the Son of God?

EOB: I don't know. That is what their teaching is, that he is the Son of God.

GB: What do you believe?

EOB: I *want* to believe that he was.

GB: Do you believe in the Real Presence at Mass?

EOB: Very often, I'm so distracted at Mass by the noise and coughing — along with the platitudes of the sermons — that I forget the sacrament itself.

GB: One last question. Suppose it's all true and you meet Jesus. When you arrive at the Pearly Gates what will you say to him?

EOB: "Bless me. Bless me throughout eternity." Thirty years ago, if I met Jesus, I might have said, "Forgive me." Not any longer. "Bless me."

EAMON DUNPHY

The Rocky Road

"'No tears and no singing!' That's what they said as I was leaving the house. And look at me. I lasted all of two minutes."

In a break in filming our interview, Eamon Dunphy had a laugh at his own expense. At the very first mention of his late parents, he had been overwhelmed by emotion. And, judging by his family's admonishments, he has form on that score. There was no singing, though, despite the musical reference contained in the title of his recent autobiography, *The Rocky Road*.

Footballers' memoirs are ten a penny, but not ones like this. There's no ghost in sight, with every page and memory slaved over — and quite possibly cried over — by the man himself. He was always more than your average footballer.

Ironically, he insists that, on the pitch, that's exactly what he was: average. And it was that self-awareness that led him to do the unthinkable, when he asked Sir Matt Busby for a transfer *away* from Manchester United, the "theatre" of his and every teenage Irish boy's dreams, once he realised that he was nowhere near the class of his peer and pal, George Best. Sir Matt thought he was mad, but nonetheless gave young Dunphy his parachute to the lower English divisions, probably enabling him to pursue a much longer career in first team football, as a journeyman striker at York City, Millwall and Shamrock Rovers — albeit one with Ireland caps.

While George Best was always happiest when he let his feet do the talking, Eamon had other options — his pen and his lip — and he can still shoot from either. At Millwall, he turned the disaster and drudgery of relegation into one of the finest sports books ever written, *Only a Game*, by telling it like it was, on the training field and in the dressing room. No player had ever spilled such honest beans before, and it was riveting stuff. No wonder, U2 and Roy Keane subsequently asked him to ghost-write books for them. And no wonder one of his Millwall teammates called him "a *Guardian*-reading poof". Social conscience and indiscretion have never played well in the Den, even if Dunphy himself did.

I was intrigued, though, by the "*Guardian*-reading" element of that ignorant insult. I wondered where Eamon's passion for reading and left-leaning politics had come from. I should have known. It comes from the same place that he does: Drumcondra. Or, more precisely, the

one-room flat just off the rocky road in from Drumcondra, where
Eamon and his brother, Kevin, were raised by their devoted parents.

Revolutionary bolshiness was, if not in the blood, certainly in the air
and the baptismal water. Eamon was named after Dev, and his brother
after Kevin Barry, by parents who sacrificed much comfort and joy to
give their beloved boys opportunities.

Cue tears.

∽

ED: My father, if he'd been doing the naming, would have named me
after Jim Larkin, so it would have been "Jim Dunphy". He didn't like
Fianna Fáil and he didn't like Dev. He was a builder's labourer, and his
best friend, Larry, was the foreman on the building site. And Larry said,
"Look, Paddy, we're going to be laying people off and the one thing that
can save you is if you join Fianna Fáil and canvass for us at the next
election. That will save your job." And my father refused. And when the
call came, my father was laid off, which, for a man in the early '50s, was
pretty shocking. He came home and told my mother, Margaret — Peg,
as he called her — and she said, "You did the right thing." [Becomes
tearful.]

GB: "You did the right thing: held on to your principles."
ED: Yeah. But it was a terrible and unforgettable moment when he came
back to the room where we lived, that night.

GB: Tell me about that room and the four of you in it, in Richmond
Road, in Drumcondra. Not pleasant . . . ?
ED: It was a rooming-house, and we had one room. We were the only
really poor family in the neighbourhood. Kevin and I slept on the floor,
and my parents were in the bed. But there was a lot of love. We said the
Rosary every night. My mother went to Mass every morning.

GB: Did you go to Mass with her?
ED: I did, yes. We went to St Alphonsus' Church.

GB: Every morning?
ED: Yeah. It was lovely, and the incense in the church and the sense of
devotion. It was a beautiful church, St Alphonsus'.

GB: Now, you say in the book that you prayed for your father's safe return every night from Macken's. Was there some sort of dangerous job he was doing?

ED: Well, he was a builder's labourer, and it was a rough old game. And, somewhere around nine or ten, I was in the grip of this morbid fear that something was wrong and that something was going to happen. And then, of course, something bad did happen. My mother got a letter one day, and she was in tears: an eviction notice. The landlord wanted us out, and I think they wanted to demolish the house. It was after the floods in 1954. And the two other families that were living in the house had accepted whatever the deal was. And my mother didn't want to. Peadar Cowan had been elected as a Clann na Poblachta TD . . .

GB: And he was a solicitor, was he not?

ED: He was a solicitor. So, my mother actually undertook to go and see him with the eviction notice. I went with her. And he said, "No one has the right to take your home away from you. We'll fight." So, we went to court and Peadar Cowan made the case. And my mother was clutching her hand, and he [the judge] said, "You're entitled to your home." And he dismissed the application to evict us.

GB: You'd kept the room . . . And Peadar Cowan, did he charge?

ED: No. She offered him a fiver — a fiver was a week's wages in those days — and he said, "Don't! . . . Say a prayer for me," which we did. [Becomes tearful.]

GB: Let us talk, now, about Mr Hayden, in school, who was one of those teachers who spotted that you were very bright, very smart, very good and gave you the confidence in later life to try things like writing.

ED: Yes, he did. He would read my essays out for the class or give me praise. And he steered me towards the library and books. And praise, at a certain moment in your life, when you're vulnerable, is so important. And I've been thinking about him for quite a long time now, how he changed my life, and how people can change your life with an act of kindness.

GB: It only takes one teacher.

ED: Yes, it does, Gay.

GB: Now, we move ahead slightly . . . Was the British Army *really* an option for you . . . ?

ED: Very much so, yeah. There was a guy called McNally, Soldier McNally, and he was the envy of the neighbourhood. He went off a kind of corner boy and came back a man with a tan, loads of money and loads of clothes. And he looked the business. I used to think, "Okay, if I don't make it in the football," — which was a slim chance — "I'm going to sign on."

GB: Can't see you as a soldier, Eamon. Can't see you in uniform, saluting corporals and sergeants, and fellas getting at you and so on . . .
ED: [Laughter.] I would have joined the army with a view to getting along and to becoming an officer.

GB: Yeah?
ED: You may not think I'm serious . . . [Laughter.] I *would* have gone into the British Army. I'd have been a good soldier. I would have polished my boots and I'd have tried to learn, and I'd have put in for promotion. And I'd have tried to be a sergeant, and then I would have tried to be an officer. And I would have had a great time.

GB: [Laughter.] Okay, let's move on to football. Not yet fifteen and Billy Behan from Man United came over and spotted you, and off you went to Manchester. This must have been any boy's dream.
ED: Yes, it was.

GB: Glamour, excitement — wonderful . . . But not quite, when you got there. Tell me about that.
ED: Well, it was two years after the Munich air crash, and Manchester United was the most written and spoken about club in the world. Manchester United was *it*. It was like going to Hollywood or winning the lotto. And I won it. But when we got there, we weren't looked after. And George Best was there. He came the year after me, and we were in digs. They were pretty lousy — eating spam and stuff. It was rough. And George and myself, we hung out together and got into scrapes and stuff.

GB: That was a learning experience for you, was it?
ED: It was, yeah. And I never encountered any anti-Irish prejudice when I went there. I liked England. I liked George. He was a lovely young guy, very quiet.

GB: It strikes me that here were a bunch of young fellas with comparatively more money in their pocket than they knew what to do with — a lot of free time and a lot of opportunities to go to snooker halls. And you took to the greyhound track.

ED: We did, yeah. I was in the dog track when I heard John F. Kennedy had been assassinated. We didn't have a lot to do, you see. You couldn't go out clubbing, because you had to be fit, and we didn't drink.

GB: You didn't drink?
ED: No, we didn't drink at all. I never really had a drink.

GB: You gambled instead . . . ?
ED: Yeah, just to get the buzz.

GB: It's not really surprising in those circumstances that Georgie Best came a cropper. What is amazing is that you didn't, although you gave it a fair whack. How was that?
ED: I don't know. I think George was very shy. I think he was catapulted from obscurity, which we lived in, to international fame overnight, which can be really seriously destabilising. And he played one game in Lisbon for Manchester United. He was sensational. And they called him "the fifth Beatle", because the Beatles were the big thing then. And that happened to him real quick. And I think he lost his bearings after that.

GB: Come back to you now, and this is extraordinary: you went, did you not, to Sir Matt and said you wanted a transfer, because you'd caught on to the fact that you were not going to be Georgie Best.
ED: Yeah. I mean, it was a kind of limbo, because I had skill, but I wasn't going to be a first team player. And he said, "Son, nobody ever asks for a transfer from Manchester United."

GB: Nobody did.
ED: But I said, "I don't mean it in a bad way. I just know that I'm never going to be good enough to play here. And you don't need me, so you can get a few quid for me" — and it *was* a few quid — "I just want to go." And then he let me go to York City. I thought, "If I go to York City, I'll work my way up." And I did, to Millwall, who are, you know, a good second division team. And I played for Ireland. I was the first York City player to be capped for any country . . . And the last, in fact. [Laughter.]

GB: But was it not in Millwall that you started to write seriously? And the amazing thing is that you had the confidence to start writing, having left school at fifteen.
ED: Yeah, I realised that football ends in your early thirties, or maybe sooner if you get an injury, so it was plan B. And I thought, "Well, I can write." So, I decided to try to write a book of six months of my life.

And, in fact, [laughs] it turned out to be a horrendous six months, so the book was called *Only a Game*. And it's the story of a has-been second division footballer about to hit the rocks. A friend helped me and put it together, and a publisher got it, Penguin, and they said, "This is amazing!" And they published it, and it was very successful.

GB: Your very nice colleague at Millwall, Mr Gilchrist, described you as a "*Guardian*-reading poof", which must have meant that he saw you as this bolshie, lefty, troublesome, trouble-making, rabble-rousing, different sort of guy. And I'm wondering where that sense of injustice came to you from, and that sense of righteousness and your outrage at the unfairness of the world. Tell me a bit about that.

ED: Well, I think, growing up, I saw it in my father's experiences, in the experiences of our family, being threatened with eviction. And I kind of had a sense of right and wrong and how the world could close in on decent people who played by the rules, which my parents were and my brother was as well. So-called "ordinary people". There are no "ordinary people": everybody is magnificent in their own way, when they're faced with sickness or illness or death or some kind of trauma.

And I always saw the power thing in soccer, where you have these buffoons in their suits — big-shot on a Saturday — and they would look at you as if you're a piece of dirt, unless you scored a hat-trick, which I didn't do very often. And there was a caste system, I think you'd call it, in soccer that I deeply resented and that most players seemed to accept. So, I had this acute sense of what was right and what was wrong, which came from my mother and father, really, and from going to Mass. I used to listen to what they said about justice, and I used to listen to what they said about goodness and about evil. And I used to absorb it, and I believed in it. I thought it was real. I thought, "This is the Gospel. This is what God wants." This was the message of their faith.

And we encountered a priest . . . My mother and father, they could never have sex, because they couldn't have another child, because they couldn't afford it. And they were in their late twenties, and they did what he said. And my father, when he told me that story later in his life, in Fagan's pub, I started to cry. You know, they did what they were told to do, what they were supposed to do. And I think most so-called "ordinary people" play by the rules, and they do what they're told is right. They do what's right by their children. They do what's right by each other.

So, I brought that with me from my childhood into my adult life: a sense that someone is being exploited here. And when you encounter it, I had the strong sense that you should stand up and say, "This is wrong. You're not doing this." I began to think, as a young man, that the left were on the side of righteousness and that the right were the baddies. And I saw life in terms of goodies and baddies. Now, of course, you grow up and learn that life is much more complex, and the left, you know, they stopped people working: they have their closed shops and they have their own rackets. But I was young then.

GB: Now, you say in the book that the matter of your marriages — your first, and your present marriage to Jane — is private and off-limits, so only answer this in terms that you choose to answer. You say that it was the disgraceful treatment by the Catholic Church, when you wanted to marry Sandra, which caused a huge rift in you.

ED: Well, we were twenty-one. And she was a lovely girl, and is a lovely woman, and, because she was a Protestant, if you were marrying a non-Catholic, you had to take counselling from the priest. And she also had to take counselling.

GB: Lest you might be corrupted.

ED: He said to me on our first meeting, "You know these Protestants aren't like us, don't you?"

GB: [Laughs.]

ED: He said, "They don't live right. She'll leave you. She'll be having affairs. They don't believe in marriage the way we do." And I was deeply shocked. I was shaking to my boots. I was shaking with anger. I was sickened. Actually, that's when I stopped going to Mass. And we got married in a "dark church", as they called it.

GB: Early in the morning.

ED: In Manchester, yeah, without the celebratory things that, particularly for a woman, I think, matter.

GB: It's called bigotry.

ED: It was bigotry, Gay, yes. And it was a defining moment for me, in terms of my religious beliefs and my, such as it was, commitment to Catholicism.

GB: What's your present situation?

ED: I've never been a secularist, Gay. I've never been down on the Catholic Church. I've never been one of those people who have hated the Catholic Church. I always recall what the faith gave to my parents and my brother and to me. I respect people's faith, whatever it is. And I find when I contemplate the cover-up in the Vatican, in particular, of the sexual abuse of children internationally — in America, Australia, everywhere the Catholic Church has power — I find it terrible — terrifying, really — that you believed in these people so much and that they betrayed us so much.

GB: Do you have any separation of faith from that?
ED: Yes.

GB: Can you separate the two?
ED: Yes, I can, and my mother could.

GB: Do you practise your faith at the moment?
ED: No.

GB: Do you pray?
ED: Yes, I do.

GB: To whom and what and when and why and for what?
ED: I pray to God.

GB: And, in your head, what is God? How do you envisage that, when you pray?
ED: When I pray, I pray for my children and for my family and for my wife . . .

GB: But how do you envisage what you're praying to?
ED: I'm praying to a caring being. It's irrational, but that's what I pray every night.

GB: Do you kneel to pray?
ED: No, I pray in my chair at night, when I'm finished watching Vincent Browne.

GB: And do you use standard prayers: Our Fathers, Hail Marys . . .
ED: No, I have my own prayers, made-up prayers. But then . . .
  Oh, Angel of God, my guardian dear,
  To whom God's love commits me here.
  Ever this day be at my side
  To light and guard, to rule and guide.
  Amen.
  [Becomes tearful.]

GB: And that brings you right back to your early days . . .

ED: It brings you back to belief that we are not guiding our own faith: we are at the mercy of forces that are greater than we are. And you can be fortunate; you can be unfortunate. I think it's terrible vanity, actually, to think, if you have good fortune, that it's down to you, because it isn't, ultimately.

GB: Okay, so you would identify somehow with Jesus, in putting up, in raising rows and fighting for righteousness. What and who was Jesus to you?

ED: I think a preacher, philosopher — someone who was crucified for his beliefs. I think an inspiration to untold numbers of people.

GB: Are you a follower of his?

ED: No. I couldn't say I was, because I'm not familiar enough with the Bible, with the Gospels. I only know of his message from how I've observed people live it who believe it and who practise it. And generally, they're good people. They're better for it.

GB: Do you think he was divine — i.e. the Son of God?

ED: I can't get to there intellectually. I'm not an atheist, but I can't get to the point where I can say that Jesus was a divine being or spirit. I believe that God is here. [Pats his heart.] Goodness is here in you. And so is the opposite: evil and badness. And there is a struggle. But I would believe that what goes around comes around, that you can manage your own spirit, your own desires, that you can pull yourself up when you're making mistakes, when you're tempted into evil. But you have to have a reason why. And I think the reason why is that you would be better if you do the right thing, in the long run. That's my faith.

GB: Your little grandson, Braiden, is seriously ill. You've prayed, I presume, for him and for alleviation of that?

ED: Yes, and my daughter, Colette, is a fantastic mother and she copes, as many, many mothers do, and many families do. But he's a brilliant boy. He's got a brilliant mind. He's nine and he's an expert on dinosaurs. And he has a lovely life, because his mother and father are good to him. And you pray for him and pray to give them strength to be what they are. They have their crosses to bear. And that's why I always say there are no ordinary people.

GB: Come back to football again now and retirement. Beckham said that he cried buckets of tears when he retired. Niall Quinn told us on this programme that he went into a deep, deep, serious depression when he came out. You retired. It doesn't seem to have affected you all that much. But you had a kind of soft landing with Johnny Giles and Shamrock Rovers, am I right about that?

ED: Yes, you are. I found it difficult, I must say, on Saturdays when I finished.

GB: And Shamrock Rovers?

ED: Shamrock Rovers was a kind of a dream: to play for a great football club here, to stop all our best young players going to England to play . . . It simply wasn't doable.

GB: But it was a lovely dream.

ED: It was. And John Giles made a huge sacrifice. I saw the writing on the wall and it said, "Get out!" And I got out.

GB: [Laughter.] Again.

ED: Again, yeah. I tell you, I wouldn't have many virtues, but one of them is in the forward-planning department.

GB: [Laughter.]

ED: I can usually see the train coming down the track and get out of the way. [Laughs.]

GB: Now, coming back to your sense of outrage and people turning against you for saying the things you did, let us be frank and say you offended a great number of people, like big Jack and your colleagues and Keano and me. In fact, it would be easier to think of people you *haven't* offended rather than people you have. And so *The Rocky Road*, which is the title of the book — a lot of those rocks would have been placed there by one Eamon Dunphy himself. Do you ever regret these comments and these things that you've said about people . . . ?

ED: Yeah, one or two I would regret. I wrote a piece about John Waters and Sinéad O'Connor for the *Sunday Independent*, because John had criticised the *Sunday Independent* when I was working there. And I would certainly regret that, because it bordered on the personal, although they were both public figures. I usually pick on the big guys: the Mary Robinsons; Seamus Heaney, when he won the Nobel Prize, not when he was a struggling writer; John Hume . . . I was very much against the Hume-Adams collaboration at a time when the IRA were killing people and committing acts of terrorism. Now, history will judge John Hume to have been a great man and right. But journalism isn't history. I was writing in the week. What would you say in the week of Enniskillen, for example, or the Shankill bombing? "Oh, okay, keep talking to them." No, I was saying, "Don't talk to them until they put the gun and bomb away." That was a point of view.

I admired journalists. I thought they were important and worked in the public interest. I kind of was romantic about journalism.

GB: What do you think happens when you die?
ED: Well, I'll tell you what I *hope* happens. I hope that you go and you're judged . . .

GB: Oh!
ED: . . . Yeah, and that you have to answer for your sins.

GB: Judged by whom?
ED: This person I pray to every night is what I'd *like* to think. My fear is that you just go up in flames and it's bye-bye. But I don't know. So, there is a mystery to life that I think is extraordinary and divine. Generosity, courage — qualities that human beings have that are divine and beautiful— I think that survives. Where it goes, I don't know. There's nothing, to me, more barren than the secular-atheist take on the world, because it discounts all that is beautiful and precious about people we know.

GB: Go back to your description of the Catholic Church at the time of your marriage to Sandra. You didn't think, at the time, "Well, this is an odd guy out. Although he may be a priest, he's a guy with problems and he's a bigot, and I'm going to ignore what he has to say"?
ED: I didn't. For sure, he was a bigot. But he was giving a message that was official Church teaching — a bad moment and a very hurtful moment, because he was talking about the woman that I loved.

GB: It was disgraceful, really, but it was so disgraceful that you would almost be inclined to say, "This guy is a nutcase. He's so outside the norm." But he's not.
ED: That was official teaching, and it was sort of rammed home to us when we got married in the dark church.

GB: When you go back, now, to your mother's faith, which was un-questioning and which was in many ways an onerous faith to carry, do you see any benefit in the consolation which she got out of that simple faith?

ED: Yes, I do. Very much so. They were people of their time. I just wonder what she would have made of all the revelations about their wealth, their abuse of people, the cover-up. I think she would have been horrified.

GB: Wouldn't have lost her faith?

ED: No, she wouldn't. She would, as many people have done, have seen beyond the representatives. And Jesus, don't forget, turned over a few temples. So that's beyond an institution or a bad man. That's something that is priceless and precious.

GB: You almost sound as if you wish you were still inside the fold?

ED: Well, I hope, in my behaviour and in my day-to-day life, I behave like a good person. And I think that that is what you're told in the Bible, that's what you're told in Islam or the Jewish faith.

GB: And when you talk about the Day of Judgement, what do you think happens to the Hitlers and the Stalins and the heavy-duty bad, bad people?

ED: I think that they'll be held to account.

GB: They'll be held to account?

ED: Well, I think their souls rot while they live. I don't think that's the way to be happy.

GB: So, you wouldn't go for Hell, or would you?

ED: I believe in redemption for everybody.

GB: Okay. Last question. Suppose it's all true, what your mother and father believed, what you were taught going to Mass every morning, and you arrive at the Pearly Gates and you are confronted by God. What will Eamon Dunphy say to God?

ED: "Are you still serving?"

GB & ED: [Laughter.]

ED: "I want to explain . . ." I'd come up with a story . . .

GB: If that's the best you can do, I wish you the best of luck . . . !

GB & ED: [Laughter.]